Conversations About Adult Learning in Our Complex World

A Volume in
Adult Education Special Topics:
Theory, Research & Practice in Lifelong

Series Editor:
Kathleen P. King, *University of South Florida*

Adult Education Special Topics:
Theory, Research, & Practice in Lifelong Learning

Kathleen P. King, Series Editor

Innovations in Career and Technical Education:
Strategic Approaches towards Workforce Competencies Around the Globe (2007)
edited by Victor C. X. Wand and Kathleen P. King

Yes We Can!
Building Workforce Competencies in Career and Technical Education (2008)
by Victor C. X. Wand and Kathleen P. King

Fundamentals of Human Performance and Training (2008)
edited by Victor C. X. Wand and Kathleen P. King

Human Performance Models Revealed in the Global Context (2008)
edited by Victor C. X. Wand and Kathleen P. King

Empowering Women Through Literacy: Views from Experience (2009)
edited by Mev Miller and Kathleen P. King

The Handbook of the Evolving Research of Transformative Learning:
Based on the Learning Activities Survey (10th Anniversary Edition) (2009)
edited by Kathleen P. King

Case Studies and Activities in Adult Education and
Human Resource Development (2010)
by Steven W. Schmidt and Kathleen P. King

Learning for Economic Self-Sufficiency: Constructing Pedagogies of
Hope Among Low-Income, Low-Literate Adults (2010)
edited by Mary V. Alfred

The Power of Learning From Inquiry: Teacher Research as a
Professional Development Tool in Multilingual Schools (2010)
by Aida A Nevárez-La Torre

Our Stories, Ourselves:
The Embodyment of Women's Learning in Literacy (2011)
edited by Mev Miller and Kathleen P. King

Conversations About Adult Learning in Our Complex World (2012)
edited by Carrie J. Boden-McGill and Kathleen P. King

DEDICATION

For those adult educators who have created and lit the pathways of life-long learning before us; may your work live and grow through our work. For those learners and adult educators who walk the pathways after us; may old wisdoms find new uses in the 21st century world and beyond.

Conversations About Adult Learning in Our Complex World

Edited by

Carrie J. Boden-McGill
Texas State University

and

Kathleen P. King
University of South Florida

Associated Edited

Lauren Merritt
University of Arkansas at Little Rock

Information Age Publishing, Inc.
Charlotte, North Carolina • www.infoagepub.com

Library of Congress Cataloging-in-Publication Data

CIP data for this book can be found on the Library of Congress website http://
www.loc.gov/index.html

ISBNs: Paperback: 978-1-62396-076-6
        Hardcover: 978-1-62396-077-3
        E-Book: 978-1-62396-078-0

Printed in the United States of America

CONTENTS

**SECTION III: PROGRAMMING FOR ADULTS—REDESIGNING
UNIVERSITY TO SERVE ADULT LEARNERS**

**SECTION IV: PROFESSIONAL DEVELOPMENT, TEACHER
TRAINING, AND LEADERSHIP DEVELOPMENT**

FOREWORD

The Adult Higher Education Alliance has evolved from a small network of colleges experimenting with alternative programs for adult learners to a membership organization engaged in action learning, reflection and discussion. Traditionally, we made available research and proceedings from our conference on our website www.ahea.org. Our history of supporting innovation and action learning for adults has culminated in this most recent venture—the publication of this volume.

Representing a range of critical issues, the work represented in this collection pushes at the existing parameters of higher education in an incredibly volatile environment. In a world of disruptive technologies, the most effective teaching and learning is responsive and sensitive to adult learners needs in a rapidly changing context. We are proud to sponsor our first peer reviewed publication which includes reflections and research on meaningful learning, leadership, authentic assessment, professional development, and intercultural competence. Join us in contemplative thought as you delve into these pages and consider the implications for your own practice and investigation!

Tessa McDonnell

Tessa McDonnell
President, AHEA—The Alliance

Conversations About Adult Learning in Our Complex World, pp. xi–xi
Copyright © 2013 by Information Age Publishing
All rights of reproduction in any form reserved.

ACKNOWLEDGMENTS

FROM THE EDITORS:
CARRIE J. BODEN-MCGILL AND KATHLEEN P. KING

Very little in an edited volume happens in isolation. There are many hands and voices that have touched this volume, and for that, we are grateful.

First, we wish to thank the AHEA Board, who at every stage provided enthusiasm, support, feedback, and guidance that was much appreciated and invaluable. We are especially grateful to Marilyn Lockhart and Carrie Johnson, who were there for the initial gleanings of an idea and stewarded through project through the obstacles to completion.

We are also thankful to the chapter authors; your conviction and enthusiasm inspired us to work when we were tired or when other obligations competed for our attention. Your voices remain with us, and we look forward to the readers and ourselves putting your words into action in the near future and, later, to seeing your research as it evolves.

Together Carrie and Kathy also wish to thank the editorial board for this volume, Teresa Carter, Thomas Cox, Jennifer Holtz, Carrie Johnson, Marilyn Lockhart, and Gabriele Strohschen, who spent their winter breaks reading with a sharp eye and offering feedback with a gentle pen. We were impressed with the level of engagement, attentiveness, professionalism, and care you gave to each manuscript. We are appreciative that you chose to offer your expertise in service to the profession though this volume.

Special thanks have been well-earned by Lauren Merritt, our editorial assistant, whose organizational savvy, adaptability, and stamina ensured that we stayed on task and on schedule. It was a pleasure to work with you as a professional—in every way.

FROM CARRIE J. BODEN-MCGILL (COEDITOR)

I appreciate Kathy King's intrepid spirit in taking on this project. Your good humor, work ethic, knowledge, and skills were all integral to the quality and timeliness of this volume. I enjoyed working with you at every step, and I could not ask for a better coeditor.

Finally, I am grateful to my family, team Boden-McGill, who supported this project in various ways, especially Isaac (Ike) Scotch McGill, whose ideas informed the design for the cover.

FROM KATHLEEN P. KING (COEDITOR)

When life is a challenge, we need faithful colleagues and friends to step forward, and we must allow them to help. A heartfelt and earnest thank you to those several people who became that support for me during a difficult time. Carrie J. Boden-McGill and this project have been critical as sustaining friends and focal points, respectively.

I appreciate the dedication, time and humility of Carrie, the editorial board, and volume contributors. Each became critical collaborators in this volume in the fullest sense. Academic collaboration, in the true sense of dialogue, give and take, and synthesis of new ideas, is more rare than we believe when we begin the journey as academics. This volume's many contributors demonstrate it is alive and well in the 21st century.

INTRODUCTION

Carrie J. Boden-McGill and Kathleen P. King

The Adult Higher Education Alliance (AHEA) is a community of scholar practitioners who "advocate for, support, and advance adults in programs of higher education" (AHEA, n.d.). One of venues through which this happens is the annual conferences. These gatherings serve as a forum for members to exchange ideas, share effective practices and current research, and engage in dialogue regarding "big questions" that the field faces. The 2011 annual conference in Indianapolis, IN, held in conjunction with the American Association of Adult and Continuing Education Conference, was themed "Adult Learning in Our Complex World," from which the title of this volume is derived. A community of scholars thoughtfully and skillfully expanded their conference presentations into book chapters for this volume; the result is a compelling collection of theories, models, strategies, cases, and examples of how adult learners and educators seek to navigate the complexities of the 21st century.

This book is unique in the world of edited volumes because we have used a double peer review system to cultivate critical contributions. The first round of peer review was at the conference level; the proposals were peer-reviewed for inclusion in the conference, and authors received feedback on their work during the conference. Next, the presenters submitted their work for the book peer review process. An editorial board of scholars from adult education, adult learning, and human resources provided detailed reviews of the submissions. In a final stage, as editors we reviewed the manuscripts, consolidated the comments of the editorial board, and requested further developmental changes from the authors. What you

Conversations About Adult Learning in Our Complex World, pp. xv–xx
Copyright © 2013 by Information Age Publishing
All rights of reproduction in any form reserved.

read here is the result of the work of a group of scholars diligently examining research, theory, and models for the critical questions of adult learning in our complex world.

Much like the wide variety of skills needed to survive in the 21st century, this book has a broad range of topics to explore the many dimensions and possibilities of adult learning today and tomorrow. As Dewey (1916) so astutely observed, "If we teach today's students as we taught yesterday's, we rob them of tomorrow." The difficult to define but essential skill, intercultural competence, appears several times in the volume for good reason. Amid the many people, careers, cultures, rapid changes, unexpected developments, and swift alterations in direction we experience in our global world, intercultural competence is rising as an essential foundation.

We offer the frame of intercultural competence to you for considering this volume. As Figure 1 indicates, these interrelated strands link together to form the basis of praxis for serving adult learners in an ever-increasingly complex landscape. Educational institutions and providers face the realities of serving multiple generations of students (Generation Y, Generation X, Baby Boomers, and Matures) from a variety of economic, cultural, and social backgrounds in the same learning spaces. In order to accomplish this goal, intercultural competence is key.

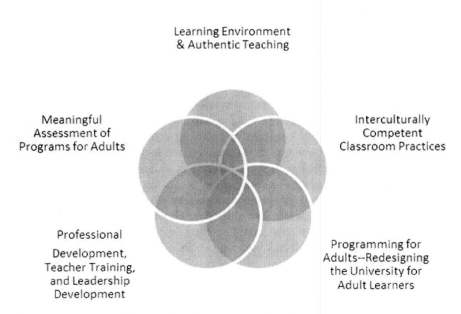

Figure 1.   Aspects of intercultural competence in education.

The chapters in this volume are arranged in five sections, each one dealing with a domain where intercultural competence and other fundamental skills may improve the learning experiences for adult learners. The sections include, The Learning Environment and Authentic Teaching, Interculturally Competent Classroom Practices, Programming for Adults—Redesigning University to Serve Adult Learners, Professional Development, Teacher Training, and Leadership Development, and Meaningful Assessment of Programs for Adults.

In the first section of the volume, the chapters focus on important aspects of the learning environment for adults as learners. Lockhart and Kelting-Gibson present findings of a study that links teacher authenticity in the classroom to teaching practices, student perceptions, and student satisfaction. The findings indicate that students place a high value on authentic teaching practices and that authenticity in the classroom is important factor for teachers to consider. Henschke presents findings from longitudinal research on the importance of trust in the learning environment. Henschke's findings echo those of others (Covey, 2006; Moehl, 2011; Stanton, 2005; Vatcharasirisook, 2011) that conclude that trust may be one of the most important factors in the learning environment, particularly teacher trust of learners. Finally, Shibata presents a model for intercultural transformative education with faculty development and training at the core of the model. Shibata suggests that a model of continual development for faculty is integral to modeling and creating inclusive, welcoming 21st century classrooms. These chapters demonstrate the many intercultural competencies that are necessary to create a productive and contemporary learning environment.

The second section focuses intercultural competencies that are present in specific classroom practices. Marsh's research focuses on the moral development of students who participate in collective decision-making processes. The findings suggest that collaborative decision-making experiences in class assignments can result in enhanced trust, stronger relationships, and a shift toward open mindedness to new ideas and possibilities. Taylor, Reynolds, Laton, and Davis explore student preferences for pedagogical and andragogical learning structure preferences. The authors propose that a number of factors influence where students fall on the pedagogy-andragogy spectrum and that most learners' preferences are somewhere in between the two extremes. Isenberg and Glancy explore generational learning preferences and the limitations of the teacher-centered model that most learning management systems follow. The authors recommend strategies for integrating andragogical principles in the online learning environment. This section concludes with a piece of action research and the presentation of a model, teaching-learning collaboration gears, that involves a blend of learning by teaching, research informed teaching, and adult self-authorship in learning. In the initial findings, Francois discovered that implementation of the model facilitates students' cognitive maturity, an integrated sense of personal identity, and mature relationships with others. The chapters in this section demonstrate that interculturally competent teaching many enhance moral development, collaboration, trust, self-direction, and self-authorship in students.

In the third section, the authors present research outlining the needs of adults as learners. These findings are critical to the understanding how best to redesign programs and universities in order to meet the needs of the adult students, who now make up approximately half of all university students (Chao, DeRocco, & Flynn, 2007; Lipka, 2012; National Center for Educational Statistics, 2007). Johnson, Richardson, and Lamczyk present findings on students' motivations to return to college and the impact that certain interventions during students' continuing education may have on quality of life. Similarly, in the next chapter, Lovell examines factors that contribute to motivation and persistence among parent and nonparent students. Several suggestions on how to structure programs and support services to help adult students succeed, as well as suggestions for practice, are offered in these chapters. Coulter and Mandell present a new model for how universities might reconfigure in order to better meet the needs of 21st century students. They point out that "The true object of adult education, the andragogical ideal, is to teach students, not what to know, but how to explore the already vast and still increasing realm of knowledge in order to pursue questions meaningful to them. This change in focus seems eminently sensible for adult students."

In the next chapter in this section, Olson weaves together the literature in the areas of first-generation college students, adult learners, and the college-to-work transition. Findings reveal that seeing possibilities, adapting, changing direction, and redefining success are key skills for adult learners. This, and the following chapter, elude to the idea that college and universities might need to change the ways in which they communicate their value in order to appeal to contemporary students. Prashun argues that the means by which credit is awarded—the credit hour—is not well suited to measure evolving instructional formats and learning, particularly in distance education settings. Prashun argues for new metric to measure and track learning outcomes and competencies. Finally, Hansman discusses how creating a community of peer mentors can be an effective measure to support students while dealing with the challenges of increased faculty workloads. This model, Hansman argues, empowers graduate students and prepares them for successful negotiation of the academic culture. The many means suggested here of redesigning university structures to serve adult students are grounded in intercultural competencies and understandings that only occur through the rich and deep listening to the needs of contemporary students.

The forth section focuses on professional development, including teacher training, and leadership development. Peno and Mangiante propose a purposeful and on-going mentoring model of professional development that provides faculty and students with an understanding of the transition from novice to expert. In another approach to professional development, McAtee and Hansman present three faculty development programs, peer coaching, learning communities, and mentoring, that address individual professional development needs. Kyobe and King present a model of culturally relevant and technologically assisted teacher training that could positively influence social and economic development in Uganda. Finally, Nanton argues that social cognitive learning is an important aspect of strategic leadership development and that leaders must leverage social media and other social learning for effective succession planning. These chapters outline the intercultural competencies of understanding the roles of individual needs, institutional culture, cultural differences, and social learning in professional development. The fifth and final section of the book focuses on the role of assessment in programs serving adults. DiSilvestro and Merrill present a longitudinal study of student perceptions of what they accomplished because of completing a degree. The benefits of the degree were measured against where students are employed, whether the degree has been of assistance in their career, as well as on graduates' reflections on the value of the degree. The students in this sample indicated that flexibility of scheduling and support from faculty, staff, and family were important factors in their success. Tweedell and Kelleher discuss a partnership, The Center for Research in Adult Learning, which was formed to measure student learning outcomes and to benchmark student retention. Two projects, one to measure persistence in adult programs and another to measure worldview of students enrolled in a Christian university, are discussed in detail. These innovative approaches to meaningful assessment provide a model for how programs might leverage data and collaborate to measure and improve student learning.

Developing solutions to cope with the challenges of learning in our complex world today and tomorrow is no simple endeavor. This volume illustrates that many adult educators approach the multitude of issues facing adult learners from different perspectives such as social work, psychology, education, administration, teaching, learning, and more. Scholars and practitioners may construct solutions independently or through intercultural or interdisciplinary collaborations and developments. Moreover, the need for adult learning is extending still further with adults encountering several new trends which prior generations did not: multiple careers, longer work careers, and longer life spans. We invite you to explore this volume to discover the many possibilities for approaching adult learning in our global, rapidly changing, and enormously exciting 21st century.

The chapters presented here represent some of the most innovative and thoughtful scholarship resulting from the work of the AHEA and, arguably, the field of adult education in the last year. Issues related to the learning environment, classroom practices, redesigning the university for adult learners, professional development, and assessment, are those that our esteemed colleagues deemed most timely and significant at this point in time. The spirit of AHEA is one that promotes cooperation, collaboration, consultation, and dialogue among professionals in the field. It is our hope that this volume functions in the same way, and that, rather than simply transmitting information, these chapters encourage, enable, and inspire you to engage in important conversations of your own. Join us in exploring adult learning in a complex world and discover new possibilities for teaching, learning, and yourself.

REFERENCES

Adult Higher Education Alliance. (n.d.). *About us.* Retrieved from http://ahea.org/about/

Chao, E. L., DeRocco, E. S., & Flynn, M. K. (2007). *Adult learners in higher education: Barriers to success and strategies to improve results:* U.S. Department of Labor, Employment and Training Administration. Retrieved from http://www.jff.org/publications/education/adult-learners-higher-education-barriers/157

Covey, S. (2006). *The speed of trust: The one thing that changes everything.* New York, NY: Free Press.

Dewey, J. (1916). Democracy and education. Englewood Cliffs, NJ: Prentice Hall.

Lipka, S. (2012). "Students who don't count." *Chronicle of Higher Education, 58,* 27, A10.

Moehl, P. (2011, July). *Exploring the relationship between Myers-Briggs type and instructional perspectives among college faculty across academic disciplines* (Unpublished doctoral dissertation). University of Missouri-St. Louis, St. Louis, MO.

National Center for Educational Statistics (2007). *Percentage distribution of undergraduates' age group and average and median age.* Retrieved from http://nces.ed.gov/das/library/tables_listings/showTable2005.asp?popup=true&rt=p&tableID=6929

Stanton, C. (2005, April). *A construct validity assessment of the instructional perspectives inventory* (Unpublished doctoral dissertation). University of Missouri-St. Louis, St. Louis, MO.

Vatcharasirisook, V. (2011, March). *Organizational learning and employee retention: A focused study examining the role of relationships between supervisors and subordinates* (Unpublished doctoral dissertation). University Missouri-St. Louis, MO.

SECTION I

THE LEARNING ENVIRONMENT AND AUTHENTIC TEACHING

CHAPTER 1

THE IMPORTANCE OF AUTHENTICITY IN THE COLLEGE CLASSROOM

Marilyn Lockhart and Lynn Kelting-Gibson

Authenticity and its importance in college teaching has been a neglected area of study (Brookfield, 2006; Cranton & Carusetta, 2004; Kreber, Klampfleitner, McCune, Bayne, & Knottenbelt, 2007). Kreber, McCune, and Klampfleitner (2010) stated that authenticity is "one of the most intriguing yet least well understood constructs in the higher education teaching and learning literature" (p. 383). While the notion of the importance of living an authentic life can be traced to Aristotle (Nussbaum, 2004), a consistent definition of authenticity in college teaching seems to be lacking. Based upon the results of a qualitative study with twenty-two educators, Cranton and Carusetta (2004) defined authenticity along five categories: self, other, relationship, context, and critical reflection. The term "active engagement with students" was an element used by other authors (Knotts, Henderson, Davidson, & Swain, 2009; Lin, 2006). "Being present in the classroom" was a component of authenticity included by Dirkx (2006), Hunt (2006), and Kornelson (2006). According to Brookfield (2006),

Conversations About Adult Learning in Our Complex World, pp. 3–13
Copyright © 2013 by Information Age Publishing

> From the student's perspective, viewing the teacher as both ally and an authority is important. Students want to know their teachers stand for something and have something useful and important to offer, but they also want to be able to trust and rely on them. (p. 5)

Brookfield defined authenticity according to four indicators (1) congruence—an instructor doing what they say they will do, (2) full disclosure—making public criteria, expectations, agendas, and assumptions that guide practice, (3) responsiveness—demonstrating clearly to students that you are teaching so as to be most helpful to them, and (4) personhood—teachers moving from formal identity to including personal aspects in the classroom. After a review of the literature pertaining to authenticity, Kreber et al. (2007) defined it according to 13 dimensions that they combined into being sincere, candid, and honest; self-reflecting, and caring for the subject and student.

All of the research found by the authors about authenticity used qualitative methods and asked faculty and/or students about their conceptualization of authenticity. Additionally, recent studies have been conducted in countries other than the United States. It is conceivable to the authors that what constitutes authenticity and the importance of it in the classroom could be a culturally influenced perspective. Kreber, McCune, and Klampfleitner (2010) wrote at the conclusion of their research about teacher and student beliefs about authenticity that "studies of how authenticity is enacted in practice will be more useful to our understanding of authenticity in teaching than studies of conceptions" (p. 396). After reviewing the research, we concluded that more practical information was needed in order to know more about adult student learning in our complex world of higher education. The purpose of this study was to (a) begin to link teacher authenticity in the classroom to practices, (b) design a survey asking students about authentic practices, (c) determine college students' evaluation of the importance of these practices and their satisfaction with these practices in their classes, and (d) compare their responses to the importance and satisfaction of authentic teaching practices to their teacher's content knowledge.

METHODOLOGY

The researchers designed a survey with a seven point Likert scale using Brookfield's (2006) four indicators as a framework for practices that constitute authenticity. The ratings were on a 1 to 7 scale, with 7 being high. The survey used Brookfield's indicators as he was the only author that we found who gave specific examples of classroom practices that reflect teacher authenticity. In addition to using Brookfield's examples of authentic classroom practices, his writings provided a model for the authors to add additional questions about each indicator.

The survey followed the format of the Adult Learner Inventory (ALI) of asking about the importance and satisfaction with each item. The ALI was developed by Noel-Levitz and the Council for Adult and Experiential Learning (CAEL) and has been used since 2003 to conduct national surveys with thousands of adult students attending over 60 higher education institutions about their priorities for their learning experiences in postsecondary education (Noel-Levitz & Council for Adult and Experiential Learning, 2011). Their survey asks about a variety of experiences in and outside the classroom such as financing, technology, student support systems, and subjects unrelated to this study. The authors of this article have used the design of asking about the importance of and satisfaction with survey items for various areas in adult education and training over the course of their combined 35 years experience practicing in the field and have found the outcomes valuable and useful in evaluating classes, workshops, and programs. The level of importance respondents place on a particular item indicates the level of expectation they assign to this area and indicates the amount of value they associate with this item. The level of satisfaction is their experience with the method. A performance gap can be calculated by subtracting the difference between the importance and satisfaction. Larger differences show larger performance gaps. Smaller differences reveal smaller performance gaps. Attention can be devoted to those items with larger performance gaps and less attention can be given to items with smaller performance gaps. Strengths can be identified by looking at high importance/high satisfaction items. Challenges are items with high importance and low satisfaction.

A class of nontraditional age graduate adult education students with experience in teaching adults and who had been studying effective classroom practices piloted the survey and made suggestions for revisions after reading and discussing Brookfield's article about authenticity. The students served as content experts as well as provided a student perspective of practices that constitute authentic teaching. Suskie (1996) recommends the use of knowledgeable students as experts to establish validity for surveys about experiences in the classroom. Based upon recommendations from the students, several teaching practices that they believed reflected authentic teaching, and a category of items reflecting instructor content knowledge questions was added. By adding the content category, the researchers were able to make a comparison with the authenticity indicators. See Table 1.1 for a list of survey items for each of Brookfield's indicators and for content items.

Table 1.1. Authenticity and Content Survey Items

Indicator	Survey Item
Authenticity Indicator 1: Full Disclosure	My instructors made clear expectations for assignments My instructors made clear criteria for grading.
Authenticity Indicator 2: Responsiveness	My instructors obtained feedback from me throughout the semester on how the course was going. My instructors used a variety of assessment tools throughout the course. My instructors learned along with the students. My instructors focused on student learning rather than teaching.
Authenticity Indicator 3: Personhood	My instructors viewed students as individuals. My instructors talked with me about my life outside of class before or after class. My instructors used autobiographical stories or examples to help illustrate course concepts or theories. My instructors shared stories of their own struggles to relate to student current struggles or fears. My instructors were interested in students' feelings about the class. My instructors learned student names. My instructors pushed students to complete assignments outside of their comfort zone. My instructors were advocates for students rather than an enforcer of institutional rules.
Authenticity Indicator 4: Congruence	My instructors were consistent with what they said they would do and what they actually did. My instructor arrived on time for class. My instructors arrived prepared for class. My instructors were available for help.
Content	My instructors were knowledgeable about the subject being taught. My instructors could answer content questions about the course.

The researchers distributed the survey to 188 freshman and sophomores during a chemistry and education class at the end of Fall semester 2010. All students in each class completed the survey. The sample was one of convenience as the faculty of these classes were colleagues of the researchers and interested in knowing more about the students in their class. Convenience sampling is recognized in the literature as sometimes being the most feasible for researchers in education survey research (Gay, Mills, & Airasian, 2012). The institution is a land-grant institution in the rural northwest with 14,000 students, most of whom are 18 to 24 years of age and native to the United States.

ANALYSIS AND RESULTS

Importance mean scores, satisfaction mean scores, and performance gap means were calculated for all students. These statistics were selected as relevant and appropriate based upon Noel Levitz using these computations and analysis for their ALI annual reports (Noel-Levitz & Council for Adult and Experiential Learning, 2011). The results are shown in Table 1.2. Indicators are listed in order of importance with greatest importance mean scores listed first.

Again, following the format and calculations of the Noel-Levitz annual national reports for ALI, main strengths and challenges were calculated. Strengths enable a professor to know what they are doing well, as students value these items and are satisfied with their experiences. Strengths (high importance/high satisfaction) were defined as items receiving an importance score of 6.0 or higher and a satisfaction score of 6.0 or higher. Performance gaps are less than 1.0. The results are provided in Table 1.3. Items are listed in descending order of performance gaps, with smallest performance gaps listed first.

Table 1.2. Summary of Authenticity and Content Items—Mean Scores and Performance Gaps

Indicator	Importance Mean	Satisfaction Mean	Performance Gap Mean
Congruence	6.46	5.75	0.71
Content	6.19	5.57	0.62
Full Disclosure	6.01	5.13	0.88
Responsiveness	5.65	4.72	0.92
Personhood	5.49	5.19	0.30

Note: N = 188. 7 = very important/very satisfied, 1 = not important/not satisfied.

Table 1.3.   Performance Gaps: Strengths

Strengths (High Importance/ high Satisfaction)	Importance Score	Satisfaction Score	Performance Gap
Congruence: My instructors arrived on time for class.	6.3	6.2	.1
Congruence: My instructors arrived prepared for class.	6.6	6.05	.55
Congruence: My instructors were available for help.	6.5	5.9	.6
Content: My instructors could answer all content questions about the course.	6.3	5.7	.6
Content: My instructors were knowledgeable about the subject being taught.	6.8	6.0	.79

Note: $N = 188$

Challenges are defined in the Noel-Levitz report as areas with high importance and low satisfaction and areas where learners expect a lot but their expectations are not being met (Noel-Levitz & Council for Adult and Experiential Learning, 2011). Noel-Levitz defines challenges as those with importance score means above the midpoint and satisfaction mean scores either below the midpoint or the top quartile of performance gaps. In this study, respondents rated all items as above the midpoint in importance and satisfaction, therefore challenges were defined as items in the top quartile of performance gaps. While this definition differs slightly from that used in the Noel-Levitz reports, the authors were looking for some indication of items of authenticity that professors could focus upon as potential areas of improvement. Results are shown in Table 1.4 and listed in descending order of largest performance gaps.

DISCUSSION AND RECOMMENDATIONS

The results revealed that these students highly value authentic practices, as defined by Brookfield (2006), in the classroom. Most important were practices reflecting the indicator of congruence, and these practices were somewhat more important than practices reflecting instructor content knowledge. Clearly, students want instructors to do what they say they will do, be available for help, be prepared for class, and arrive on time for

Table 1.4.   Performance Gaps: Challenges

Challenges (High Importance/Low Satisfaction)	Importance Score	Satisfaction Score	Performance Gap
Full Disclosure: My instructors made clear expectations for assignments.	6.6	5.2	1.4
Full Disclosure: My instructors made clear criteria for grading.	6.5	5.1	1.4
Responsiveness: My instructors focused on my learning rather than their teaching.	6.2	4.9	1.3
Congruence: My instructors were consistent with what they said they would do and what they actually did.	6.6	5.4	1.2
Responsiveness: My instructors obtained feedback from me throughout the semester on how the course was going	5.5	4.4	1.1

Note: N = 188

class. Full disclosure practices such as following the syllabus, making expectations and criteria for assignments and grading clear, and following these expectations, was also very important to students. To a somewhat lesser degree, responsiveness, which is instructors obtaining feedback from students during the semester, using a variety of assessment tools, focusing on student feedback, and learning along with students, was important.

Given what the literature says about the importance of teachers showing they are a "real person," it was surprising that the importance mean for practices reflecting personhood was one point lower on the seven point Likert scale than that for congruence. The personhood importance mean of 5.4 was the lowest mean of all the indicators, making it easier, compared to the other indicator means, for this to be an area that met student expectations. A closer examination of the data showed that 20% of the students marked the item "My instructors talked with me about my life outside of class before and after class" as "not applicable." This led us to question if perhaps these freshman and sophomore students who are beginning to establish their independence and autonomy did not expect or want college instructors to talk with them about their lives. Some of the faculty in Cranton and Carusetta's (2004) qualitative study viewed students' personal lives outside of the classroom as being outside of their concern, so this may be an area that has varied perspectives of importance by students and faculty alike. However, with 20% of the students not answering this particular item in personhood, the implication of the somewhat lower mean score of this indicator is uncertain.

The largest indicator mean performance gap, experienced by students, .92, defined by the difference between importance and satisfaction with experiences, was in the area of responsiveness. Within this indicator, rating the instructors as focusing on their own teaching rather than student learning, with a gap of 1.3, reflected the largest performance gap of an item in this indicator. This area is one that faculty at our institution should direct additional effort and concentration to, especially with recent calls from accrediting bodies and the public to increase student learning.

Examining largest performance gaps for individual items, defined as challenges, reveals additional areas for attention. Instructors should make clear expectations for assignments and criteria for grading.

The greatest strengths of instructors were in the content and congruence areas. Students' expectations and experiences of instructors arriving on time for class (gap of .1), being prepared for class (gap of .55), available for help (gap of .6), knowledgeable about the subject (gap of .7) and answering content questions (gap of .6), were more closely matched than other items in those and other indicators.

The results of this survey can be used by faculty at our institution for examination for areas of strength and areas to study for improvement. The results of this study are not generalizable to students at all institutions. However, according to the position of Gay, Mills and Airasian (2012), results of studies intended to develop deeper understanding of a concept may be transferable. Readers of this study may find the following recommendations relevant as they try to better understand the individuals in their classrooms and aspire to be more authentic teachers.

1. Concentrate on student learning and the teaching practices that maximize student outcomes in classes rather than what *you* believe is good teaching. Authentic teachers are responsive to and focused on students in the classroom rather than themselves.

2. Ensure that behavior is consistent with what you say you will do. Aligning written and oral expectations with classroom practice is important and shows that you are trustworthy and can be depended upon.

3. Make expectations and criteria for assignments and grading clear. Disclosing guidelines creates an open environment and removes uncertainty for students.

4. Obtain feedback throughout the semester on how students are doing and what they are learning. Providing the opportunity for students to give feedback enables teachers to be responsive to students and make changes to the course as the semester progresses.

5. Use a variety of assessment tools. Students learn and prefer to learn in a variety of ways. Teachers can respond to these differences by incorporating various assessment strategies such as case studies, small group work, independent work, role play, etc.

6. Learn along with the students. Teachers can remain current and keep a fresh perspective by discovering new research and electronic sources and by conducting their own research in class related projects. Problem based learning projects, in which students work to study and propose recommendations for real-life situations, is an example of a teacher being considered a partner in learning.

7. Consider letting students see you as a "real person" by sharing your own experiences with the topic and perhaps some of your own challenges and struggles. The importance placed on this by students in your class may vary, but given what other qualitative research studies have found, this practice is most likely appreciated by many.

Some may react that the recommendations are standard good teaching practices, as per Davis (2009) and Svinicki and McKeachie (2010), and the authors agree. Certainly it is reassuring to recognize that much of what has been written about excellent teaching may also be viewed by students as authentic teaching. Based upon the results of this study, there is still work to be done to improve student satisfaction with what occurs in the classroom.

Future work using the survey can be considered. Revisions to the survey could add items based upon the writings of others. Faculty in Cranton and Carusetta's (2004) study stated that the context of a class impacted their view of authenticity. Adding items regarding class size, discipline of the course, and physical arrangement of the class and then analyzing their relationship to results could be of value. Further depth to the survey could be accomplished by asking students about the importance of authentic or "real life" learning experiences or assessments such as service learning projects, case studies, or projects. Another dimension to authenticity would be added by asking students if they believe their instructor's teaching is a good fit with their personality, and if they appeared to care about the subject matter. Analyzing data according to native culture and college major could reveal differences in perspectives. Graduate students and undergraduate students may place different levels of importance to items, as may traditional and nontraditional age students.

Instructors could consider administering a similar survey asking solely about importance of practices to their own classes early in the semester. By discovering the rating for each practice, faculty could emphasize those areas with greatest importance for that specific group of students. Giving the survey again with the additional "satisfaction" dimension at midterm would accomplish a formative midterm assessment.

Several authors have written about the importance of faculty self-reflection as a key component of authentic teaching (Brookfield, 2006; Cranton, 2010; Kreber, 2010). College teachers could use this survey for reflection on their own practices by comparing student level of importance and their own perceived level of practice for each item. Performance gaps would reveal their personal strengths and challenges. New questions relating to Kreber, McCune, and Klampfleitner's (2010) "being true to oneself" and "being mindful of what is happening in the classroom" (p. 190) would expand their self-reflection.

In conclusion, we echo previous authors that authenticity in the college classroom is important for teachers to consider and that it is a complex concept deserving further study. It is hoped that this work serves the purpose of relating the concept of authenticity to practice and that future research will extend this work.

REFERENCES

Brookfield, S. (2006). Authenticity and power. In P. Cranton (Ed.), *New Directions for Adult and Continuing Education: Authenticity in Teaching 111*, 5-16.

Cranton, P. (2010), Formal and implicit conceptions of authenticity in teaching. *Teaching in Higher Education, 15*(4), 383-397.

Cranton, P., & Carusetta, E. (2004). Perspectives on authenticity in teaching. *Adult Education Quarterly, 55*(1), 5-22.

Davis, B. (2009). *Tools for teaching* (2nd ed.). San Francisco, CA: Jossey-Bass.

Dirkx, J. M. (2006). Authenticity and imagination. In P. Cranton (Ed.), *New directions for Adult and Continuing Education: Authenticity in Teaching, 111*, 27-39.

Gay, L., Mills, G, & Airasian, P. (2012). *Educational research: Competencies for analysis and application*. Upper Saddle River, NJ: Pearson.

Hunt, R. (2006). Institutional constraints on authenticity in teaching. In P. Cranton (Ed.), *New Directions for Adult and Continuing Education: Authenticity in Teaching, 111*, 51-62.

Knotts, G., Henderson, L., Davidson, R. A., & Swain, J. D. (2009). The search for authentic practice across the disciplinary divide. *College Teaching, 57*(4), 188-196.

Kornelson, L. (2006). Teaching with presence. In P. Cranton (Ed.), *New Directions for Adult and Continuing Education: Authenticity in Teaching*, *111*, 73-82.

Kreber, C. (2010). Academics' teacher identities, authenticity, and pedagogy. *Studies in Higher Education*, *35*(2), 171-94.

Kreber, C., Klampfleitner, M., McCune, V., Bayne, S., & Knottenbelt, M. (2007). What do you mean by "authentic?" A comparative review of the literature on conceptions of authenticity. *Adult Education Quarterly*, *58*(1), 22-43.

Kreber, C., McCune, V., & Klampfleitner, M. (2010). Formal and implicit conceptions of authenticity in teaching. *Teaching in Higher Education*, *15*(4), 383-397.

Lin, L. (2006) Cultural dimensions of authenticity in teaching. In P. Cranton (Ed.), *New Directions for Adult And Continuing Education: Authenticity in Teaching*, *111*, 63-72.

Noel-Levitz & Council for Adult and Experiential Learning (2011). National adult learners satisfaction-priorities report. Retrieved from https://www.noellevitz.com/documents/shared/Papers_and_Research/2011/ALI_report%202011.pdf

Nussbaum, M. (2004). *Upheavals of thought*. Cambridge, England: Cambridge University Press.

Suskie, L. (1996). *Questionnaire survey research*. Tallahassee, FL: Association for Institutional Research.

Svinicki, M., & McKeachie, W. (2010). *McKeachie's teaching tips: Strategy, research, and theory for college and university teachers* (13th ed.). Belmont, CA: Wadsworth.

CHAPTER 2

TRUST IN LEARNING—
MAKES ALL THE DIFFERENCE

John A. Henschke

What are the necessary major elements for an adult educator to practice in the field? What significance does trust between facilitator and learner have on learning? How does the presence of trust or the absence of trust impact the learning process? In 1987, after 22 years practicing adult education relating to a variety of subject matters, these were a few of the questions I was asking. Through these questions, the rich literature in the field and my own research, I discerned the necessary major elements for adult educators to practice in the field. This lead to my developing a model which identified five major elements: (1) beliefs and notions about adult learners; (2) perceptions concerning qualities of effective teachers of adults;(3) phases and sequences of the adult learning process (as identified by andragogy assumptions & processes [perceptions from my studies with Malcolm Knowles] as depicted in Table 2.1,); (4) teaching tips and adult learning techniques; and, (5) implementing the prepared plan.

As I published and presented this model, there were opportunities to take a step toward finding out the spectrum of important characteristics for adult educators to possess. Henschke (1989) found emphasis placed on: the adult teacher identifying her/himself as a colearner with other learners; the actions of the adult teacher in the conduct of the classroom activities; competencies for adult educators; and, philosophy knowledge

Conversations About Adult Learning in Our Complex World, pp. 15–31
Copyright © 2013 by Information Age Publishing
All rights of reproduction in any form reserved.

of the adult teacher. Although these are individually worthy of consideration, each leaves a gap in necessary abilities of adult educators. Nonetheless, when taken together, these ideas have some cohesion. This scope of characteristics would include: (1) solid connection with a context, which is dynamic; (2) behaviors of the teacher being crucial in relationship to the learning process; (3) generation of various feelings in her/himself (*the teacher*) or the learners depending on the level of functioning; and, (4) undergirding beliefs which in turn guide professional practice. Thus, a study was launched that would address the following question: What beliefs, feelings, and behaviors do adult educators need to possess to practice in the field of adult education?

BACKGROUND

I had been practicing in the field of adult education for over 2 decades, drawing upon adult education literature, observing the practice of others in the field as well as developing and testing ideas of my own. In 1987, out of the known practice of a variety of adult educators, the rich literature in the field as well as my own adult education practice relating to a variety of subject matters and my own research, I developed a model that identified five major elements as being necessary for an adult educator to practice in the field.

I published "Training Teachers of Adults" and "Preparing Non-Experienced Teachers of Adults"; both articles investigated the known practice of a variety of adult educators including Cochran, Custer, Dirkx, Ellington, Hoffman, and Knowles and others (as cited in Henschke, 1987a, 1987b). These articles furthered my research and contributed to the development of an instrument to address the best organization of the 50 items identified (10 for each of five main elements necessary for adult teachers to possess) dividing the items between positive and negative characteristics.

Following is a detailed description of the study resulting in an instrument used in multiple countries, dissertations, workshops, and seminars. This study was initiated to answer the following question: what beliefs, feelings, and behaviors do adult educators need to possess to practice in the emerging field of adult education? The purpose was to take some major steps toward developing an assessment instrument.

Methodology-First Round

To achieve balance in developing the original instrument, five negative and five positive questions were generated for each of the five major

Table 2.1.   Andragogy Assumptions and Process

Assumptions of an Andragobical Model of Learning	
About	*Androgogical*
Need to know reason for learning something	Reason that makes sense to the learner
Concept of learner	Increasingly self-directed
Learner's experience	Rich resource for learning by self and others
Readiness to learn	Develops from life task and problems
Orientation to learning	For immediate application
Motivation	by internal
Process Elements of an Andragogical Model of Learning	
About	*Androgogical*
Preparation	Gain insight, understand of what is to come
Climate	Relax, trusting, mutually respectful, informal, warm, collaborative, supportive, fun, openness, authenticity, humanness, pleasure
Planning	Mutually by learners and facilitators
Diagnosis of needs	Mutual assessment by learners and facilitators
Setting of objectives	Mutual negotiation by learners and facilitators
Designing learning plan	Learning contracts, learning projects, sequenced by readiness
Learning activities	Inquiry projects, independent study, experimental techniques
Evaluation	By learner-collected evidence, validated by peers, facilitators, experts. Criterion-referenced

elements: (1) beliefs and notions about adult learners; (2) perceptions concerning qualities of effective teachers of adults; (3) phases and sequences of the adult learning process; (4) teaching tips and adult learning techniques; and, (5) implementing the prepared plan, for a total of 50 questions. When the 50 items were developed, it became apparent that there was not a clear separation of each of the five elements. There were ideas from all elements that overlapped into other elements. Also, it became clear that some of the ideas needed to be categorized as beliefs, others as feelings, and still others as behaviors. They were not all just action or learning, or competencies, or philosophical knowledge.

However, this then became problematic in that the original five categories did not hold if the inventory were to emerge-into a useful instrument. The best organization of the items at that stage of development was to divide the items between positive and negative characteristics. The result became 33 positive and 17 negative characteristics.

The instrument was developed into a Likert type scale. Each question became "How frequently do you...?" The answer for each item had four choices: Never, Rarely, Sometimes, and Often; with the numerical value of 1, 2, 3, 4 given respectively.

The opportunity came to test the instrument with nearly 600 adult educators. Three hundred eighty-nine of those were adult learning specialist (ALSP) instructors in one major institution. They completed these forms voluntarily. These instructors taught in the Adult Basic Education (ABE), General Educational Development (GED), and/or the English as a Second Language (ESL) programs at the Chicago City Colleges. These programs were conducted both on and off all the campuses in the system.

After the data was generated, the positive characteristics measured to 3.3 on the 4.0 scale, and the negative characteristics measured a 2.2 on the 4.0 scale. Although this indicated a general direction desirable, more for the positive and less for the negative characteristics to be scoring on the scale, the meaning of these positive and negative measures seemed somewhat vague unless one looked at each item separately.

Findings-First Round

As a result, it was decided at this point to conduct a factor analysis on the data gathered from the 389 adult educators involved with teaching at the Chicago City Colleges. Seven factors emerged from that analysis (see Table 2.2).

A quick observation from this profile of adult educators shows that this group is mainly concerned with benefits to the learners rather than themselves. This kind of professional attitude would be the desire of any organization wishing to serve people well.

The top ranking item for each factor are shown in Table 2.3.

It must be noted that in the factor analysis the highest scoring item for each factor was positively correlated with the factor with the exception of factor number seven. The highest scoring item for factor seven was negatively correlated with the factor. In fact, although there were three items that clustered in factor seven analyses on teacher trust of learners, the first two items were negatively correlated and the third item positively correlated with the factor. That positive item was: How frequently do you purposefully communicate to learners that each is uniquely important?

Table 2.2. First Round IPI Factors

Factors	Mean	Standard Deviation
1. Planning and delivery of instruction	3.50	0.39
2. Learner-centered learning processes (experience-based learning techniques)	2.75	0.51
3. Teacher centered learning process	1.89	0.53
4. Teacher empathy with learners	3.79	0.29
5. Teacher insensitivity towards learners	2.86	0.58
6. Accommodating learner uniqueness	3.28	0.24
7. Teacher trust of learners	3.53	0.46

Table 2.3. First Round IPI: Top Ranking Item for Each Factor

Factor	Item Asking "How Frequently Do You"
1.	Integrate teaching techniques with subjective matter content
2.	Conduct role plays
3.	Believe that your teaching skills are as refined as they can be
4.	Express appreciation to learners who actively participate
5.	Have difficulty getting your point across to learners
6.	Expect and accept learner frustration as they grapple with problems
7.	Demonstrate specific skills for learners

Methodology—Second Round

Following the factor analysis, eleven out of all 50 items were dropped because they did not fit into any of the seven factors. It was felt that for the sake of instrument brevity, as well as maintaining the strength, validity, and integrity of each factor, no more than five items were necessary for any one factor. To further strengthen and refine the instrument each factor that had more than five items, the lowest scoring items were eliminated. Any items negatively correlated with a factor it was clustered with were also eliminated. There was one item negatively correlated with factor six and two items negatively correlated with factor seven.

New items were developed to strengthen factors five, six, and seven. It was felt that for each new item needed to survive a subsequent factor analysis process, a minimum of two and a desired three items needed to be developed and included. Consequently, the first four factors needed no additional items. Factors five and six each had four new items developed and added. Factor seven had ten new items added; the revised assessment form then had a total of 45 items.

The process by which the new items were added was as follows: for each item needed, three statements/questions were developed relating to that category. For instance, for factor number five, Teacher insensitivity toward learners, there were two new items needed. Hence, six items were developed. The items were then submitted to members of a 1989 winter semester graduate adult-education course entitled "Foundations of Adult Education" at the University of Missouri-St. Louis. This population represented beginning as well as advanced practitioners in the adult education field. They were asked if each statement/question reflected a clear focus on the particular factor in question. Answers were to be "YES or NO." Any answer that received more than two "No" responses was eliminated.

The second group which was available to use the assessment instrument was two hundred ten of the teachers/faculty members at the St. Louis Community College (SLCC). The participants taught in the regular daytime program and taught in a wide variety of subject matter areas. There are three campuses within the SLCC system.

Findings-Second Round

A factor analysis was conducted with the data, which was gathered with this group of 210 teachers. As shown in Table 2.4, five factors emerged.

A quick observation from this profile of community college teachers shows the group as being very sensitive toward learners and possesses high trust in the learners. There is a strong showing that these teachers think it important that they (the learners) are in control of the teaching/ learning process.

The top ranking item for each factor are shown in Table 2.5.

Following the factor analysis, 6 out of the total of 45 items were dropped because they did not fit into any of the five factors. Again, any items negatively correlated with a factor it was clustered with were eliminated. There was only one item which was negatively correlated with any factor and that was number four.

APPLICATIONS OF THE FINDINGS TO PRACTICE

The purpose of this study was to take some major steps towards developing an assessment instrument to answer the following question: What beliefs, feelings, and behaviors do adult educators need to possess to practice in the field of adult education? The final instrument included the

Table 2.4.   Second Round IPI Factors

Factors	Mean	Standard Deviation
1. Teacher trust of learners	3.45	0.66
2. Experience-based learning techniques	2.70	0.82
3. Teacher insensitivity towards learners	2.42	0.68
4. Sensitivity to learner differences	3.82	0.46
5. Teacher centered learning process	3,10	0.79

Table 2.5.   Second Round IPI: Top Ranking Item for Each Factor

Factor	Item Asking "How Frequently Do You"
1.	Promote positive self-esteem in learners
2.	Use buzz groups (learners grouped together to process information from lectures)
3.	Have difficulty with the amount of time learners need to grasp various concepts
4.	Establish instructional objectives
5.	Believe that your teaching skills are as refined as they can be

following factors in no particular order: Teacher empathy with learners; Teacher trust of learners; Planning and delivery of instruction; Accommodating learner uniqueness; Teacher insensitivity toward learners; Learner-centered learning processes (experience-based learning techniques; and, Teacher-centered learning processes (Henschke, 1989, 1994). The instrument was initially labeled "Instructor Perspectives Inventory" (IPI).

The strongest factor that came out of both rounds of analyses was "teacher trust of learners." Despite the strongest factor being "teacher trust of learners," in the first round there were only three items included in the strongest factor with two of them negative and one of them being positive. Thus, there was a need to eliminate the negative items and add positive ones. Twelve items were added for a total of 13 items in the second round. On the second round, only 2 of the 13 were eliminated, thus leaving a total of 11 items that came into the final version of the factor labeled "teacher trust of learners" (Henschke, 1989). Henschke (1989, 1998) identified the 11 items that comprise this factor and illustrate those facilitators of learning who believe, internalize, and enact the foundation of trust will:

- Purposefully communicate to learners that each is uniquely important;

- Express confidence that learners will develop the skills they need;
- Trust learners to know what their own goals, dreams, and realities are like;
- Prize the learners' ability to learn what is needed;
- Feel learners need to be aware of and communicate their thought and feelings;
- Enable learners to evaluate their own progress in learning;
- Hear what learners indicate their learning needs are;
- Engage learners in clarifying their own aspirations;
- Develop supportive relationships with learners;
- Experience unconditional positive regard for learners; and,
- Respect the dignity and integrity of learners.

The factor analysis of the IPI was validated a number of times and later in this chapter, statistics will be presented on three of those validations.

In practice, I have administered the IPI to adult educators in workshops that I have conducted in the United States, and the universities where I have taught. I have also administered the IPI in numerous countries around the world: Germany, Austria, Hong Kong, Peoples' Republic of China, South Africa, Brazil, Thailand, and the United Kingdom. Almost without exception, in these situations, the strongest factor in the instrument has remained "teacher trust of learners."

Initial Research Using the IPI With Doctoral Dissertations

The instrument became known in the field of adult education and was presented at the 1994 Commission of Professors of Adult Education (CPAE) Conference in Nashville, TN (Henschke, 1994). In 1995, the IPI was used for the first time in a doctoral dissertation (Henschke, 2011). At this writing it has been used in a total of 14 doctoral dissertations (see Table 2.6).

Without exception, in each of these 14 completed dissertations the strongest factor remained "teacher trust of learners." The instrument is currently in the process of being used in another eight doctoral dissertations. Although I have granted permission for using the IPI instrument in these eight dissertations as they are progressing, I am not on any of the dissertation committees. Consequently, I am unaware of exactly how the instrument is being used in each dissertation. I have full confidence and trust that the instrument will be used appropriately.

Table 2.6.   Completed Doctoral Dissertations Using IPI/MIPI

Date of Dissertation	Author	Title
1995	Thomas, E.	An identification of the instructional perspectives of parent educators
1997	Seward, S.	An identification of the instructional perspectives of Kansas parents as teachers educators
1997	Dawson, S.	Instructional perspectives of nurse educators
2003	Drinkard, G.	Instructional perspectives of nurse educators in distance education
2005	Stanton, C. (First to modify instrument)	A construct validity assessment of the Instructional Perspectives Inventory (IPI)
2006	Stricker, A.	Learning leadership: An investigation of principals' attitudes toward teachers in creating the conditions conducive for learning in school-based staff development
2007	Reinsch, E.	The relationship among lifelong learning, emotional intelligence and life satisfaction for adults 55 years of age or older
2007	McManus, L.	The instructional perspectives of community college mathematics faculty
2007	Rowbotham, M.	Teacher perspectives and the psychosocial climate of the classroom in a traditional BSN program
2009	Ryan, L.	Adult learning satisfaction and instructional perspective in the foreign language classroom
2010	Manjounes, C.	An adult accelerated degree program: Student and instructor perspectives and factors that affect retention
2011	Vatcharasirisook, V.	Organizational learning and employee retention: A focused study examining the role of relationships between supervisors and subordinates
2011	Jones-Clinton, T.	Principals as facilitators of professional development with teachers as adult learners
2011	Moehl, P.	Exploring the relationship between Myers-Briggs Type and Instructional Perspectives among college faculty across academic disciplines

Adult Education Literature Surrounding Trust

In seeking to foster self-direction in human beings, Combs (1966) asserted that we need to believe self-direction is important, trust that the human organism is able to exercise self-direction, be willing to experiment with self-direction, and provide opportunity for self-direction to be practiced and learned.

Neibuhr (1981) suggested that a renewal of traditional institutions is critical to their becoming effective learning agencies of self-directed development with individuals carrying forward their learning, since life guidance services are blossoming almost spontaneously into a resurgence of caring for the development of others. Additionally, he believed it to be possible that if we can promote this guidance and trust in self-directed development between teacher and student, supervisor and employee, friend and friend, parent and child, we will be well on the way to the new self-directed learning paradigm of achieving a coherent and balanced strategy or theory of living.

Knowles (1996) looked at trust from the standpoint of a professor and an employer who works with adults in their learning. He very clearly explained that in a climate of mutual trust, people learn more from those they trust than from those they are not sure they can trust. Educators of adults [ones who seek to help adults learn] need to prove themselves to be trustworthy. The same thing is true with employers who need to prove themselves to be trustworthy with their employees. Professors and employers will do well to present themselves as a human being rather than as an authority figure, to trust the people they work with and to gain their trust.

In 1997, an international doctoral student of Knowles found that Knowles possessed a very deep reliance on trust in people. The student shared with Knowles what she described as "an extremely unpleasant experience" with another professor, who implied that the time the student had taken away from her doctoral assistantship for her father's funeral (the international culture expected one month of mourning) was excessive and costly to the professor. After experiencing the critical incident, the student shared the unpleasant incident with Knowles. Knowles responded to the student with compassion and peace, "No matter what, we still need to choose to believe and trust other human beings" (Han & Henschke, 2012 p. 7).

Peale (1996) added another dimension to trust by identifying a device within each of us (he called it a "censor") which he believes all people are endowed with, it is not only a natural part of a human being, but also something God put in each of us in order to hear His voice. "Your 'censor' knows-trust it." If you follow it, he adds, this is one of the safest principles for making things go well for you. People who think that this concept is outmoded, or who assume they can have an easy, bendable moral attitude and get away with it forever, always find otherwise. Adherence to a proven moral code does not guarantee sweetness and light. But it does promise an enveloping feeling of rightness much more surely than when we bend the laws for pleasure. (p. 172)

Billington (2000) characterized an atmosphere of trust in highly effective adult learning programs: if present, adults learn and grow; if absent, adults regress and do not grow. The key characteristics are: class environment of respect, abilities and life achievements are acknowledged, intellectual freedom with experimentation and creativity encouraged, adults treated as intelligent and whose opinions are valued, self-directed learning encouraged and practiced, class is an intellectual challenge, interaction promoted with instructor and between participants with them trying new ideas in the workplace, regular and timely feedback from the instructor, and learners treated fairly by instructor who listened, responded, and made adequate changes. Bell (2002) in looking at the partnership between mentor and mentee claimed that if protégés see their mentors providing a climate of taking risks and experimenting, they will follow suit. Thus, this kind of partnership which is full of trust becomes one in which error is accepted as a necessary step on the path from novice to master. Enlow (2008) leans in the direction of differentiating between the left brain and the right brain, but believes they are connected by masses of nerve fibers, which allow messages to pass between them. The left brain is verbal and processes information analytically and sequentially, and the right brain is visual and processes information intuitively and simultaneously. The left brain listens to *what* is said and communicated verbally and the right brain listens to *how* something is said, aiding our vocal inflection and mannerisms. In all the considerations about the right and left brain in learning, it appears that both are important to contribute to the balance. The right brain is more oriented toward trusting the human being to carry forward the creative growth and maturing aspects of learning. The function of the left brain in the balance appears to be more of a governor to place some definite boundaries around what transpires when creativeness goes beyond the growth and maturing protocol norms of the culture.

Each of these references serves to strengthen the importance of the idea of "teacher trust of learners." Combined, they add to what the use of the IPI in dissertation research continues to make as a stronger case for considering the value of trust in facilitation of an andragogical learning process, or what Neibuhr (1981) referred to as promoting guidance and trust between teacher and student, supervisor and employee, friend and friend, parent and child.

Another Perspective in Trust

As I progressed in my use of the IPI and found trust as being a very critical and increasingly important element of my University of Missouri-St. Louis and Lindenwood University classroom teaching process, one day I happened across a book (Covey, 2006) that supported what I had been researching, theorizing, and practicing in adult education since the late 1980s (Henschke, 1989).

Trust in learning and in every relationship, team, family, organization, nation, economy, and the world, is the one common thing that changes everything in our current era. It is considered by some as the key leadership competency, belief, feeling, and behavior vital in our personal, professional, and interpersonal well-being on the global scene (Covey, 2006). Covey (2006) made the bold claim that trust is the one thing that changes everything and makes all the difference—but when absent, nothing else makes a difference. He says that there are five waves of trust-self (personal/individual), relationship (between two or more people), organizational (group of people with common goal), market (constituencies served), societal (world community), and for trust to be extended, it needs to be inspired. These five waves could develop in sequential order, but it is more likely that each wave will develop simultaneously with the other ones, but will develop with its own unique characteristics. For Covey, within trust there are four cores of credibility within one's self-integrity, intent, capabilities, and results. Additionally, in relationships there are 13 behaviors—talk straight, demonstrate respect, create transparency, right wrongs, show loyalty, deliver results, get better, confront reality, clarify expectations, practice accountability, listen first, keep commitments, and extend trust. In organizational trust, there is the principle of alignment. In market trust, there is the principle of reputation, and in societal trust, there is the principle of contribution. Within all of this, the thing that is clear is that all of which Covey is speaking is only behavior. Even in credibility, he shows the metaphor of a tree, with integrity and intent being below ground in the roots, and capabilities and result being in the branches and the leaves.

The parable of the sower and the seed (Matthew 13, circa 80) indicates that there are four different kinds of ground into which the seed is sown. First, is where the seed falls on the ground and the birds come and take it away and eat it. Second, is where the seed is sown and it immediately springs up but has little root, so when the sun gets very hot, the seed is parched and dies. Third, is where the seed is sown and begins to grow, but thick weeds begin to grow within the field and it chokes out the plants and takes over the field. Fourth, the seed is sown and takes good root and produces some 30, some 60, and some 100 fold. Nonetheless, Covey (2006) never addresses the kind of ground (Matthew 13, circa 80) in which his tree metaphor on trust is anchored. With his metaphor, the tree could be suspended in midair. There is no belief system that governs the relationship of trust that has to do with the nature of the trust behaviors.

At the 2011 American Association for Adult and Continuing Education (AAACE) Conference where I presented the initial concept of what is in this chapter, one person present said that in light of our discussion on this concept of trust and the perspective of the scope of andragogy, it looks like pedagogy is about to be swallowed up by andragogy. Another person present indicated that she and personnel from the corporation where she worked had participated as an organization in a Covey workshop on the "Speed of Trust." When asked about the results, she without hesitation said something like the following. "When the Covey workshop was completed, there was not more trust prevalent in and between the people than before. It made no difference. Mistrust and suspicion was still there just as it was prior to the workshop." The workshop had been planned and implemented for the purpose of having trust permeate the atmosphere and the operational work of the corporation, but at least one person within the organization did not see more trust than before the workshop. Thus, although the Covey workshop perspective added some useful activities that have to do with trust, I assert the foundation of the trust is rooted in the factor comprised of the eleven beliefs of Henschke's (1989) research on "teacher trust of learners." Consideration is given to the fact that these comments are limited to individual perception on the subject and in the case of the Covey workshop it is only one individual's opinion of the workshop. However, it is important to keep in mind that this is an example of an individual who participated in the workshop, but "believed" that the trusting outcomes intended for the workshop were not met, thus, emphasizing belief is a strong factor in trust.

Modified Instructional Perspectives Inventory (MIPI) Validated Three Times

The original IPI was changed by Stanton (2005) from a 4-point Likert scale to a 5-point Likert scale, becoming the Modified Instructional Perspectives Inventor (MIPI). The MIPI was validated numerous times and statistics are presented below on three of them—Stanton (2005), Moehl (2011), and Vatcharasirisook (2011). Stanton and Moehl worked with the wording of the factors such as "Teacher Trust of Learners." This wording was focused on groups that were in an educational setting. Vatcharasirisook worked with the wording of the factors such as "Supervisor Trust of

Subordinates." The reason for the change of wording on the last one was that it was focused on groups that were in a work setting. So to replace the word *teacher*, the word *supervisor* was used. To replace the word *learner*, the word *subordinate* was used. Nevertheless, the same validation technique was used in each instance. The results show that it was equally valid to use the different terminology to designate the various roles and situations people were fulfilling.

Figure 2.1 shows Cronbach's alpha coefficient calculations for the three dissertations that validated the instrument.

The Modified Instructional Perspective Inventory factors follow:

Factor 1. = Teacher/supervisor empathy with learner/subordinates

Factor 2. = Teacher/supervisor trust of learner/subordinates

Factor 3. = Planning and delivery of instruction

Factor 4. = Accommodating learner/subordinates uniqueness

Factor 5. = Teacher/supervisor insensitivity toward learners/subordinates

Factor 6. = Learner/subordinate-centered processes

Factor 7. = Teacher/supervisor-centered processes

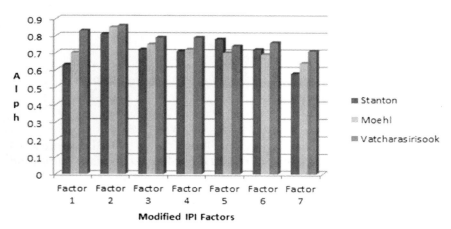

Figure 2.1.   MPI validity calculations.

Vatcharasirisook (2011) translated the MIPI into the Thai Language. She used it with 523 employees of banks, hospitals, and hotels in Thailand to help determine the level of their job satisfaction and their willingness to stay with the company. The *Supervisor trust of subordinate's* factor significantly predicted a major part of the *Subordinate's job satisfaction*. In turn, the *Subordinate's job satisfaction* was found to have a strong positive effect on the *Subordinate's intention to remain in the company*. The eleven ingredients or beliefs that form the foundation of trust have been worded differently with the *Supervisor's trust of subordinates* (instead of Teacher's trust of learners). Thus, supervisors who espouse, internalize, and enact the foundation of trust will demonstrate and express their belief as follows:

- Purposefully communicate to subordinates that each is uniquely important;
- Express confidence that subordinates will develop the skills they need;
- Trust subordinates to know what their own goals, dreams, and realities are like;
- Prize the subordinates' ability to learn what is needed;
- Feel subordinates need to be aware of and communicate their thoughts and feelings;
- Enable subordinates to evaluate their own progress in learning and working;
- Hear what subordinates indicate their learning and working needs are;
- Engage subordinates in clarifying their own aspirations;
- Develop supportive relationships with their subordinates;
- Experience unconditional positive regard for their subordinates; and,
- Respect the dignity and integrity of their subordinates.

CONCLUSION

This chapter started with my seeking the necessary elements for an adult educator to practice in the field. Using the philosophy of andragogy, an instrument (the Instructor Perspectives Inventory [IPI]) was developed and tested. It was found that Teacher Trust of Learners was its strongest factor. The IPI was administered in the United States and various countries around the world to encourage individual evaluation and reflection on personal practice. It was also used as a research instrument in 14 doctoral dissertations with Teacher Trust of Learners remaining the strongest factor. Supporting literature on trust was included. Covey (2006) offered that trust makes a difference in everything, and if absent, nothing else makes a difference. His perspective is weak in that it only considers behavior and not beliefs and feelings as the Henschke (1989) IPI does. The IPI was modified for doctoral dissertation work originally by changing the Likert scale from 4 points to 5 points and then in additional studies by word variations (teacher to supervisor, learner to subordinate) the instrument has been validated by three different researchers: Stanton (2005), Moehl (2011), and Vatcharasirisook (2011), with Teacher Trust of Learners maintaining its very strong position. The Trust element even contributed to workers job satisfaction in banks, hotels, and hospitals in Thailand, and in turn, contributing to the workers wanting to stay with their corporations.

In a world of ever increasing technology, where core values of previous generations are less reflected in popular culture such as television and video games, where trust effects not only our personal lives, but also our success and satisfaction in learning and in our work, the relationship of mutual trust between teacher and learner is of particular value and concern.

In the 23 years since the IPI was developed, the world view of trust has undergone many changes. These changes can be seen at the airport, on the nightly news reports, the games (video) our children play, popular music, and television programming available in primetime. Trust is not a word that means the same to every individual, it is very subjective; however, trust is the foundation of relationships and for learning to be successful trust as researched and exemplified through the IPI must be a dominate factor.

I invite you to take the MIPI for yourself, to evaluate and reflect on your level of trust in learners. If you wish to have a copy of the MIPI and scoring scale, please e-mail me at the following address jhenschke@lindenwood.edu. You are a model for those who come to you in order to learn. You have within your grasp the ability to empower learners, to promote lifelong learning, and to demonstrate and model trust.

REFERENCES

Bell, C. R. (2002). *Managers as mentors: Building partnerships for learning* (2nd ed.). San Francisco, CA: Berrett-Koehler.

Billington, D.D. (2000). Seven characteristics of highly effective adult learning programs. *New Horizons for Learning*. Seattle, WA: New Horizons. Retrieved from http://www.education.jhu.edu/newhorizons/lifelonglearning/workplace/articles/characteristics/index.html

Combs, A. W., (1966). Fostering self-direction. *Educational Leadership, 23*, 373-387.

Covey, S. (2006). *The speed of trust: The one thing that changes everything.* New York, NY: Free Press.

Enlow, J. (2008). *The seven mountain prophecy.* Lake Mary, FL: Creation House.

Han, P., & Henschke, J. (2012). Cross-cultural learning and mentoring: Autoethnographical narrative inquiry with Dr. Malcolm Shepherd Knowles. *International Journal of Adult Vocational Education and Technology.*

Henschke, J. (1987a). Training teachers of adults. In C. Klevins (Ed.), *Materials and methods of adult and continuing education* (4th ed., pp. 414-422). Los Angeles, CA: Klevens.

Henschke, J. (1987b). Preparing non-experienced teachers of adults. In S. J. Levine (Ed.). *Proceedings of the Sixth Annual Midwest Research-To-Practice Conference in Adult and Continuing Education* (pp. 2-8). East Lansing, MI: Michigan State University.

Henschke, J.A. (1989). Identifying appropriate adult educator practices: Beliefs, feelings and behaviors. In C. Jeffries (Ed.), *Proceedings of the Eighth Annual Midwest Research-To-Practice Conference in Adult, Continuing and Community Education* (pp. 89-95). St. Louis, MO: University of Missouri.

Henschke, J.A. (1994). Development and use of the Instructional Perspectives Inventory in graduate adult education. In C.J. Polson & F.M. Schied (Eds.), *Proceedings of the Commission of Professors of Adult Education Conference* (pp. 74-80). Nashville, TN.

Henschke, J.A. (1998). Modeling the preparation of adult educators. *Adult Learning, 9*(3), 11-13.

Henschke, J. A. (2011, November). *Trust in learning-makes all the difference; if absent, nothing else makes a difference.* Presentation at the American Association for Adult and Continuing Education Conference, Indianapolis, IN.

Knowles, M. S. (1996). Adult learning. In R. L. Craig (Ed.), *ASTD Training Development Handbook: A Guide to Human Resource Development* (4th ed.) New York, NY: McGraw-Hill.

Matthew 13:1-9, 18-23. (circa, 80). Parable of the sower and the seed. *New Testament Scriptures of the Bible.* King James Version, 1611.

Moehl, P. (2011, July). *Exploring the relationship between Myers-Briggs type and instructional perspectives among college faculty across academic disciplines* (Unpublished doctoral dissertation). University of Missouri-St. Louis, St. Louis, MO.

Neibuhr, H., (1981, Jan.). Teaching and learning in the eighties: The paradigm shifts. *Phi DeltaKappan, 62*(5), 367-368.

Peale, N. (1996). *The power of positive living.* New York City, NY: Peale Center for Christian Living.

Stanton, C. (2005, April). *A construct validity assessment of the instructional perspectives inventory* (Unpublished doctoral dissertation). University of Missouri-St. Louis, St. Louis, MO.

Vatcharasirisook, V. (2011, March). *Organizational learning and employee retention: A focused study examining the role of relationships between supervisors and subordinates* (Unpublished doctoral dissertation). University Missouri-St. Louis, MO.

CHAPTER 3

FACULTY DEVELOPMENT FOR INTERCULTURALLY TRANSFORMATIVE EDUCATION

Anne M. Shibata

Whether online, crossing time zones and national borders, or on college campuses with increasingly diverse demographics, the population of students is changing drastically (Imbra & Rallis, 2002; Stanley, 2002; Warren, 2002). Accreditation bodies and institutions list commitment to diversity as a core value. However, it is frequently left to faculty and faculty developers to ascertain how to create learning spaces, both face to face and online, that welcome all individuals.

Many faculty still lack support, experience and training in intercultural education, and as a result may be uncomfortable teaching or facilitating in classrooms with diverse students (Gopal, 2011). In addition, colleges, medical schools, law schools, and other institutions express values about diversity and multiculturalism, but a look at mission statements of various colleges show many different definitions (or none at all) of what this means. Some define diversity primarily as racial or ethnic differences (Gurin, n.d., para 1).

In this chapter, the author suggests a broad definition of diversity, reviews the theoretical underpinnings for transformative education, and introduces a three step process for interculturally transformative educa-

Conversations About Adult Learning in Our Complex World, pp. 33–45
Copyright © 2013 by Information Age Publishing

tion using critical reflection. While the framework is described in the terminology of higher education, the principles could be applied to intercultural education in all groups and institutions. Using this process will enable faculty to increase their intercultural awareness, efficacy, and comfort in the increasingly complex and diverse 21st century adult classroom.

CAMPUS DIVERSITY

What do we mean by diverse? College mission statements as well as accreditation agencies reference fostering diversity awareness in students and on campus as important goals. In fact, the Higher Learning Commission of the North Central Association of Colleges and Schools (2011) has listed diversity as a core component of accreditation:

Core Component 1b

In its mission documents, the organization recognizes the diversity of its learners, other constituencies, and the greater society it serves.

Examples of Evidence

• In its mission documents, the organization addresses diversity within the community values and common purposes it considers fundamental to its mission.
• The mission documents present the organization's function in a multicultural society.
• The mission documents affirm the organization's commitment to honor the dignity and worth of individuals.
• The organization's required codes of belief or expected behavior are congruent with its mission.
• The mission documents provide a basis for the organization's basic strategies to address diversity. ("Criteria for Accreditation," para. 3)

However, note that the definition of diversity is left to individual institutions.

Demographics in all areas of postsecondary education are undergoing rapid changes. For example, according to a recent report by the U.S. Department of Education, enrollment in institutions of higher education in the United States is projected to increase by the following racial percentages between 2007 and 2018: 4% for White students; 26% for Black students; 38% for Hispanic students; 29% for Asian/Pacific Islanders; 32%

for American Indian/Alaskan Natives, and 14% for nonresident aliens (Institute of Education Sciences [IES], 2009, p. 10).

Online Learning and Diversity

Making the issue of creating inclusive classrooms more complex, the increasing acceptance and availability of online learning is accelerating the pace of more diverse people meeting in an educational environment than ever before, and the physical anonymity of the environment means that diversity is not immediately (or sometimes ever) apparent.

Aside from the convenience of anytime, anywhere study, online learning is an educational modality better suited to some learners than the face to face classroom, giving educational opportunities to students who might not otherwise have pursued them (Pallof & Pratt, 1999). For example, students who are deaf and hard of hearing can study online without interpreters. Blind students can study without having to navigate a physical campus, with the help of dictation software like Dragon Naturally Speaking. Students who have social anxiety disorders or other mental health issues can avoid attending physical classes, students who have attention deficit disorder or attention deficit hyperactivity disorder can study in short bursts at their own paces with fewer distractions, and students who speak English as a second language and find it easier to read and write rather than to participate in spoken conversations are just some of the many students who find the online classroom a welcome alternative to the traditional face to face classroom. As an online instructor, this author has interacted with students with all of these characteristics, as well as U.S. military service people who were studying while posted at bases worldwide, some in active combat areas.

According to the Sloan Consortium survey on online education, published annually, students at American colleges taking at least one online class numbered 6.1 million as of 2010, an increase of 10% over the prior year (Allen & Seaman, 2011). Students from all over the world, of all ages, ethnicities, nationalities, ableness and so forth are interacting in the online classroom, and the numbers are increasing each year.

Adult Learners

The perceived need for an undergraduate or graduate degree is increasing the number of adult learners returning to school. The U.S. Department of Education estimates that enrollment of adult students of all ages will far outpace that of traditional (18-22) aged students (IES,

2009). This trend is likely to continue well into the 21st century. The Georgetown University Center on Education and the Workforce estimates that more than 60% of American jobs will require some form of postsecondary education by 2018 (Merisotis, 2011, para. 4).

All of these dynamics are causing shifts in the demographics of the population of students at U.S. colleges, making the student body the most diverse we have ever seen. Therefore, this author proposes that the term "diversity" be used in the broadest sense: encompassing varied ages and generations of students, (often to generationally as Baby Boomers, Gen-Xers, Millennials, and so forth), ethnicities, races, religions, sexual orientations, gender expressions, thinking and learning styles, and ableness.

INTERCULTURALLY TRANSFORMATIVE TEACHING FRAMEWORK

Transformative learning theory in adult education has been researched for more than 25 years (Taylor, 2007). Mezirow (1996, 1997) defined transformative learning as a process that effects a change in an individual's frame of reference. This paradigm shifting can only happen when there is a space created in the classroom. The old educational model was the "sage on the stage." The 21st century instructor must adopt the attitude of the "guide on the side." The instructor then becomes a facilitator for the student process, helping students to reflect on, interpret, process, and apply new ideas, becoming a colearner in the process.

Frames of reference encompass two dimensions: habits of mind and point of view (Mezirow, 1997). Habits of mind are "broad, abstract, orienting, habitual ways of thinking feeling and acting ... that constitute a set of codes" (pp. 5-6). Habits of mind then translate into an individual's point of view: "the constellation of belief, value judgment, attitude, and feeling that shapes a particular interpretation" (p. 6). Frames of reference can be changed through a process of critical reflection, which allows us to change our habits of mind and transform our points of view. This connotes an active approach to learning and is a continuous process of refinement rather than a one-time shift.

Competencies faculty need to effectively facilitate learners' intercultural growth include a high degree of self-awareness, self-reflectiveness, awareness of cultural norms and learning styles, sensitivity, and an ability and willingness to keep learning about the individuals they interact with in the classroom (Paige, 1993). In a longitudinal study, Cranton and Carusetta (2004) found that teachers who are working towards authenticity were more likely to critically reflect on self and other. Research supports the premise that critical reflection is crucial to the process of shifting frames of reference (Taylor, 2008; Taylor, Fischer, & Taylor, 2009). Being an effective intercultural educator in the complex classroom requires active self-reflection on the part of instructors.

Interculturalists, according to Bennett (1998), focus less on differences than on how these differences affect interactions. In diverse classrooms the focus should be on educators and students shifting frames of reference to be broader and more inclusive, becoming more aware of our individual points of view through the process of critical reflection and challenging ourselves and each other to expand our frames of reference.

Becoming interculturally transformative educators can be accomplished through an ongoing and imperfect three-step process: cultivating self awareness and reflectiveness, (and creating opportunities for students to do so), seeking feedback regularly, and increasing knowledge of the various cultural groups students identify with.

Cultivate Reflective Self-Awareness

Regular self reflection and self awareness are crucial to being a transformative educator. In order to develop intercultural competency, instructors must understand their own teaching and learning style preferences (Kolb, 1984) and their assumptions about cultures to identify what strengths and weaknesses they bring to the classroom.

For example, does the instructor prefer students who are proactive and take responsibility for their own learning or expect that students will need a lot of support and contact? Does the instructor consider students who frequently ask for feedback to be "high maintenance" or welcome this as a natural part of the learning process? Does the instructor expect students to communicate in a linear and direct fashion or in an indirect, circumspect way? Unconscious, unexamined expectations and assumptions about culture and the educational process will affect how an instructor interacts with students and influence the classroom climate.

Is the instructor aware of various learning disabilities and how students with those disabilities are likely to experience a classroom setting? Do discussions about racial issues make the instructor uncomfortable? Lesbian, gay, bisexual, and transgender students are increasingly embracing their sexual orientation and gender expression (Imbra & Rallis, 2002). Is the faculty member comfortable acknowledging this in the classroom? Instructors need to have high levels of self-awareness to be competent facilitators (Paige, 1993).

Are there certain groups about which the faculty member unconsciously or tacitly tolerates bias? Self reflection may uncover some of this. For example, some people who would not dream of making a racial or ethnic "joke" tacitly approve disparaging remarks about people who are poor, homeless, or obese (Puhl & Brownell, 2001), from a particular regional area of the country (Sweeney, 2001), or affiliated with a particular religion or political party. A commonly unexamined bias is the use of Native Americans as mascots in the local sports community (the Cleveland Indians and the cartoonish and insulting Chief Wahoo, for example), or to sell products in the supermarket (Munson, 2010).

Instructors must learn what preconceived ideas they have about other cultures and uncover their own hidden biases while modeling this process for their students. Ways to uncover assumptions and preferences include journaling, reading, seeking additional training and support from campus faculty development specialists, and discussing issues with fellow faculty and students. An excellent way to examine one's own learning style is to take the Kolb Learning Style Inventory (Kolb, 1984). An Internet search will identify some versions available free, online. Also, instructors can assess their thinking style preferences (Sternberg, 1996, 1997). In addition, they can learn more about important cross-cultural differences in the way people learn to think (Nisbett, 2003). The instructor can make these a part of the explicit curriculum of the class in subtle ways by encouraging students to examine their own thinking and learning preferences and introducing them to the idea that such variations exist.

Use Active Means to Help Students Develop Self-Awareness

There is sometimes a naïve idea that mere exposure to different cultures will foster intercultural competence (Seelye, 1993). Unfortunately, this rarely occurs. However, intercultural competence can be developed via activities that challenge perceptions and allow for paradigm shifting. One effective technique for promoting student self-awareness, adapted from various communication and psychology models (Broadbent, 1987) helps students identify their perceptual filters. Preface the activity by explaining to students that each person takes in information through various filters, and these filters affect how we interpret meaning. We all have filters that differ in various ways, and some are more important at times than others, and these become our frames of reference. The context of the communication situation frequently affects which filters are prominent.

First, have the class collectively brainstorm some of the filters together. Table 3.1 includes a list of some perceptual filters. It is not necessary to elicit all of them, in fact, generating a partial list together works better. List them on the board or a flip chart.

Then, have students list theirs in specific individual terms and see if they can generate other categories on their own as well. Have them use specific descriptors rather than the general categories, for example,

Table 3.1.   Perceptual Filters

Gender	Past experiences
Sexual orientation	Personal history
Age	Political persuasion
Physical state (height, weight, state of health, ableness)	Socioeconomic status
Ethnic background	Family of origin culture/customs
Race	Religion/Beliefs
Language	Fears
Educational level	Superstitions
Role/position in the communication process	Values

married, single, in a relationship, straight, gay, bisexual, republican, democrat, libertarian, independent, and so forth. The faculty member should share some of his or her own filters to model for students and promote an atmosphere of self-disclosure. It is important to be explicit that students do not have to reveal any information that they are prefer not to share, and the instructor should heed this same advice. The point of the exercise is to encourage reflection and allow students to see what parts of themselves they identify with, *and are comfortable sharing,* not to force self-disclosure.

The next step in the activity is to ask students to share their filters in pairs or small groups and then discuss as a class: Were they surprised at any of the filters on their lists or their classmates' lists? Why? How do these different filters affect how we communicate? How do they lend themselves to better communication or poorer communication? Can we control how someone else "gets" our communication once it starts moving through those filters? Ask students if someone else has ever misinterpreted their communication or taken something they said "the wrong way!" Since this is fairly universal, many students will raise their hands. It is a good way to illustrate that our different filters strongly affect how we experience the world.

The point of the exercise is to demonstrate that everyone begins with different points of view, and everything we experience is filtered through these frames of reference. Some of these frames are changeable, (educational level, socioeconomic status, experiences, and even gender) and others are fixed (race, ethnicity, generation, etc.) While this is a simple exercise, for some students it becomes an "aha" moment, particularly for ones who have oversimplified and naively believed that everyone shares similar perspectives and interprets information the same way. It broadens their worldview and gives them more material to use to reflect critically on their own and others' experiences of the world. "We cannot critically reflect on an assumption until we are aware of it. We cannot engage in discourse on something we have not identified. We cannot change a habit of mind without thinking about it in some way" (Cranton, 2002, p. 65).

This type of activity can be used as an introduction to more complex assessments for specific interactions, depending upon the subject matter. One example is the CHAT (Cultural Health Beliefs Assessment Tool), a simple questionnaire for medical students and clinicians to explore what culturally related health beliefs their patients hold (Rosen et al., 2004). Again, rather than focusing on learning all about specific cultural beliefs, this is a method used to find out what an individual thinks in order to facilitate intercultural awareness.

In addition, the faculty member should actively challenge students to think deeply. What strategy does the faculty member use if a student makes an inappropriate joke or comment in his or her presence or in an online discussion? Directly challenge it? Ignore it? Use it as a teachable incident? One way to handle these moments is to reflect back to the student, "I'm curious— why do you think the comment you just made is appropriate?" This requires the student to self-reflect and respond thoughtfully, and sometimes leads to more flexibility in the student's thinking.

Seek Feedback Regularly

Another way to create a transformative learning environment and let students know they are valued is by creating opportunities for them to give regular feedback, both openly and anonymously. This allows students to convey what they are thinking and feeling and to share issues or questions about the explicit or implicit curriculum. There are several techniques an instructor can use:

Course Introduction Assessment Surveys

Ask students to complete a questionnaire at the beginning of a course. The instructor can ask students to comment on their comfort level with or prior knowledge of the material, why they are taking the class, etc. One question that has elicited the most interesting responses is: "What do I need to know about you to help you be successful in this course?" This can also be one place where the instructor introduces the idea of learning styles, by asking students to reflect upon their own learning or thinking style preference. Simply by asking for feedback, an open and welcoming dynamic is established (Shibata, 2007).

Daily or Weekly Feedback Cards

Ask students to, anonymously, write what they do not understand or need help with on index cards. Because some students are uncomfortable asking questions in class or admitting that they do not understand, this written format allows them to ask for clarification or share an insight or a concern with the instructor in a candid manner. The instructor can address the issues in the next class.

Take-Aways

Ask students what they are taking away from a particular class or unit of study. This is best accomplished by quickly going around the room at the end of a class, allowing the instructor to clarify points as necessary and to assess the effectiveness of the lesson. Because this activity does not require much self-disclosure, it may be done verbally.

Midterm Course Assessment Surveys

A slightly more formal method of seeking feedback is a written anonymous survey where students are asked about their perceived grasp of the subject matter so far, as well as being given the opportunity to give feedback regarding classroom climate issues or any other concerns they may have. Because this is done halfway through the semester (or sooner if the instructor deems it necessary), there is still ample course time to address any issues that arise, rather than have instructors receive this information after the end of the course when it is too late to address.

By collecting and responding to student feedback, instructors demonstrate a genuine interest and can address concerns and clarify issues. Each of these techniques provides instructors with more material for their own critical reflection as teachers, particularly in getting to know students as individuals and transcending boundaries with them. Students likewise have an opportunity to self-reflect on their own learning process while simultaneously observing the instructor model critical reflection.

Increase Knowledge Areas

To be a competent interculturally transformative educator, an instructor must learn about the various cultures with which students identify. There are many good resources available to assist in this quest, such as books, articles, and studies. Such research is a great opportunity for faculty to learn, but we must be judicious with the information and remember that our students are *individuals* who identify with particular cultures or groups, and a s such, will express themselves uniquely. For example, it is helpful for an instructor to learn about Japanese culture, but is the student in class an international exchange student from Japan here in the U.S. for the first time? Or is she raised here in the United States but of

Japanese ethnicity? Perhaps she is binational Japanese and another nationality and has lived internationally? Or maybe to this student, the identifying factor you see may not be the one she identifies with most closely. Identity negotiation is a complex process; therefore, as facilitators we must be open to the multiple perspectives that exist in the intercultural classroom (Ting-Toomey, 2005). The best way to learn about your individual students is to communicate with them using some of the techniques outlined here.

Interculturally transformative facilitating helps instructors and students focus on how differences shape our interactions and to change our frames of reference and move towards new frames that are more self-reflective and inclusive (Mezirow, 1997). Creating opportunities for learners to engage in practices such as journaling, dialogue, and critical questioning are important to this critical reflective practice (Taylor, 2008), which leads to gradual transformation and improved competence for instructors and students.

We cannot learn the cultural characteristics of every group. And even if we could, we are dealing with people in our classrooms, not "group members." When we classify and think of people by their labels, intercultural transformation is not possible. Nor do we want to ignore differences, however so politely. Students know they are gay/deaf/biracial, and what they value, people talk about (Imbra, & Rallis, 2002). Acknowledging differences is important because that also acknowledges the individual and his or her unique characteristics, while at the same time developing understanding of all students as individuals helps us transcend the differences.

The way we use language also shapes perceptions. Note the terminology and construction in this chapter: *students who* are deaf; *students who* have learning disabilities, students who are of a particular religion. This adjectival format puts the person first, rather than identifying students by a condition or group affiliation, such as "deaf students" or "gay students" and so forth (American Psychological Association, 2010). Modeling this language in the classroom is subtle, yet important. It shows that we see students as individuals first, and the overlapping group identifications, while meaningful, as secondary to that.

CONCLUSION

Faculty have a key responsibility in both the explicit curriculum (what is taught), as well as the implicit curriculum (the educational environment where the explicit curriculum is delivered) (Grady, Powers, Despard, & Naylor, 2011). As practitioners of interculturally transformative teaching, we recognize this approach continues to develop in an ongoing process.

We will continue to have students in our classes that will challenge and stretch our boundaries; therefore, we need to be flexible and open to always learning more about our students and ourselves.

Ultimately, intercultural sensitivity is a result of developing cognitive complexity (Bennett, 1993). We can develop this complexity as we strive to treat our students as individuals with varying needs and identities, seek feedback individually and collectively on a regular basis, and continuously assess and reflect on our teaching practices. We need not worry that it is also an imperfect process because by modeling intercultural transformation, in its complexity and imperfection, we are teaching students "how to learn" about relating to other individuals and striving to create inclusive, welcoming 21st century classrooms.

REFERENCES

Allen, I. E., & Seaman, J. (2011). *Going the distance: Online education in the U.S. 2011* (Annual Report). Retrieved from http://sloanconsortium.org/publications/survey/going_distance_2011

American Psychological Association. (2010). *Publication manual of the American Psychological Association* (6th ed.). Washington DC: Author.

Bennett, M. J. (1993). Towards ethnorelativism: A developmental model of intercultural sensitivity. In R. M. Paige (Ed.), *Education for the intercultural experience* (2nd ed., pp. 21-71). Yarmouth, ME: Intercultural Press.

Bennett, M. J. (1998). Intercultural communication: A current perspective. In M. J. Bennett (Ed.), *Basic concepts of intercultural communication* (pp. 1-34). Yarmouth, ME: Intercultural Press.

Broadbent, D. E. (1987). Perception and communication. Oxford, England: Oxford University Press.

Cranton, J. (2002, Spring). Teaching for transformation. *New Directions for Adult & Continuing Education, 93*, 63-71.

Cranton, P., & Carusetta, E. (2004). Perspectives on authenticity. *Adult Education Quarterly, 55*(1), 5-23.

Gopal, A. (2011). Internationalization of higher education: Preparing faculty to teach cross-culturally. *International Journal of Teaching and Learning in Higher Education, 23*, 373-381. Retrieved from http://www.isetl.org/ijtlhe/

Grady, M. D., Powers, J., Despard, M., & Naylor, S. (2011, Fall). Measuring the implicit curriculum: Initial development and results of an MSW survey. *Journal of Social Work Education, 47*(3), 463-487.

Gurin, P. (n.d.). New research on the benefits of diversity in college and beyond: An empirical analysis. Retrieved from http://www.diversityweb.org/digest/sp99/benefits.html

Imbra, C., & Rallis, H. (2002). What we value, we talk about: Including lesbian, gay, bisexual and transgender people. In K. H. Gillespie, L. R. Hilsen, & E.

C. Wadsworth (Eds.), *A guide to faculty development: Practical advice, examples and resources* (pp. 227-249). San Francisco, CA: Anker.

Institute of Education Sciences. (2009). Projections of education statistics to 2018: Thirty seventh edition (NCES 2009-062). Washington, DC: U.S. Government Printing Office.

Kolb, D. A. (1984). *Experiential learning.* Englewood Cliffs, NJ: Prentice Hall.

Merisotis, J. P. (2011). House testimony on keeping college within reach: Discussing ways institutions can streamline costs and reduce tuition. Retrieved from http://www.luminafoundation.org/about_us/president/speeches/2011-11-30.html

Mezirow, J. (1996). Contemporary paradigms of learning. *Adult Education Quarterly, 46*(3), 158-172.

Mezirow, J. (1997, Summer). Transformative learning: Theory to practice. *New Directions for Adult and Continuing Education, 74,* 5-12. doi:10.1002/ace.7401

Munson, B. E. (2010). Teach them respect, not racism: Common themes and questions about the use of "Indian" logos. In C. R. King (Ed.), *The Native American mascot controversy: A handbook* (pp. 13-18). Lanham, MD: Scarecrow Press.

Nisbett, R. E. (2003). *The geography of thought: How Asians and Westerners think differently ... and why.* New York, NY: Free Press.

Paige, R. M. (1993). Trainer competencies for international and intercultural programs. In R. M. Paige (Ed.), *Education for the intercultural experience* (2nd ed., pp. 169-199). Yarmouth, ME: Intercultural Press.

Palloff, R. M., & Pratt, K. (1999). *Building learning communities in cyberspace: Effective strategies for the online classroom.* San Francisco, CA: Jossey-Bass.

Puhl, R., & Brownell, K. D. (2001). Bias, discrimination and obesity. *Obesity Research, 9*(12), 788-803.

Rosen, J., Spatz, E. S., Gaaserud, A. M., Abramovitch, H., Weinreb, B., Wenger, N. S., & Margolis, C. Z. (2004).A new approach to developing cross-cultural communication skills. *Medical Teacher, 26,* 126-132. doi:10.1080/01421590310001653946

Seelye, H. N. (1993). *Teaching culture: Strategies for intercultural communication* (3rd ed.). Chicago, IL: National Textbook Company.

Shibata, A. M. (2007). Exploring intercultural communication issues in online classes: Where theory and teaching meet. *Explorations in Media Ecology,* 139-148.

Stanley, C. A. (2002). Conceptualizing, designing, and implementing multicultural faculty development activities. In K. H. Gillespie, L. R. Hilsen, & E. C. Wadsworth (Eds.), *A guide to faculty development: Practical advice, examples and resources* (pp. 194-213). San Francisco, CA: Anker.

Sternberg, R. J. (1996). *Successful intelligence.* New York, NY: Simon & Schuster.

Sternberg, R. J. (1997). *Thinking styles.* New York, NY: Cambridge University Press.

Sweeney, G. (2001). The trashing of white trash: Natural born killers and the appropriation of the white trash aesthetic. *Quarterly Review of Film and Video, 18*(2), 143-155. doi:10.1080/10509200109361520

Taylor, E. W. (2007). An update of transformative learning theory: A critical review of empirical research (1999-2005). *International Journal of Lifelong Education, 26*, 173-191. doi:10.1080/02601370701219476

Taylor, E. W. (2008). Transformative learning theory. *New Directions for Adult and Continuing Education*, 5-15. doi:10.1002/ace.301

Taylor, M. A., Fischer, J. M., & Taylor, L. (2009). Factors relevant to the affective content in literature survey: Implications for designing an adult transformational learning curriculum. *Journal of Adult Education, 38*(2), 19-31.

The Higher Learning Commission (2011). *Criteria for accreditation.* Retrieved from http://www.ncahlc.org/Information-for-Institutions/ criteria-for-accreditation.html

Ting-Toomey, S. (2005). Identity negotiation theory: Crossing cultural boundaries. In W. B. Gudykunst, (Ed.), *Theorizing about intercultural communication* (pp. 211-256). Thousand Oaks, CA: SAGE.

Warren, L. (2002). Methods for addressing diversity in the classroom. In K. H. Gillespie, L. R. Hilsen, & E. C. Wadsworth, (Ed.), *A guide to faculty development: Practical advice, examples, and resources* (pp. 214-226). San Francisco, CA: Anker.

SECTION II

INTERCULTURALLY COMPETENT
CLASSROOM PRACTICES

CHAPTER 4

BUILDING AN ETHIC
OF COLLABORATION

Moral Development In and Out of
the Classroom

Catherine McCall Marsh

As this chapter is written, the stock market has had another volatile day and news commentators suggest that the United States may be in for the dreaded double dip recession. The United States Congress is firmly entrenched in partisan politics, and the good of the American people seems to have been long forgotten. The evening news features the plight of the starving Somalis, relocated to refugee camps, as the warring tribes within their own nation sabotage efforts to spread food, water, and medication to thousands of their fellow citizens. Margaret Wheatley's (2005) words strike a familiar chord. She states,

> We have a great need to remember the fact of human goodness. Today, human goodness seems like an outrageous "fact." Every moment we are confronted with mounting evidence of the great harm we so easily do to one another. We are bombarded with global images of genocide, dislocations caused by ethnic hatred, and stories of individual violence committed daily in communities around the world. The word evil comes easily to our lips to

Conversations About Adult Learning in Our Complex World, pp. 49–60
Copyright © 2013 by Information Age Publishing
All rights of reproduction in any form reserved.

explain these terrible behaviors. And in our day-to-day lives, we are directly confronted by people who are angry, deceitful and interested only in their own needs. In organizations and communities, we struggle to find ways to work together amidst so much anger, distrust and pettiness. (p. 55)

In the next paragraph however, Wheatley (2005) articulates hope for humanity and hope for the future, if we would but look around us at the behaviors of those who have not been defeated by despair. She proffers,

> I know that the only path to creating more harmonious and effective workplaces and communities is if we can turn to one another and depend on one another. We cannot cope, much less create, in this increasingly fast and turbulent world, without each other. We must search for human goodness.... We can do the impossible, learn and change quickly and extend instant compassion to those suffering from natural and political disasters. (p 55)

As Wheatley calls us to learn to depend upon one another's goodness, Robert Wright, in *The Moral Animal* (1994), suggests that there is scientific basis for Wheatley's plea. He purports that "altruism, compassion, love, conscience, the sense of justice—all of these things, the things that hold society together" (p. 12) have a firm genetic basis across humanity. He offers that today's Darwinian, not to be confused with Social Darwinian, anthropologists "focus less on surface differences among cultures than on deep unities" (p. 7). Taking poetic liberty, Wright describes that which binds the world's people together as the "dense and intricate web of human nature" (p. 8).

Steven Pinker (2011), although critical of Wright's tendency to assign a sacred order to the universe, suggests that that perhaps human history is evolving in a direction of moral truth. He meticulously documents the decline of violence and ascribes critical import to the unfolding of new patterns of human behavior. Supporting his case that the human condition has indeed improved, Pinker, much like Wright, underscores the accelerating growth of the web of human connection.

Although optimistic, a positive outcome is not guaranteed by Wheatley (2005), Wright (1994), or Pinker (2011). Pinker indicates that "motives such as greed, fear, dominance, and lust keep drawing us toward aggression" (p. 695). He continues by explaining that while ongoing aggression continues to bring us to the negotiation table, due to our human striving to perpetuate our species, negotiations often end in miscalibrated compromises that can in actuality perpetuate the cycles of feuding. Similarly, Wright warns that our moral sentiments may indeed have an adverse impact on the evolution of our species in that they can be "switched on and off in keeping with self interest; and how naturally oblivious we often are to this switching" (p. 13).

Martin Nowak and Roger Highfield, in *Super Cooperators* (2011) do not completely disagree, but they emphasize the view that our moral sentiments may well have evolved for the good of the species and that cooperation and survival go hand in hand. They insist that although the danger facing us is very real, that rapid advances in technology that link us together can work for us. Their plea is that we expedite our search for other novel ways to support our attempts to work in harmony.

This chapter is written as an appeal to adult educators to join in that search and participate in creative exploration of possibilities to enhance collaboration in and out of the classroom. The author investigates collaboration as an essential aspect of moral development and a critical ingredient on the adult education agenda. As our economic and political tensions appear to heighten our sense of competition over cooperation, the accelerated growth of the dense and intricate web of human connection (Nowak & Highfield, 2011; Pinker, 2011; Wright, 1994) may provide a bridge to an alternative reality.

PURPOSE STATEMENT AND RESEARCH QUESTION

This study seeks to understand the experiences of adult business and nonprofit management students who perceive themselves to have matured in their moral development as a result of participating in intensive collaborative experiences that were embedded in the curriculum of two courses in graduate program. Beginning with the desire to understand what had changed for these students, the research expanded its focus to include the extent to which group collaborative educational experiences are perceived to be beneficial to each student's development as an individual as well as a manager. This study is an early exploratory study that will eventually become a part of a larger case study. The following research question was formulated: How can collaborative decision-making experiences promote moral development?

THEORETICAL FRAMEWORK

Carol Gilligan's (1982) moral development framework on the Ethic of Care together with Alasdair MacIntyre's perspective on virtue ethics provide a strong theoretical support in investigating the supposition that the an ethic of collaboration may indeed be viable. To understand Gilligan, it may be necessary to first investigate the moral development theory developed by Lawrence Kohlberg (1973). Strongly influenced by the cognitive theories of Jean Piaget and John Dewey, Kohlberg proposed that children develop modes of moral reasoning through their experiences, and as they mature, they begin to understand complex moral concepts such as justice, rights, equality, and human welfare (Trevino & Nelson, 1999). Kohlberg, unlike previous cognitive theorists, posited that the attainment of moral maturity was a lengthy and gradual process that moved beyond childhood into adulthood. Kohlberg suggested that there is a universal good, and that if individuals were morally advanced, they would operate from that universal perspective–which Kohlberg associated with justice (Kohlberg, 1973).

Known for her disagreement with many aspects of Kohlberg's theory, Carol Gilligan, stresses that Kohlberg's psychological levels of moral development is biased in favor of the ethics of justice which excludes dimensions of "moral experience, such as contextual decision making, special obligations, the moral motives of compassion and sympathy, and the relevance of considering one's own integrity in making moral decisions" (Calhoun, 1988, p. 451). Gilligan indicates that morality is founded in a sense of concrete connection and direct response between persons, a direct sense of connection which exists prior to moral beliefs about what is right or wrong or which principles to accept. Moral action is meant to express and sustain those connections to particular other people through an ongoing openness to dialogue and learning what it means to care for one another (Gilligan, 1982). While Kohlberg's theory pointed to a linear hierarchical progression or morality, Gilligan's views support a nonlinear organic web of connections that bind us together as we grow in our relationships.

Closely aligned with Carol Gilligan's view of moral development is Alasdair MacIntyre's (1984) perspective on virtue ethics. MacIntyre asserts that current ethical theory and practice are in a state of grave disorder brought on by the liberal individualism of the Enlightenment. A critical tenet offered by MacIntyre's theory is that we discover our virtuous character only in acting it out in relationship within community—it is only through our association with virtue that we can become virtuous. Hence, moral education and development is at the heart of ethics. This is a strong point of congruency between MacIntyre's approach to virtue ethics and Gilligan's perspective on moral development. MacIntyre (1999) states,

> To participate in this network of relationships of giving and receiving as the virtues require, I have to understand that what I am called upon to give may be quite disproportionate to what I have received and that those to whom I am called upon to give may well be those from whom I shall receive nothing. And I also have to understand that the care I give to others has to be in an important way unconditional, since the measure of what is required of me is determined in key part, even if not only, by their needs. (p. 108)

Gilligan and MacIntyre both emphasize the web of relationship and the intricate ties that bind us together in community as that which freights the good or ethical behavior. Perhaps structured collaborative activities used in the classroom can not only add to the skill set of adult business and nonprofit management students but can also serve to strengthen the relational web that enhances the vision of thriving in community rather than competing for individual success.

METHODOLOGY

The methodology of this research is the case study, involving an examination of students who participated in a common management curriculum. For this qualitative study, the researcher avoided beginning the study with a hypothesis or structured interview questions. This is what Yin (1994) considers an exploratory case study, where the data is collected prior to the definition of the research questions and hypotheses. Qualitative research is inductive, with the study structuring the research, rather than preconceived ideas or a specific research design (Bogdan & Bilken, 2006).

The case study is a thorough description and analysis of a phenomenon or social unit, seeking to describe the situation in depth (Merriam & Associates, 2002). The goal of learning in a specific case study is to strive to understand a particular situation bounded by time and activity, rather than seek to apply the learning to other contexts; indeed the value of the case is its context (Stake, 1995). A case study investigates contemporary phenomenon within its real-life context, especially when the boundaries between phenomenon and context are not clearly evident. While an experiment intentionally separates a phenomenon from its context, the case study method would be used when the researcher believes that contextual conditions might be highly relevant to the phenomenon of the study (Yin, 1994).

The contextual conditions relevant to this case are the intensive collaborative nature of the curriculum of two courses in a graduate business curriculum and the desire of a number of former students to share their stories and encourage the growth of collaborative learning across business school curricula. The social unit under examination in this case study consists of adult students who completed the team building and or the negotiations courses in the graduate business and nonprofit management curriculum at a small private Midwestern liberal arts university located in an exceptionally diverse urban area during the 2010-11 academic year. The instruction in both courses was conducted primarily through experiential group activities followed by extensive reflection, with minimal lecture and presentation by the course facilitator.

Open-ended questions were asked of 15 students over a 1 month period. Participants were nominated based on their self identified interest in participating in the study and to represent demographic (age, race, gender) diversity of the student population. The selection was based on purposeful sampling (Maxwell, 1996). Purposeful sampling is a deliberate sampling technique that chooses participants based on the belief that the person is capable of supplying important information. Further, the nomination technique of purposeful sampling (Goetz & LeCompte, 1984) provides access to individuals who have expertise in the area being studied. Approval was received from the university's institutional review board and the participants gave consent to have their interview data used in the study. Data was collected and the constant comparison technique (Bogdan & Biklen, 2006) of qualitative data analysis was performed until themes emerged that could be developed into a framework for transferring the responses into case study format. To prevent conflict of interest, the students had all completed all course work with the instructor who conducted the research.

FINDINGS

Four themes arose from the data collected. As a result of the intensive course work participants perceived that: (1) the individual's need to compete can get in the way of collaborative efforts; (2) the development of trust allowed them to reduce competitive behavior and fostered the desire to work collaboratively (3) relationship outcomes became equal in importance to task outcomes; and (3) their worldview had shifted; transformative learning occurred.

Competition Can Block Collaborative Efforts

Twelve of the 15 students expressed that their cultural upbringing and their work and academic environments rewarded competition. A young Caucasian female student studying for a master's in nonprofit administration stated,

> I strive to work as a team at work and in school, but I'm paid as an individual and my performance appraisal, which is linked directly to my pay increase, is based on what I do—not what my team has accomplished. I try to step back and let my team take control, but in worrying about my raise at work, and my final grade at school, I am tempted to step in and take control because the team outcome could detract from my individual success.

A middle aged Black male student studying for an MBA shared, "To trust in my team I must allow myself to become vulnerable and let go of control; that conflicts with the image I have tried to maintain of being confident and in charge." A young Hispanic male student pursing a masters degree in nonprofit administration admitted, "At work I'm expected to collaborate as a member of a team, but in my culture a man can appear weak if he allows women to control outcomes." Similar statements from many of the other students underscore the cultural and structural forces at play that can complicate, and possible defeat, collaborative efforts.

Successful Collaboration is Built on Trust

All but one of the study participants mentioned that the development of trust was essential if collaborative efforts were to succeed. Tied closely to the comments about the benefits of competitive behavior were statements about the necessity of trust. The middle aged Black male business student, mentioned above, stressed the benefit of allowing himself to become vulnerable. He admitted,

> When working with the other people in my group I had to humble myself and admit that I didn't have all the answers, and in some instances I didn't even know the questions, and that I was relying on them for insight on how to handle a given situation. I found out that when I allowed myself to become vulnerable, I started to learn more. I grew. And I accomplished more.

A middle aged Black female student, taking business courses to satisfy leadership requirements for the master's of nursing degree, shared her experience. She disclosed,

> I know I had matured when I trusted someone else enough to let them put together the group paper or the group's slides. I didn't have to do it myself. I could contribute, but I didn't have to dominate. I didn't have to make it happen. I participated in making it happen but I was not alone. I didn't have to be in control. What a relief. What a release.

A number of the students added that while trust was critical, it took time to build trust, and that some team members might need more time than others, dependent upon personality and past experience. Nonetheless, for collaborative efforts to succeed, it was agreed that slowing down and focusing on the relationship, as well as the task, was essential.

Relationship Is As Important as Task

Each of the study participants emphasized the importance of relationship building when working collaboratively. A young eastern European female business student working on an MBA emphasized,

> We had to take time to get to know one another as people. We had to appreciate one another as individuals before we could trust one another to accomplish a task. When the task was done, I did not want the team to disband. The relationships had become as important as our task.

A middle aged Caucasian female nonprofit student shared, "Each team I worked with offered me new potential to learn and grow from the differences of their diverse mixtures. In my team development process, I experienced the formation of a mutual support system." She continued, "Throughout the process, I witnessed complete strangers evolve from focusing on the me and I to the we and us. Individuals bonded together and started to care emotionally about each other." She compared team membership with motherhood, "It was similar to the natural phenomenon of a mother protecting her babies. The longer the team worked together the more natural the bond became." A young Hispanic male student working toward an MBA observed,

> If I know I can't do it alone, I make myself work with others. The bigger the task, the more important the relationships, and the more work has to go into building those relationships, and that takes time. We had to get along. We had to appreciate each member's contribution if we were going to help each other get the job done. In the end, while the good job was the expected reward, the new relationships were the unexpected reward.

There appeared to be mutual agreement among all the study participants that tasks requiring collaboration demanded enhanced relationships. They believed that relationship could not be assumed and that time had to be spent on building and nurturing those relationships. It was also agreed that strengthened relationships added to the satisfaction of task completion.

Worldview Shifted

Seven of the 15 study participants made remarks that indicated that, in some way, their learning had shifted their view and approach to work and life; transformational learning had occurred. Baumgartner (2001) indicates that "transformational learning is not an independent act but is an interdependent relationship built on trust" (p. 19). With the construction of relationships built on trust, the study participants allowed themselves to advance developmentally by moving toward greater meaning perspectives (Mezirow, 1991). A young Hispanic male working toward an MBA indicated that he had never before experienced the rewards of service.

> I'm no longer just concerned about my work and my family. I want to find ways to be of service—to connect with others—to open myself to participate with others in helping build my community. I know I won't, and can't do it alone, but I found out that I can make a difference when I work with others.

A middle-aged Caucasian studying for a masters in nonprofit administration divulged, "My moral development was sharpened because I no longer saw black and white. She specified, "In fighting with others for workable solutions, instead of fighting against others to win, I began to see all the shades of gray." In conclusion, she emphasized, "I realized that notions of right and wrong were irrelevant to our common future." An older Caucasian female studying for a degree in nonprofit administration indicated, "I learned the power of a collaborative effort and it changed my life. I quit trying to change the world myself." She continued, "My view of the world changed because I learned that small groups of people could have a huge impact."

In summary, the data suggests that collaborative decision-making experiences, although challenging due to societal and cultural expectations of individual success, can result in enhanced trust, stronger relationships, and a shift of mindset that encompasses a wider range of views and possibilities than previously considered. In alignment with Gilligan's theory on moral develop and MacIntyre's view on ethics, the growth and strengthening of the web of relationship opened the students to an expanded understanding of self in relationship to others and greater opportunities to both give and receive from those who are located within the widening circumference of the web. If moral development can be equated to the expansion of the web and the development of reciprocal caring relationships across the web, exercises in collaborative decision-making may be seen to enhance moral development.

CONCLUSION

Organizational theorists project the possibility for a more collaborative future. Hatcher (2002) explains that today's complex problems, arising from our diverse and complicated world, are forcing us to examine alternatives that will require us to connect to and rely upon one another. Wheatley (2005) emphasizes the importance of interconnections. She stresses, "Our safety and future depend on each of us stepping outside the lines and participating intelligently in this complex world of interconnections" (p. 206). Echoing Wheatley, O'Brien (2008) indicate that while the individual's relentless desire for happiness remains intact, and that the fulfillment of potential is core to that search, potential cannot be achieved in isolation but only in conjunction with others.

In apparent support of the suppositions of Hatcher (2002), Wheatley (2005), and O'Brien (2008), Sowa (2009) reports that nonprofit collaborative service delivery ventures are increasing across the human services and other policy fields. She indicates that in the nonprofit arena, oftentimes there is no choice but to collaborate; collaboration may be the only means to survival. In fact, collaborative service delivery ventures are increasing across the human services and other policy fields and collaboration could be perceived as a rising trend. Warm (2011) writes about collaborative efforts in local government indicating that such efforts are an, "increasingly pervasive approach to addressing community challenges. It has evolved from interlocal, bilateral and targeted cooperative arrangements to include complex relationships involving multiple partners and various sectors focused on achieving long-term outcomes" (p. 60).

The findings of a qualitative study, such as this one, are descriptive, not prescriptive. The findings do not indicate what should be true, rather, they describe what is true for the participants engaged in the study (Tsang, 1997). The intent of this study was not external generalizablity, rather it was an attempt to understand a particular phenomenon, through the use of case study (Stake, 1995), within a particular, internally generalizable, context (Maxwell, 2002). It should not be construed, however, that the findings are not meaningful. The findings lay a foundation for future experimentation with intensive experiential collaborative learning activities and continued research on transformational learning and moral development.

This research project has highlighted recent research on collaboration in light of moral development theory, heard from students who believed themselves to have grown through collaborative experiences, and highlighted trends in business and nonprofit management. In conclusion, the words of Dr. Martin Luther King, Jr., in his 1963 letter from the Birmingham jail, provide a context for moral development through the building of an ethic of collaboration:

> All men are caught in an inescapable network of mutuality, tied in a single garment of destiny. Whatever affects one directly affects all indirectly. I can never be what I ought to be until you are what you ought to be, and you can never be what you ought to be until I am what I ought to be. (King, 1963)

As adult educators, let us work together to bring to light the inescapable network and assist with a mutual becoming.

REFERENCES

Baumgartner, L. M. (2001). An update on transformational learning. *New Directions for Adult and Continuing Education, 89,* 15-24. doi:10.1002/ace.4

Bogdan, R. C., & Biklen S. K. (2006). *Qualitative research in education: An introduction to theory and methods* (5th ed.). Boston, MA: Allyn & Bacon.

Calhoun, C. (1988). Justice, care, gender bias. *The Journal of Philosophy, 85*(9), 451-463.

Gilligan, C. (1982). *In a different voice.* Cambridge, MA: Harvard University Press.

Goetz, J. P., & LeCompte, M. D. (1984). *Ethnography and qualitative design in educational research.* New York, NY: Harcourt Brace Jovanovich.

Hatcher, T. (2002). *Ethics and HRD: A new approach to leading responsible organizations.* Boulder, CO: Perseus.

King, M. L (1963). *Letter from a Birmingham jail.* Atlanta, GA: Estate of Martin Luther King, Jr.

Kohlberg, L. (1973). The claim to moral adequacy of a highest stage of moral judgment. *The Journal of Philosophy, 70*(18), 630-646.

MacIntyre, A. (1984). *After virtue* (2nd ed.). Notre Dame, IN: University of Notre Dame Press.

MacIntyre, A. (1999). Establishing a tradition of practical rationality. In K. Knight (Ed.), *The MacIntyre reader* (pp. 105-155). Notre Dame, IN: University of Notre Dame Press.

Maxwell, J. A. (1996). *Qualitative research design: An interactive approach.* Thousand Oaks, CA: SAGE.

Maxwell, J.A. (2002). Understanding and validity in qualitative research. In A. M. Huberman & M. B. Miles (Eds.), *The qualitative researcher's companion* (pp. 37-64), Thousand Oaks, CA: SAGE.

Merriam, S.B. & Associates (2002). *Qualitative research in practice: Examples for discussion and analysis.* San Francisco, CA: Jossey-Bass.

Mezirow, J. (1991). *Transformative dimensions of adult learning.* San Francisco, CA: Jossey-Bass.

Nowak, M., & Highfield, R. (2011). *SuperCooperators: Altruism, evolution and why we need each other to succeed.* New York, NY: Free Press.

O'Brien, W. J. (2008). *Building character at work: Building prosperity through the practice of virtue.* Mahwah, NJ: Paulist Press.

Pinker, S. (2011). *The better angels of our nature: Why violence has declined.* New York, NY: Viking Press.

Stake, R. E. (1995). *The art of case study research.* Thousand Oaks, CA: SAGE.

Sowa, J.E. (2009). The collaborative decision in nonprofit organizations: Views from the front lines. *Nonprofit and Voluntary Sector Quarterly, 38*(6), 1003-1025.

Trevino, L. K, & Nelson, K. A. (1999). *Managing business ethics: Straight talk about how to do it right* (2nd ed.). New York, NY: John Wiley.

Tsang, E. W. K. (1997). Organizational learning and learning organization: A dichotomy between descriptive and prescriptive research. *Human Relations, 50*(1), 73-89.

Warm, D. (2011). Local government collaboration for a new decade: Risk, trust and effectiveness. *State and Local Government Review, 43*(60), 60-65.

Wheatley, M. (2005). *Finding our way: Leadership for an uncertain time.* San Francisco, CA: Berrett-Koehler.

Wright, R. (1994). *The moral animal: Why we are the way we are.* New York, NY: Random House.

Yin, R. K. (1994). *Case study research designs and methods* (2nd ed.). Thousand Oaks, CA: SAGE.

CHAPTER 5

THE LEARNING ENVIRONMENT PREFERENCE INVENTORY

Measuring Pedagogy, Mesagogy, and Andragogy in a Community College Setting

**Jonathan E. Taylor, Joseph H. Reynolds,
David E. Laton, and Ted N. David**

A great deal of attention has been given to the work of Malcolm Knowles (1970, 1980, 1984). Whether positive regard (Brockett, 1983; Pratt, 1993; St. Clair, 2002) or leveled criticism (Alfred, 2000; Brookfield, 1986; Davenport & Davenport, 1985; Elias, 1979), there is an undeniable Knowlesian heritage in the field of adult education. Knowles' ideas of andragogy were met with great interest at the time of their unveiling (Brookfield, 1986), but based on contemporary scholarship in the field, have been discounted and perhaps even ignored in the years since. His ideas served as the impetus of great passion and excitement, but as the field has matured, his work has become less salient. As Knowles' ideas developed in his later work, he reframed the overly simplistic idea that children are collectively characterized by a specific set of learning principles (pedagogy), while adults, across-the-board, were characterized by another (andragogy). He acknowledged that while the spectrum was related to learner maturity, it

Conversations About Adult Learning in Our Complex World, pp. 61–76
Copyright © 2013 by Information Age Publishing

was not solely determined by one's status as a child or an adult (Knowles, 1980; Knowles, Holton, & Swanson, 2005). Beyond this, Knowles indicated that there might be a number of contextual factors that could influence where one fell on that pedagogy—andragogy spectrum.

These theoretical adjustments may have led to a strengthened theory but did not stanch the loss of energy surrounding Knowlesian thought. There are probably many reasons for this, and a full discussion of them is outside the scope of this chapter; however, one possible reason for the loss of status is the increased focus, over the past several decades, on research-based literature in the field. One of the larger criticisms lodged against Knowles' ideas of andragogy, has been the dearth of empirical evidence available to support it (Jarvis, 1984; Merriam, Caffarella, & Baumgartner, 2007; Rachal, 2002). It may be that the very quality that caused the andragogical principles to be an overnight sensation—the anecdotal nature and face-value validity—is also the quality that led to their marginalization in the field over time.

One very noteworthy exception, in terms of research, is self-directed learning. While not the primary foci, Knowles is an important seminal figure in self-directed learning scholarship. There have been numerous successful efforts to measure learner self-direction, with three of the most widely used inventories being the Oddi Continuing Learning Inventory (OCLI) (Oddi, 1986; Oddi, Ellis, & Roberson, 1990), the Self-Directed Learning Readiness Scale (SDLRS) (Guglielmino, 1977), and the Personal Responsibility Orientation Self-Direction in Learning Scale (PRO-SDLS) (Stockdale & Brockett, 2011).

It is important to note, however, that learner self-direction is only one of the six principles of adult learning that Knowles proposed (Knowles et al., 2005). When looking at the andragogical principles as a whole, there is relatively little empirical work to be found (Merriam et al., 2007). Measurement is a chief culprit in this gap because in order to find evidence of just how much of any given principle can be observed in a given adult learner, one must be able to accurately measure that construct.

Knowles himself developed an instrument for measuring andragogical principles but constructed it in such a way that it would measure the teacher's view on these principles rather than the students' (Knowles et al., 2005). Hadley (1975), similarly examined pedagogy and andragogy from the perspective of the teacher, and Christian (1982) modified Hadley's inventory into a measure of student perspective, using it to look at military and civilian personnel. Also, using Christian's SOQ, Davenport and Davenport (1984) examined personal and contextual variables among university students. Henschke (1989) developed the Instructional Perspectives Inventory (IPI), which also focused on an educational perspective. None of the inventories appears to have been widely used, and taken together represent, in terms of volume, a somewhat limited amount of empirical work (Merriam et al., 2007) over a 40 period.

PURPOSE

In this chapter, we describe the development and testing of an inventory that measures Knowles' ideas of pedagogical and andragogical learning structure preferences, and all the space between those two polar, hypothetical constructs. There has been some debate about whether the relationship between pedagogy and andragogy is linear (and dichotomous). Delahaye, Limerick, and Hearn (1994) proposed that the relationship between pedagogy and andragogy was less linear and more orthogonal. As such, they proposed that one could be both pedagogical and andragogical. While this work was conducted, at least in part, in answer to some of the contentions that the proposed linear relationship (continuum) was overly simplistic (Cross, 1981), it is our view that, practically speaking, the orthogonal and linear views represent the same dynamic. We will discuss this at length when we address our theoretical framework.

Much less emphasis is given to Knowles' ideas in contemporary scholarship in the field, but the implications of his work can still be observed in many, if not most classroom contexts. Merriam et al., (2007) claim that practitioners continue to use Knowles' andragogy to understand learners, and in our experience many practitioners do one of three things with regards to Knowles' assertions. Practitioners either (a) operate as if all, or even most, adults are fully andragogical, (b) operate as if all learners are pedagogical, or (c) operate as though everyone is somewhere in that range. This, of course, is not to say that everyone explicitly subscribes to these views, but that in practice, practitioners approach the learning situation as if one of these three were the case. Of these three possibilities, the third—everyone on the continuum—is the safest but also possibly the least useful. It permits the teacher to embrace academic moderation and avoids some of the sticky contentions of Knowles' ideas, but it also stops short of offering any specific course of action in the classroom.

Our purpose in the development of the Learning Environment Preference Inventory (LEPI) was threefold. First, we hoped to add to the literature by providing additional empirical evidence regarding the six andragogical assumptions (Knowles, 1980; Knowles, Holton, & Swanson, 2005). Also, by using a bipolar format, the constructs of pedagogy, mesagogy, and andragogy could be measured simultaneously. This is also a noticeable distinction from the other existing measures. Second, we hoped to indicate empirically that there was, indeed, a substantial group residing in the middle of the continuum, referred to as *Mesagogy* by Reynolds, Laton, Davis, and Stringer (2009). Our third objective, and perhaps the most far-reaching, was to provide an accurate measure of Knowles' ideas of pedagogy, andragogy, and Reynolds' et al. conception of mesagogy, so that meaningful research could be conducted and data could be collected to provide information about learning preferences and the interaction of contextual layers with those preferences. Do learners automatically become more independent, self-directed, and intrinsically motivated in a linear fashion as they mature? Do learners tend toward more tightly structured, teacher-controlled environments (move toward pedagogy) when facing a difficult subject? Does one's gender, occupation, and social status affect one's preferences? With the exception of one of the six andgragogical assumptions (self-directedness), there is a distinct gap in the literature in terms of empirically supported answers to these questions. Most simply put, this study is an inaugural effort to devise a reliable, valid instrument to measure students' pedagogical, mesagogical, or andragogical proclivities. It is our hope that through these efforts, we may be able to provide new tools to further and more fully utilize extant theory to address the complexities of our present time.

THEORETICAL FRAMEWORK

Pedagogy and Andragogy

The studies described in this chapter and the newly constructed inventory which served as the focus of the studies, are based upon two related lines of thought. Knowles' (1984) expanded list of six principles of adult learning provides the outer limits of the continuum used for the design of the LEPI. One could certainly call into question the terminology used (i.e., pedagogy and andragogy) as being somewhat vague and unspecified, but we are using Knowles' original terms for the sake of clarity. When we use the word pedagogy, we are referring to Knowles' ideas of child learners, or, in the very least, less mature learners. Likewise, we are using the term andragogy in the sense that Knowles meant it in his original work. A list of Knowles's six assumptions of the adult learner is provided below:

1. Adults need to know why they need to learn something.
2. Adults have a need to be self-directed; to be responsible for their own learning.
3. Adult enter a learning situation with a unique set of experiences that are rich sources for learning.

4. Adults become ready to learn things that they need to know for their real-life situations.

5. Adults are life-centered, rather than content or subject-centered.

6. Adults are more driven by internal motivation than external factors. (paraphrased from Knowles et al., 2005, pp. 64-68)

As previously mentioned, Delahaye et al. (1994) contested the linear nature of the pedagogy/andragogy relationship, instead suggesting it is a more complex, orthogonal relationship, permitting a learner to be both andragogical and pedagogical. They made a sound mathematical case, and we do not disagree, in a technical sense. However, one of the primary benefits of their proposal seems to be to enable a learner to be both pedagogical and andragogical at the same time. They identify four categories of learner preferences, the third being "High Andragogical/High Pedagogical" (p. 195). They described this as a stage in which the learner is beginning to rebel against the pedagogical model but is still fearful of adopting the andragogical model and all the freedom and ambiguity that it can bring to the learning situation. This is similar, in many ways, to the construct of *mesagogy* that we propose in this chapter.

The idea that there may be elements of both pedagogy and andragogy, even in large volume, in a learner simultaneously is, in our view, much like identifying (accurately enough) that one can have hot water and cold water in the same container simultaneously. However, when purely hot water is mixed with purely cold water, the result is warm water. While the term *warm* might be an oversimplification, since it is really a mix of hot and cold, it is, nonetheless, a very practical term and lends itself readily to many applications. In other words, to step away from the metaphor, if one has a large degree of pedagogical preference at the same time as a large degree of andragogical preference, it may be that the mixture ends up being, in terms of practice, almost the same as a learner existing roughly in the middle of the continuum between pedagogy and andragogy. One of the purposes of models is to provide a simplified explanation (for a simplified understanding) of a complex reality. So long as one accepts the limitations of that simplification, it may be more efficient and practicable to utilize the simplification. It is for these reasons that we have chosen to base our inventory on the more traditional continuum.

Mesagogy

At some interval in many students' lives, there is an unhurried yet discernible transition where they mature as learners and embark on more rewarding, personally gratifying academic pursuits. This transition stage has been identified by Reynolds, Laton, Davis, and Stringer (2009) as *mesagogy* to parallel Malcolm Knowles' work where pedagogy and andragogy are juxtaposed through various learning assumptions. Conceptually, mesagogy is suggested as a component of a Teaching-learning continuum depicted in Figure 5.1, which illustrates learner maturation, regardless of age, and the role teachers assume in that process. For a detailed discussion on the implications of mesagogy for practice, see Reynolds, Taylor, Laton, and Davis (2013).

We propose that the continuum harmonizes various ideas regarding learning maturation, that it provides a macrolevel understanding of the teaching-learning transaction, and that it assists both teacher and learners in understanding their various roles in the transaction (see Reynolds et al., 2009). Though it appears in Figure 5.1, the heutagogic component was not considered in this study. For a description of heutagogy, see Hase and Kenyon (2000).

When these conceptions are overlaid, a fluid and logical spectrum presents itself. This continuum, ranging from pedagogical, to mesagogical, to andragogical, serves as the frame for the inventory designed in this study. Taking into account Delahaye et al.'s (1994) third category, in which learners embrace both pedagogy and andragogy, the mesagogy construct pro-

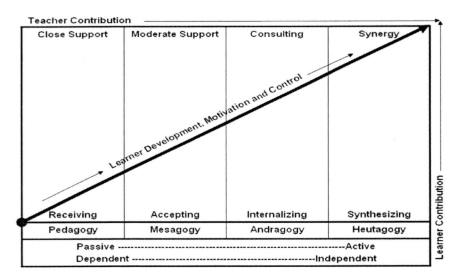

Figure 5.1.   The teaching-learning continuum.

vides a similar demarcation but is more easily understood and more practically employed by both teachers and learners in a learning situation.

METHOD

For our studies, we used a survey design, attempting to construct an inventory with sound psychometric properties. We chose this method because of our desire to measure large numbers of participant learners using a standardized inventory. We named the inventory the LEPI due to its purpose of measuring, at least broadly, the learning structure preferences individual learners have within a specific learning context. It is designed with a bipolar format (i.e., Likert scale rests between two contrasting statements), and consists, in its present form, of 12 items, but is being tested with a larger number with the aim to include 20-25 items. During the design, construction, and validation and reliability testing of this inventory (LEPI), we collected and analyzed two rounds of data and revised the instrument accordingly along the way.

Population and Sample

The population for both studies was beginning students in various programs of the 2-year colleges within the Alabama community college system (ACCS). Participants ranged from traditional freshman college students just completing secondary education to more mature students. The average age of students in the ACCS is 27. Students were a mix of male and female with a slightly higher female population. Students were from a variety of disciplines offered at the college. Demographic information is addressed in the results section and presented in Tables 5.1 and 5.2. The sample sizes for the two studies were, 142 and 136, respectively. While the actual number of scores utilized for various statistical tests varied according to what data were missing from individual inventories, even the lowest number (e.g., 73 in Study # 1 to determine learning structure preference) was in keeping with Nunnally's (1967) standard of at least a five to one ratio of participants to number of items in a scale.

Ethical Considerations

All research complied with the institutional review boards for both the researcher's university and the ACCS. All participants completed the inventory voluntarily and were clearly informed of their right to abstain both verbally and in the form of an attached information/informed consent sheet indicating that completing the inventory was an expression of their consent to participate. Participants did not put names on the inventories and were provided contact information for the researchers in the event that there were concerns that needed to be addressed.

Instrument Development

The basis for instrument development were Knowles' six pedagogical and andragogical assumptions (Knowles et al., 2005), and subsequent adaptation of these assumptions into the mesagogical domains. The theory of a construct guide the creation of individual items within the scales, and clearly specifying a construct leads to the creation of stronger items (Lounsbury, Gibson, & Saugardas, 2006). Using the theoretical frameworks already provided in this chapter, we developed clear item construct specifications (i.e., definitions, relevant domains, operationalized behaviors) to guide the constructions of individual scale items.

Because the construct of mesagogy, as presented here, exists somewhere in the range between pedagogy and andragogy, any attempts to measure it make it necessary to measure both pedagogy and andragogy simultaneously. That is to say, the existence of mesagogy is represented by participants' indicating somewhere in the middle of the continuum. To address the problem of the midpoint in unidimensional scales noted by Kaplan (1972), and following a format used by other researchers (e.g., Lounsbury, Loveland, Sundstrom, Gibson, Drost, & Hamrick, 2003), we employed a bipolar format for our response scales.

We chose a bipolar scale with each item's extremes representing purely pedagogical or purely andragogical learning preferences. Instrument design centered on the idea that there would be three learning preference inclinations: pedagogical and andragogical, represented by the polar ends of the scale, and mesagogical, represented by the midpoint between these two polar constructs. Logic based on the theory was used to divide scores into thirds. The lowest third represented pedagogical preferences, the middle third represented mesagogical preferences, and the highest third represented andragogical preferences. The initial instrument was composed of 37 items.

Reliability and Validity

Validity and reliability were addressed across two studies. Reliability was addressed through internal-consistency coefficients (Cronbach's alpha).

Both content validity and known-group validity were addressed in this study. Validity will be further addressed in the subsequent sections.

Content validity. Before the pilot, we sent an initial draft of the instrument to three subject-matter experts for review. Each of the three reviewers returned the draft with ample feedback, and with a few justifiable exceptions, we took expert advice and items were adjusted to accommodate recommendations. This feedback was related primarily to the specific wording of items, and suggested minor changes to avoid potential response bias, reduce ambiguity, and improve logical clarity.

Known-group validity. The PRO-SDLS (Stockdale & Brockett, 2011) was embedded in the instrument for the second study for the purpose of establishing known-group validity. The PRO-SDLS measures levels of learner self-directedness, and theory would reasonably suggest that there would be a significant positive correlation between self-directedness and preferences for loosely structured (andragogical) learning environments. The PRO-SDLS has 25 items and a reported reliability coefficient of $\alpha = .92$.

Study # 1 (Pilot). After subject matter expert review, the improved instrument consisted of 30 items and was prepared for administration at a 2-year college within the ACCS. The sample was one of convenience, but it was also chosen because the original concept of mesagogy was born, in part, out of experience within the 2-year college system (ACCS). Convenience samples are commonly used in educational research and acceptable in the face of the difficulties of obtaining large enough randomized samples (Gall, Gall, & Borg, 2003). The sample consisted of students just entering the college setting who were required to take the institution's orientation class. The selected college was a technical rather than a community college, and the primary difference between the two is that the required academic credentials of technical college faculty are lower. Because faculty was not involved in this study and students were surveyed early in their program, it was felt that this would have no major bearing on the study. Faculty influence over students is minimal at this point; further, faculty did not preview the survey.

One hundred forty-two students in 10 classes participated and were told "As you take this survey, please think back to a formal learning experience (high school or college) during which you felt the most comfortable or which you felt was the best fit for you." We designed this statement to establish a consistent context among all participants. There was no time limit for instrument completion, and after initial instructions, participants were directed to complete a short demographics portion before completing the items. Completion times ranged from 10 to 20 minutes.

Study # 2 (Validation). After the first study, the instrument was refined to 20 items. In addition, to address known-group validity, the 25 item PRO-SDLS (Stockdale & Brockett, 2011) was included.

The improved 20 item instrument and PRO-SDLS were administered within the same context as the first pilot study. The sample consisted of students just entering the college setting who were required to take the institution's orientation class. One hundred and thirty-six students in twelve different classes participated.

RESULTS

Results from both the pilot and validation studies are provided in this section.

Study # 1 (Reliability Pilot)

In the first study, 141 participants completed the instrument. Of those, 39 were removed from the data because they were completed incorrectly (i.e., not filled out all the way, multiple boxes checked for individual items). Demographics are included for the full 141 but subsequent statistical analysis included anywhere from 73 to 102, depending on what data was missing from the individual inventories (e.g., reliability analysis utilized 102, while the total scores listed to determine whether the learner was pedagogical, mesagogical, or andragogical utilized only 73). As previously noted, using even the smallest number (73), the sample size for this reliability study was sufficient (Nunnally, 1967).

Demographics. Demographics for the first study are displayed in Table 5.1.

Descriptive statistics and reliability. After conducting item analysis and deleting items with a corrected item-total correlation below .3, the scale had 14 items. For the 14 item scale, the mean was 59.74 (SD = 11.81). Scores of 54 and 68 were the first and third quartiles, respectively. Reliability for the scale was $\alpha = .783$.

Measures of pedagogy, mesagogy, and andragogy. In study # 1, 4 participants fell within the pedagogical category (14-37), 32 fell within the mesagogical category (38-61), and 37 fell within the andragogical category (62-85). Those in the mesagogy category represented roughly 44% of the scores utilized.

Table 5.1.   Study # 1 Demographics

Demographic	Number of Participants	Percentage of Sample
Gender		
Female	81	57%
Male	58	41%
Not Specified	2	2%
Age		
<18	1	<1%
18-21	62	44%
22-30	21	15%
31-39	23	16%
>40	34	24%
Race/Ethnicity		
White	59	42%
African American	75	53%
Asian	1	<1%
Native American	1	<1%
Not Specified	5	3%
GPA		
<1.5	0	–
1.5-2.49	10	7%
2.5-3.49	29	20%
3.5-4.0	49	35%
Not Specified	53	38%

Study # 2 (Validation)

In the second study, 136 participants completed the instrument. Of those, 14 were removed from the data because they were completed incorrectly (i.e., not filled out all the way, multiple boxes checked for individual items). Demographics are included for the full 136 but subsequent statistical analysis included 121.

Demographics. Demographics of study # 2 are displayed in Table 5.2.

Descriptive statistics and reliability. After conducting item analysis and deleting items with a corrected item-total correlation below .3, the scale had 12 items. For the 12 item scale, the mean was 56.04 (SD = 8.78). Scores of 50 and 63 were the first and third quartiles, respectively. Reliability for the scale was $\alpha = .782$.

Measures of pedagogy, mesagogy, and andragogy. In study # 2, 2 participants fell within the pedagogical category (12-31), 30 fell within

Table 5.2.   Study #2 Demographics

Demographic	Number of Participants	Percentage of Sample
Gender		
Female	94	69%
Male	39	29%
Not Specified	3	2%
Age		
<18	0	-
18-21	68	50%
22-30	38	28%
31-39	14	10%
>40	14	10%
Not Specified	2	1%
Race/Ethnicity		
White	33	24%
African American	94	69%
Asian	1	<1%
Native American	2	1%
Not Specified	6	4%
GPA		
Unknown	31	23%
<1.5	0	–
1.5-2.49	21	15%
2.5-3.49	58	43%
3.5-4.0	26	19%

the mesagogical category (35-51) , and 89 fell within the andragogical category (52-72). Those in the mesagogical category represented roughly 25% of the participants.

Validity. To establish known-group validity, a valid and reliable measure of learner self-direction was included in the second round of data collection. The PRO-SDLS (Stockdale & and Brockett, 2011) was included because of the strong emphasis on learner self-directedness in Knowles' adult learning principles.

We hypothesized that there would be a strong positive correlation between the andragogy end of our scale (high scores), and measures of learner self-direction as indicated by the PRO-SDLS. In Study # 2, the PRO-SDLS was administered along with our scale and there was a statistically significant positive correlation as hypothesized ($r = .522$, $p = .000$, two-tailed).

DISCUSSION

The purpose of these studies was threefold. The first was to provide reliable and valid measures that would indicate where learners were positioned in terms of Knowles' six principles of adult learning. The second was to demonstrate, empirically, that a substantial number of learners reside somewhere roughly in the middle of the pedagogy-andragogy continuum. Third was to develop and validate an instrument that could be used in future research studies to be able to determine what, if any, influence a number of different factors might have on the learner's preference.

The first goal was realized, at least to a large extent, and learners' preferences were measured in terms of pedagogical and andragogical characteristics. Certain aspects of the inventory remain problematic, some of which may have resulted in such large numbers of learners being at the middle and andragogical end of the scale, and so few being on the pedagogical end. Certainly this supports Knowles' claims, but it is also possible that response bias errors may be affecting the data. This will be discussed further on because of its relation to our third goal.

The second goal was met as the results of these studies indicate that many learners fall somewhere between the two polar extremes originally framed by Knowles as pedagogy and andragogy. Those falling into the Mesagogy category did not constitute a majority in either study, but represented, practically speaking, a substantial group of learners in both. While this is not necessarily surprising, it is based on empirical data rather than theory, which makes it noteworthy. To disregard these results would require an adult educator to disregard at least a full quarter of his or her students, and possibly as many as half.

Our third goal was to construct a valid and reliable pedagogy-mesagogy-andragogy measurement instrument. While validation is a continuous process that requires a preponderance of evidence, the inventory constructed and tested in both iterations of this study is supported by adequate internal consistency coefficients, and the early attempts to validate the instrument using expert opinion and known-group validation (PRO-SDLS) provide support for valid instrumentation. Further validation studies are required to provide greater support and several such studies are already being planned.

As a reliable and valid instrument that measures the learning environment structure preferences of adult learners, the LEPI could be a valuable resource for further empirical investigations into how learners' preferences for structure are influenced by personal characteristics (i.e., personality, self-efficacy, age, gender, vocation), disciplinary venues (i.e., mathematics, English, philosophy, workplace training), and a wide range of other potential factors. In our present studies, we did not find any significant relationships between demographics and one's score on the inventory.

LIMITATIONS

Our study was focused, from the beginning, on students enrolled in the ACCS, and because of this, cannot be generalized to the greater population. Particularly, more evidence is necessary to extend the findings to the 4-year university student, the workforce development student, or the professional workplace training and education student.

The pedagogy range had a very small showing, which may, of course, indicate that very few college-age learners fall into Knowles' ideas of pedagogical learning. It is likely, however, that the wording of certain items facilitated a response bias from the participants. For instance, while one might behave as if only the grade matters, one might realize that it does not sound very astute, or socially acceptable to admit that "What I learn should be relevant in school but not necessarily in real life." This type of social desirability bias is a legitimate threat to validity in scaling and should be taken seriously (Lounsbury et al., 2006). We can address this in the continued design of the inventory by writing items that more indirectly measure the ideas. The behavioral implications of the belief need to be measured rather than the explicit statement of the belief itself.

The structure of the scale itself could be improved by constructing more items. Twelve items falls at the very low end of acceptable for broad constructs (Lounsbury et al., 2006), but a moderately larger number of items could be beneficial. Reversely coded items did not, as a general rule, work in the bipolar format, which resulted in having to remove several items.

CONCLUSION AND RECOMMENDATIONS FOR FUTURE RESEARCH

There are a number of improvements that need to be made on the inventory. The present scale is reliable and has initial indications of validity, but validation requires multiple studies over a period of time. There are a number of interesting questions for which the LEPI can be used to find answers. Among these, some of the more interesting may be related to potential differences between gender, age, career path, success in elementary or secondary school, difficulty of subject matter, and many other such factors. Additionally, a more wide-spread administration of this inventory can ultimately provide a rich and detailed empirical basis for understanding the full scope, both limitations and utility, of Knowles' ideas of Andragogy. This contemporary understanding of Knowles' classical work can provide Adult Education scholars and practitioners with valuable and practical insight in dealing with the complexities of our present world.

REFERENCES

Alfred, M. V. (2000). Philosophical foundations of andragogy and self-directed learning: A critical analysis from an Africentric feminist perspective. In M. Glowacki-Dudka (Ed.), *Proceedings of the 19th Annual Midwest Research to Practice Conference in Adult, Continuing, and Community Education* (pp. 21-26). Madison, WI: University of Wisconsin.

Brockett, R. G. (1983). Self-directed learning and the hard to reach adult. *Lifelong Learning: An Omnibus of Practice and Research, 7*(5), 16-18, 28.

Brookfield, S. D. (1986). *Understanding and facilitating adult learning: A comprehensive analysis of principles and effective practices* (1st ed.). San Francisco, CA: Jossey-Bass.

Christian, A. C. (1982). *A comparative study of the andragogical-pedagogical orientation of military and civilian personnel* (Unpublished doctoral dissertation). Oklahoma State University, Stillwater.

Cross, K. P. (1981). *Adults as learners* (1st ed.). San Francisco, CA: Jossey-Bass.

Davenport, J., & Davenport, J. A. (1985). A chronology and analysis of the andragogy debate. *Adult Education Quarterly, 35*(3), 152-159.

Delahaye, B. L., Limerick, D. C., & Hearn, G. (1994). The relationship between andragogical and pedagogical orientations and the implications for adult learning. *Adult Education Quarterly, 44*(4), 187-200.

Elias, J. I. (1979). Andragogy revisited. *Adult Education, 29*(4), 252-256.

Gall, M. D., Gall, J. P., & Borg, W. R. (2003). Educational research (7th ed.). Boston, MA: Allyn & Bacon.

Guglielmino, L. (1977). *Development of the self-directed learning readiness scale.* (Unpublished dissertation). University of Georgia, Athens.

Hadley, H. N. (1975) *Development of an instrument to determine adult educator's orientation as andgragogical or pedagogical* (Unpublished doctoral dissertation). Boston University School of Education, Boston, MA.

Hase, S., & Kenyon, C. (2000). *From andragogy to heutagogy.* Ultibase, Australia: RMIT.

Henschke, J. A. (1989). Identifying appropriate adult educator practices: Beliefs, feelings and behaviors. In C. Jeffries, (Ed.), *Proceedings of the Eighth Annual Midwest Research-To-Practice Conference in Adult, Continuing and Community Education* (pp. 89-95). St. Louis, MO: University of Missouri.

Jarvis, P. (1984). Andragogy: A sign of the times. *Studies in the Education of Adults, 16*, 32-38.

Kaplan, K. J. (1972). On the ambivalence-indifference problem in attitude theory and measurement: A suggested modification of the semantic differential technique. *Psychological Bulletin, 77*, 361-372. doi: 10.1037/h0032590

Knowles, M. (1970). *The modern practice of adult education: Andragogy versus pedagogy.* New York, NY: Cambridge Books.

Knowles, M. (1980). *The modern practice of adult education: From pedagogy to andragogy.* New York, NY: Cambridge Books.

Knowles, M. (1984). *The adult learner: A neglected species.* Houston, TX: Gulf.

Knowles, M. S., Holton, E. F., & Swanson, R. A. (2005). *The adult learner* (6th ed.). New York, NY: Elsevier.

Lounsbury, J. W., Gibson, L. W., & Saudargas, R. W. (2006). Scale development. In F. T. L. Leong & J. T. Austin (Eds.), *Psychology research handbook: A guide for graduate students and research assistants* (2nd ed., pp. 125-146). Thousand Oaks, CA: SAGE

Lounsbury, J.W., Loveland, J.M., Sundstrom, E., Gibson, L.W., Drost, A.W., & Hamrick, F. (2003). An investigation of personality traits in relation to career satisfaction. *Journal of Career Assessment, 11(3)*, 287-307.

Merriam, S. B., Caffarella, R. S., & Baumgartner, L. M. (2007). *Learning in adulthood: A comprehensive guide* (3rd ed.). San Francisco, CA: Jossey-Bass.

Nunnally, J. C. (1967). *Psychometric theory.* New York, NY: McGraw-Hill.

Oddi, L. F. (1986). Development and validation of an instrument to identify self-directed continuing learners. *Adult Education Quarterly, 36(2)*, 97-107.

Oddi, L. F., Ellis, A. J., & Roberson, J. E. A. (1990). Construct validity of the Oddi continuing learning inventory. *Adult Education Quarterly, 40(3)*, 139-145.

Pratt, D. D. (1993). Andragogy after twenty-five years. *New Directions for Adult and Continuing Education, 57*, 15-23.

Rachal, J. R. (2002). Andragogy's detectives: A critique of the present and a proposal for the future. *Adult Education Quarterly, 53(3)*, 210.

Reynolds, J., Laton, D., Davis, T., & Stringer, D. (2009). From pedagogy to heutagogy: A teaching-learning continuum. *Selected Papers from the 20th International Conference of College Teaching and Learning.* Florida Community College at Jacksonville.

Reynolds, J. H., Taylor, J.E., Laton, D. E., & Davis, T. N. (2013). A practical teaching/learning continuum for theorists and practitioners. Manuscript submitted for publication.

St. Clair, R. (2002). *Andragogy revisited: Theory for the 21st century? Myths and realities.* Columbus, OH: ERIC Clearinghouse on Adult Career and Vocational Education.

Stockdale, S. L., & Brockett, R. G. (2011). Development of the PRO-SDLS: A measure of self-direction in learning based on the personal responsibility orientation model. *Adult Education Quarterly, 61(2)*, 161-180.

CHAPTER 6

THE NEW CLASSROOM OF MULTIGENERATIONAL LEARNERS

Using Andragogical Principles in 21st Century Online Learning

Susan Isenberg and Fletcher Glancy

The higher education classroom is making history. For the very first time, four generations of adult learners are in college all at the same time (Coates, 2007). New times call for new strategies to address the needs of all the generational cohorts of learners: Matures born 1900-1946, Baby Boomers born 1947-1964, Generation X born 1965-1982, and Generation Y born 1983-1991 (also called Millennials) (Oblinger & Oblinger, 2005). Year ranges differ slightly among sources.

Members of cohorts tend to share common characteristics and outlooks due to common historical and societal experiences. The term Baby Boomers became popular in the 1960s and was used to distinguish rebellious children from their parents (Reeves & Oh, 2008). Then, in the 1980s, Generation Xers were in the news because of their independence

Conversations About Adult Learning in Our Complex World, pp. 77–90
Copyright © 2013 by Information Age Publishing
All rights of reproduction in any form reserved.

and distrust of authority (Debard, 2004). Now, Generation Y is the focus of discussion in the workplace and on college campuses because of their shear numbers and among other distinguishing characteristics, an expectation for connectivity and technology (Coates, 2007). They compare to Baby Boomers in size and dwarf Generation X (Coates, 2007; Howden & Meyer, 2011). Generation Yer's early and extensive use of technology gives them a desire for connectedness that challenges higher education to develop new instructional strategies and education technologies while still meeting the needs of other generational cohorts. Generation Xers tend to be technologically conservative and less connected (Werth & Werth, 2011) and Baby Boomers tend to be even less technologically sophisticated than Gen Xers (Reeves & Oh, 2008).

A practitioner concern has emerged over the seeming inability to engage all learner cohorts in a higher education online learning environment with current learning management systems (LMSs) that seem to be teacher-centered instead of learner-centered. Holtrum (2005) argued that online learning is impeded because instructors design their courses to fit the LMS instead of the needs of their students. Additionally, many online instructors try to replicate their face-to-face (FtF) teaching strategies that are less effective in the online environment (Holtrum, 2005). This chapter discusses the differences and commonalities among the four learning cohorts, the challenges of helping each learn, the use of technology and andragogy in online education, and the results of prototyping a new strategy for online education that begins to address the limitations of LMSs.

LEARNER COHORTS

The differences in the four learner cohorts can be summarily compared: The Mature Generation tolerates technology, Baby Boomers use technology, Generation X embraces technology, and Generation Y assumes technology (Scheef & Thielfoldt, 2004). The Mature generation is the smallest group and includes those who either fought in World War II or were children during the war. They tend to follow rules, have great communication skills, demand quality, and see no need to customize. Baby Boomers struggle to be on time, manipulate rules to their benefit, are optimistic, like to be in control, and seek immediate gratification. Generation Xers reject rules, want control of their time, trust people, distrust organizations, and are productive. Generation Yers rewrite rules, seek work-life balance, and are civic-minded, inclusive, and impatient (Coates, 2007; Forbus & Gomes, 2009; Scheef & Thielfoldt, 2004; Werth & Werth, 2011). There is little substantive research on the learner cohort differences, but generational differences could be problematic in traditional higher education classrooms and perhaps impede learning.

Instructional strategies for Generation Y are

- use experimental learning,
- encourage learning communities,
- provide structure (what is expected, by when),
- provide lots of feedback,
- use technology (so that learning is like every other part of their lives),
- make it fun,
- be relevant (allow skipping steps they already know),
- utilize their talents (help others students),
- allow for creativity and be creative,
- be visual (stronger visual learners than other cohorts),
- be smart (to this generation, being a good teacher is more important than knowing everything),
- be organized (they are more prolific readers and expect more learning resources),
- provide respectful learning environment,
- social interaction is important to their memory and learning,
- allow focus time (attention span declines after 15-20 minutes), and
- make learning relevant. (Coates, 2007, p. 137)

Strategies for Generation Yers seem to make sense and are likely important to all learning cohorts, but the difference is that the Matures, Baby Boomers, and Generation X may not expect these strategies to be used in education because of their traditional classroom experiences in the past. Generation Yers assume these strategies will be used in their education in the same way they are used in other aspects of their lives (e.g., banking, voting, communication, research, social networking, etc.). The other cohorts have made accommodations to be successful in the traditional university learning environment. Generation Y has not made the same accommodations. The technology that Generation Y grew up with has greatly increased globalization and the complexity of the world. The role technology played in the 2011 Arab Spring is evidence of the generational differences in the use of technology (Dunn, 2011).

Learning in a Complex World

Because of globalization and the ubiquity and transparency of information, learning has become more complex than ever before. Complexity of learning increases as media choices take it beyond simply acquiring information. Online media can connect people in new ways that promote learning, motivate, inspire, and transform those who participate. Adult learners now more than ever see themselves as members of a global family due to the instant communication flow around the world. The national education system must "overcome the desire to simplify" (Friedman, 2011, p. 238), because there is no easy way to approach learning to solve complex problems. Online educators may be simplifying when they control the course content and the media and teach the way they were taught. Giving control to the learners, using a student-centered approach, can foster the critical innovation that is needed; however, it is messy and unpredictable. Many professors lack the tolerance and skill required to work within a student-centered online learning environment

The "Big Tent" is a group of international community university research and engagement networks that organized to dialogue about three phenomena: young citizens' movements around the world, the fast increasing demand for postsecondary education, and expression of the need to transform society to address poverty, peace, and social justice (Osborn, 2011). The common element of all these phenomena is youth. Present day higher education does not understand young learners and is not prepared to meet their needs. The "Big Tent" (Osborn, 2011) idea is to transform universities by 2030 to reach all learners and "become postcosmopolitan centers of social thinking renewal creating cultural and social capital and active citizenship" (p. 3). This will be accomplished through such things as collaborative dialogue with the community on complex issues, community partnerships, science shops for action research, experiential learning in community settings, educator development, and collaborative publishing between community practitioners and university academics (Osborn, 2011). Such radical thinking must be accepted by educators before they will be able to convince higher education institutions to change. Only then will traditional universities learn to think differently about the youngest learner cohort and the role of the university in the world.

In the next decade, Friedman (2011) predicts innovation will focus on improving and finding new applications for current technologies (Internet, computers, cell phones, etc.). Computers remain simply a means for transmitting and manipulating information. Even so, educators who know their students, the content, and the learning process can push the limits of online learning for all generational cohorts. Living knowledge thinking (Osborn, 2011) must replace fixed knowledge thinking to create a mature and questioning citizenry. Online learning that allows learners to actively manipulate data to change reality (real innovation) will be the next phase of computing (Friedman, 2011). These technologies are being developed for online learning today (Glancy & Isenberg, 2011).

Learning Technologies

Learning technologies have routinely been thought to be those technologies that are used in the classroom. Microsoft PowerPoints slide presentations with animation can enhance a learning experience. Learning technologies also include learning management systems (LMS) such as Blackboard that allow the educator to use the computer and Internet to organize and facilitate student learning. They allow the educator to share content, assign work, administer tests, give feedback, and post grades. Learning technologies are not limited to those that are directly controlled by the educator such as LMS. Any technology that is used to communicate information, concepts, or ideas is potentially a learning technology (Dennis, Fuller, & Valacich, 2008; Glancy & Isenberg, 2011). Educators need to use this broad definition of learning technology to keep up with the technology the students use and expect. These technologies may allow for synchronous or asynchronous communication. Most are Internet enabled. An example of asynchronous online learning technology was introduced by American educator Salman Khan (2011) of Khan Academy who has produced more than 2,700 free educational videos for children in math, science, and the humanities. The curriculum videos have *flipped* (Khan, 2011) the classroom with YouTube video lectures being the homework (watched alone with the ability to replay them over and over until understood) and the homework being the class work (done together, learning from the teacher and from each other), which allows the teacher to help students individually and in small groups apply what they learned at home instead of spending all the class time teaching the lesson. Allowing the teacher to mentor rather than lecture is the basis for Khan Academy's claim that technology can be used to humanize the classroom (Khan, 2011). Education is not limited to the classroom. Peer-to-peer education takes place on social networking sites. One-to-one instant messaging (IM) as well as one-to-many IM through sites such as Twitter can be used for education. Search engines provide information on any subject imaginable through searches that return millions of items in fractions of a second. An open source encyclopedia such as Wikipedia brings together experts from across the world to provide information on a wide variety of topics. The educational technologies also include the devices that allow the exchange of information. These devices include not only desktop computers in the classroom but have moved beyond the classroom to mobile devices such as e-readers, smart phones, and Internet enabled tablet computers. The generational cohorts are not all moving at the same rate. Generation Y is leading the movement in mobile technologies.

Generation Y and Learning Technologies

Generation Y has never known a time when the Internet did not exist. Many Generation Yers have had mobile computing technology from the time they entered grade school. Some characterize themselves as less comfortable in FtF social situations and more comfortable in electronically connected ones. They are connected through social networks, posting many times daily, using IM to send text messages one-to-one and through one-to-many websites. This generation does not go to the library to search for information, but instead searches the Internet on smart phones and expects the technology to work and to bring the information on demand all the time, as if it is a part of them. A professor of freshman college students recently told the story of how two students were noticeably distraught in his on ground class. When queried about their appearance of being lost, one volunteered that they both forgot to bring their cell phones. "It was as if they were missing an arm" (A. Smith, Notes from a lecture on students, teachers, and the digital divide. November 23, 2011, Lindenwood University, St. Charles, MO).

Impatient Generation Yers are fast multitaskers (Forbus & Gomes, 2009) rapidly shifting between tasks and technologies. They are socially connected and learn peer-to-peer through the social network. New information is shared immediately through IM, often one-to-many. Among the learner cohorts, Generation Yers are the earliest adopters of new technology, not only to learn and communicate, but also to be involved activists. The overthrow of the Egyptian government in 2011 was enabled by Generation Yers' use of mobile technology (Dunn, 2011).

PRACTITIONER CONCERN

Generation Yers are early adopters of online higher education courses and programs. The other cohorts are following their pattern, and at the same time online courses are proliferating (Allen & Seaman, 2010). Educators who value student-centered teaching and learning and are responsible for, engaged in, or plan to teach higher education online courses using an LMS, may be concerned about how to make a teacher-centered LMS more student-centered to fulfill the complex learning aspirations all adult learners, especially Generation Y. LMS are extremely helpful tools for organizing content, managing instructional media, and communication. However, LMS have been inherently teacher-centered, giving control over content and process to teachers instead of the learners.

METHODOLOGY

A new learner-centered instructional strategy was proposed (Glancy & Isenberg, 2011) titled Conceptual E-Learning Framework (CELF) based on andragogy principles (Knowles, 1980), informed by transformative learning theory (Mezirow, 1981), and aligned with the concepts of conveyance and convergence contained in media synchronicity theory (Dennis, Fuller, & Valacich, 2008). The CELF conceptual framework allows the learner to obtain information from the educator, the Internet, peers, and expert sources. The learner can follow his/her own path to information that is conveyed through any appropriate media, reflect on the information, can use discourse to increase understanding, and through convergence and assessment achieve integration of the new knowledge. This integration modifies the learner's frame of reference; and through the modified frame of reference, the learner becomes more flexible and better prepared for future learning. The CELF is illustrated in Figure 6.1.

Hevner, March, Park, and Ram (2004) suggested several evaluation methods for design science. The evaluation method chosen was for the CELF was prototype evaluation, which first required creating a prototype. The prototype was then evaluated using action research methodology (O'Brien, 2001). In action research, practitioners study their own practice and identify problems and possible solutions that are evaluated (Fraenkel & Wallen, 2009). A prototype of the CELF was innovated that challenges the teacher-centered limitations of the LMS and builds on Generation Y's intrinsic bias toward interconnectivity. The case study was on an LMS graduate course, *Applying Andragogical Principles to Internet Learning* at a midsized Midwestern university during the spring (12 students) and summer (6 students) 2011 semesters. Most students were in the Instructional Leadership Doctor of Education—Andragogy Emphasis Area Specialty program and took the course as an elective, but some were taking it at the master's level out of interest in the topic. Five students in the summer session were professors in the university's school of business and entrepreneurism taking the course for no credit as preparation for converting FtF courses to online courses in their new online master's of business administration (MBA) program. Students designed and created their own courses as the final project that applied andragogical principles using an LMS course shell within the instructor's LMS course, which had never been done before at the university. Students in this course first had to learn about andragogy, the art and science of helping adults learn (Knowles, 1980). The instructor modeled andragogy (Henschke, 1998) and how to apply it to Internet learning by attending to andragogy's eight process elements. The first is preparing the learner (Knowles, 1995). The other seven are having a mechanism of mutual planning, involving the learners

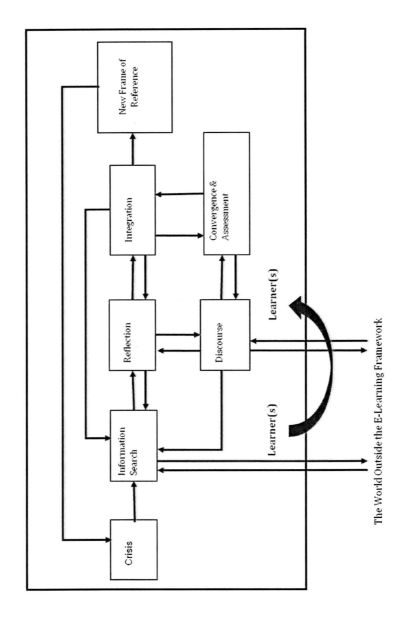

Figure 6.1.   Conceptual E-Learning Framework.

84

in diagnosing their own learning needs, formulating their own program objectives that will satisfy their needs, designing a learning plan with appropriate learning experiences, conducting these learning experiences with suitable techniques and technologies, and involving the learners in evaluating and reassessing their learning (Knowles & Associates, 1984). The instructor also modeled an understanding of the assumptions about adult learners through her course design and tone. The assumptions are increasing self-directedness, learners are a rich resource for learning, learning readiness is related to developmental tasks of social roles, immediacy of application, and problem-centeredness (Knowles, 1973).

The student LMS course shells were set up inside the instructor's LMS course and appeared on the instructor's course homepage. The student courses had the same title as the instructor's courses with one exception, the student's course titles ended with their last names. Students were given instructor rights to create and change content and media (going outside the LMS and bringing content and media into the course without going through the instructor) for their own course and teacher assistant (TA) rights for their fellow students' courses. With TA rights, students could visit other students' courses, respond to their directions, and post feedback in existing discussion threads. In other words, the students designed and built their online courses together within the instructor's LMS course, giving each other feedback along the way. The instructor did not have instructor rights in the student courses, only TA rights. Online students' (especially Generation Y) interconnected activity and satisfaction increased during the activity in the second half of the semester as measured by the amount of course-within-a-course activity and the number and content of the student postings. They expressed feeling empowered to go outside the LMS to bring in media content without going through the instructor.

Generation Y and Andragogy

There seems to be a natural fit between Generation Y and andragogy—more so than the other generational cohorts. Table 6.1 illustrates how several of the Generation Y instructional strategies seem to align with several of the andragogy process elements and adult learner assumptions.

Andragogy describes a way to think about adult learners and a process to engage them in learning that is aligned with the instructional strategies recommended for Generation Yers based on their generational characteristics and outlook. Perhaps andragogy has already "flipped" the adult classroom (Kahn, 2011). In other words, in andragogy courses, students engage in learning at home (reading material, planning what they will

**Table 6.1.   Aligning a Sampling of Generation Y
Instructional Strategies and
Andragogy's Process Elements and Learner Assumptions**

Generation Y Strategies	Andragogy Process Elements and Assumptions
Encourage learning communities—social interaction is important	Experience is a rich resource for learning from each other (assumption)
Be relevant (allow skipping steps they already know)	Problem-centeredness and immediacy of application (assumption)
Be organized (they are more prolific readers and expect more learning resources)	Formulating their own program objectives that will satisfy their needs (process element)
Provide structure (what is expected, by when)	Preparing the learner (process element)
Utilize their talents (to help others students)	Increasingly self-directed (assumption)
Provide respectful environment	Providing an environment conducive to learning (process element)
Be smart (to this generation, being a good teacher is more important than knowing everything)	Conducting learning experiences with suitable techniques and technologies (process element)
Provide lots of feedback	Involving learners in evaluating own learning (process element)

Note: Compiled from Coates (2007, p. 137) and Knowles (1980)

learn and how they will learn it) and apply it (homework) in the classroom through student facilitated discussions, presentations, and other experiential learning opportunities. Online educators who apply andragogical principles understand the limitations of the LMS and take responsibility to create a climate of openness and respect that empowers learners to use their preferred learning strategies. Andragogy seems to humanize learning not just for Generation Y, but for all learners; and therefore, may humanize technology in online learning. Perhaps Generation Y and andragogy are a kickback to the old one-room school where students of all ages learned all together, but not all the same.

RESULTS

Students in the online course, *Applying Andragogical Principles to Internet Learning* were required to design and build their own online course as a final project that applied andragogical principles. In prior semesters, students in this course were forced to go outside the Blackboard course and find their own way to build an online course. Some had means to acquire an LMS shell from their employer such as university professors, but most did not. Those who had no access to a LMS were only required to describe how they would do it in a narrative report. Some drew pictures of what the homepage would look like and wrote about the hyperlinks they would create, and so on.

The first course that provided a course-within-a-course surprised the students. It was a new experience, even for those who were professors who had previously taught online. Students were well prepared for the build-a-course assignment in the first 2 weeks even though the official start of building the courses together did not begin until the second half of the semester. The youngest learners were drawn to their courses like magnets and started playing around—pulling in content from the Internet and experimenting with making assignments. Students' (especially Generation Y) activity and satisfaction level increased while they were building their courses, as measured by the amount of course-within-a-course activity and the number and content of the student postings.

In addition to level of activity and content of postings in the second half of the semester, students completed a five-question midterm course evaluation and e-mailed them back to the instructor. All the cohorts were represented in the two courses except for the Matures (8 Generation Yers, 7 Generation Xers, 3 Baby boomers, 0 Matures). End of course evaluations were anonymous; and therefore, could not be sorted by generational cohort. However, an analysis of the identifiable midterm evaluation comments revealed themes among the cohorts illustrating their differences, which are supported in the literature.

Baby boomers seemed frustrated—frustrated having constant difficulty accessing content, and frustrated not being able to make their course-within-a-course do what they learned about in the class and that there was little they could do about it. Generation Xers seemed surprised and overwhelmed. They were surprised that they were annoyed with the people in the class whom they had not known prior to this online course, that co-learners in the class did not question anything, but surprised at how engaging they found Blackboard to be. The Xers seemed overwhelmed with the number of messages and replies on the discussion boards when they checked it (sometimes only once a week) and frustrated with the significant time they spent away from the content due to lack of time, work, and family commitments. Generation Yers seemed eager, impatient, engaged, and surprised. They were eager to learn, explore the Blackboard course-within-a-course, and to read extra articles beyond what was required. They were impatient for clear direction and for feedback. They were engaged when actively building the Blackboard course and surprised that building a course-within-a-course was more creative than expected.

All generational groups were characteristic of their generation. Lack of immediate gratification frustrated Baby Boomers; Generation Xers were overwhelmed by the time commitment, trusted only individual people, and were surprised to be the only questioners. Last, Generation Yers' comments were on target for their cohort with their eagerness, impatience, and engagement. As Coates (2007) found, there seems to be great value in matching teaching strategies to generation-based learning styles, characteristics, and outlooks.

CONCLUSION

Complex learning is the key to an intelligent society (Friedman, 2011; Osborn, 2011). Online learning is growing as rapidly as the number of Generation Yers on college campuses (Allen & Seaman, 2010). The CELF was proposed to address the educator centeredness that limits a traditional LMS and to enable learner-centered education (Glancy & Isenberg, 2011). The CELF prototype surprised all cohorts, and it demonstrated that learner-centered education is appropriate for all age groups. Of all of the cohorts, Generation Yers were energized the most by the CELF prototype because it was learner-centered. Generation Yers are the generation that has grown up always having technology available. They expect technology to be used in their education and expect it to be available on demand. Generation Y is the cohort that is demanding that educators rethink their teaching methods and give up control to the learner. Online education using the CELF can give the Generation Y what they expect from an online education environment and meet the online educational needs of all of the generational cohorts. Additional testing of the CELF model will further refine it and improve the CELF's ability to support complex learning.

REFERENCES

Allen, I. E., & Seaman, J. (2010). *Learning on demand: Online education in the United States, 2009* Retrieved from http://sloanconsortium.org/publications/survey/pdf/learningondemand.pdf

Coates, J. (2007). *Generational learning styles*. River Falls, WI: LERN Books.

Debard, R. D. (2004). Millennials coming to college. In R. D. Debard, & M. D. Coomes (Eds.), *New Directions for Student Services, 106*, 33-45. doi:10.1002/ss.123

Dennis, A. R., Fuller, R. M., & Valacich, J. H. (2008). Media, tasks, and communication processes: A theory of media synchronicity. *MIS Quarterly, 32*(3), 575-600.

Dunn, A. (2011). Unplugging a nation: State media strategy during Egypt's January 25 uprising. *The Fletcher Forum of World Affairs, 35*(2), 15-24.

Retrieved from http://fletcher.archive.tusm-oit.org/forum/archives/pdfs/35-2pdfs/Dunn_FA.pdf

Forbus, R., & Gomes, S. (2009, August). *Generation gap: "The doctors are in" elected standing committee on teaching.* Paper presented at the American Association for Education in Journalism and Mass Communication (AEJMC) Conference. Boston, MA. Retrieved from http://www.aejmc.com/home/wp-content/uploads/2010/12/Generation-Gap.pdf

Fraenkel, J. R., & Wallen, N. E. (2009). *How to design and evaluate research in education* (7th ed.). Boston, MA: McGraw-Hill Higher Education.

Friedman, G. (2011). *The next decade: Where we've been and where we're going.* New York, NY: Doubleday.

Glancy, F. H., & Isenberg, S. K. (2011, May). A conceptual e-learning framework. *Proceedings of the European, Mediterranean, and Middle Eastern Conference on Information Systems, Athens, Greece.*

Henschke, J. A. (1998, Spring). Modeling the preparation of adult learners. *Adult Learning,* 11-13.

Hevner, A. R., March, S. T., Park, J., & Ram, S. (2004). Design science in information systems research. *MIS Quarterly, 28*(1), 75-105.

Holtrum, M. (2005). Technical evaluation report 44: Breaking down the LMS walls. *The International Review of Research in Open and Distance Learning, 6*(1). Retrieved from http://www.irrodl.org/index.php/irrodl/article/view/212/295

Howden, L. M., & Meyer, J. A. (May, 2011). *Age and sex composition: 2010.* 2010 Census Briefs (*C2010BR-03*), *U.S. Department of Commerce Economics and Statistics Administration.* Retrieved from http//census.gov/prod/cen2010/briefs/c2010br-03.pdf

Khan, S. (2011, March 9). *Salman Kahn talk at TED 2011* [ted.com]. Retrieved from http://www.youtube.com/watch?v=gM95HHI4gLk

Knowles, M., & Associates (1984). *Andragogy in action: Applying modern principles of adult education.* San Francisco, CA: Jossey-Bass.

Knowles, M. S. (1973). *The adult learner: A neglected species.* Houston, TX: Gulf Publishing.

Knowles, M.S. (1980). *The modern practice of adult education.* Englewood Cliffs, NJ: Cambridge.

Knowles, M. S. (1995). *Designs for adult learning: Practical resources, exercises, and course outlines from the father of adult learning.* Alexandria, VA: American Society for Training and Development.

Mezirow, J. (1981). A critical theory of adult learning and education. *Adult Education, 32*(1), 3-24.

Oblinger, D., & Oblinger, J. (2005). Is it age or IT: First steps toward understanding the net generation. In D. Oblinger & J. Oblinger (Eds.), *Education the Net Generation* (pp. 2.1-2.20). Boulder, CO: Educause. [Educause ebook.] Retrieved from http://content.imamu.edu/sa/Scholars/it/net/onedayv2-ho.pdf

O'Brien, R. (2001). Um exame de abordagem metodológica da pesquisa ação [An overview of the methodological approach of action research]. In R. Richardson (Ed.), *Teoria e Prática da Pesquisa Ação* [Theory and practice of action research]. João Pessoa, Brazil: Universidade Federal da Paraíba. (English version), Retrieved from http://www.web.ca/~robrien/papers/arfinal.html

Obsorn, M. (2011). Community-university engagement in 2030: A scenario. *Perspectives from the "Big Tent" global dialogue on community-university research and engagement, OsbornObservatory.org*. Retrieved from http://Osbornobservatory.org/library/big-tent-ii-community-university-engagement-2030-scenario

Reeves, T., & Oh, E. (2008). Generational differences. In J. M. Spector, M. D. Merrill, J. van Merrienboer, & M. P. Driscoll (Eds.), *Handbook of research on educational communications and technology* (pp. 295-303). New York, NY: Taylor & Francis Group.

Scheef, D., & Thielfoldt, D. (2004). *What you need to know about mentoring the new generations*. The Learning Café and American Demographics Enterprising Museum. Retrieved from http://www.TheLearningCafe.net

Werth, E. P., & Werth, L. (2011). Effective training for the millennial students. *Adult Learning, 22*(3), 12-19.

CHAPTER 7

BLENDING "LEARNING BY TEACHING" AND "RESEARCH INFORMED TEACHING" FOR ADULT AUTHORSHIP IN LEARNING

A Collaborative Learning Experience of Undergraduate Students in a Human Service Program

Emmanuel Jean Francois

Nontraditional students have become the new trend in U.S. colleges and universities (National Center for Education Statistics, 2011). These post-secondary institutions tend to focus on administrative and student service strategies that can contribute to recruitment and retention of nontraditional students (Brown, 2002). The challenge is to accommodate the effective learning of such nontraditional students through innovative ways of teaching (Bland, 2003). Part of meeting such challenge includes an understanding of the perceptions of nontraditional students about their

Conversations About Adult Learning in Our Complex World, pp. 91–106
Copyright © 2013 by Information Age Publishing
All rights of reproduction in any form reserved.

teaching and learning experience (Bierema, 2002). This demarche may enable to adapt innovative approaches in instructional activities involving nontraditional students. This chapter suggests a model that involves a blend of learning by teaching and research informed teaching collaborative approach. Consequently, the reader of this chapter will be able to: (1) Review the main theoretical and conceptual framework of learning by teaching (LBT), research informed teaching (RIT), and adult self-authorship in learning (ASL), (2) Explore the implications of collaboration between adult educator and adult learner for effective teaching and learning processes; (3) Explore the potential of the teaching-learning collaboration gears approach to foster better learning experience for adult students in our complex 21st century world.

BACKGROUND AND CONCEPTUAL FRAMEWORK: THE TEACHING-LEARNING COLLABORATION GEARS!

The background and conceptual framework of this chapter draws from what I called the "Teaching-Learning Collaboration Gears." Simply put, a gear is a toothed part of a machine that can mesh or work together with another toothed part to alter motion, or change the speed or direction of a driving mechanism. In other words, a set of gears can be adjusted to provide specific outcomes based on how the teeth successively engage each other. The term is used in this chapter to refer to the interactive motion among the concept of teaching, learning, and research in a curriculum and instruction process, involving adult learners.

The concept "Teaching-Learning Collaboration Gears" is based on seven assumptions that guided the experience inspiring the present chapter. The assumptions were that: (1) Knowledge and academic background of the instructor alone is not enough to translate into learners that are knowledgeable of course contents; (2) Knowledge of course contents without critical thinking and ability to apply in real life experience is quasi-useless; (3) The benefits of structured learner empowerment are more likely to outweigh the disadvantages; (4) Learning motivation is more likely to increase if the teaching and learning process combines challenges, fun, and relevance; (5) Learners are more likely to better value what they learn when it is confirmed by more than one source; (6) Learners are more likely to appreciate what they learn when they have to pause and reflect on how they are learning; (7) and students are more likely to be willing to participate when accountability is clearly defined and expectations are realistic.

As Figure 7.1 illustrates, the collaboration rooted in the assumptions outlined in the previous paragraph suggested three gears. The *first gear* in

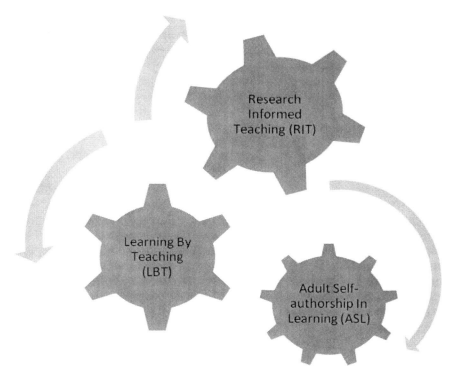

Figure 7.1.   The Teaching-Learning Collaboration Gears.

the model aims to ensure internal collaborations (learning by teaching) between the instructor and the learners (learner as coinstructor), and among learners (learner as instructor to other learners). In other words, the instructor plans and implements instructional activities that empower the learner to learn by being a coinstructor (e.g., codesigns syllabus, develops lesson plan, teaches a sequence, and contributes to course assessment) and by teaching other learners. The *second gear* is external collaboration (research informed teaching) between the learner, the scholarship, and the course contents, and between the learner and the empirical world (community). Through the second gear, the instructor empowers the learner to learn through inquiry-based activities (e.g., literature review, empirical data collection, research synthesis, and reporting). The *third gear* (adult self-authorship in learning) is envisioned to maintain and control the velocity of the two other gears. With the third gear, learners are engaged in reflection and self-reflection activities that challenge their assumptions and critical thinking in a way that gives them shared decision making power and shared-ownership over the teaching and learning process. The syllabus, course contents, in-class and out-of-class activities, and all the stakeholders involved in the teaching learning process (instructor, students, guest speakers, community members interviewed) constitute the teeth of the collaborative gears. More specifically, the teaching-learning collaboration gears involve TBL and RIT, in order to foster (ASL).

Learning By Teaching

Learning by teaching (LBT) consists primarily of empowering the students to become partners and active agents who take control of their learning (Pratt & Nesbitt, 2000). Husson and Kennedy (2003) argue that "adults need more interactive and participatory components with fewer lectures" (p. 52). Okita and Schwartz (2006) conducted an experiment study testing a "learning by teaching" model on 40 adults, and found that the approach had positive and long lasting influence on student learning experience. Several other studies found that learning by teaching contributes to student motivation and self-efficacy (Gordon & Fittler, 2004; Sherin, 2002).

Research Informed Teaching

Research-informed teaching (RIT) involves linking teaching practices with research, as a strategy to enhance student learning experience through disciplinary-based inquiry (Healey, 2005). According to Griffiths (2004), teaching can be research-led (learning through research findings), research oriented (curriculum focused on research process and research ethos), and research-based (learning as researcher through inquiry-based activities). This strategy enables instructors to enhance student learning experience through disciplinary-based research and active inquiry.

Adult Self-Authorship in Learning

Adult self-authorship (ASL) is based on the assumptions that college student success depends on their cognitive maturity, integrated sense of personal identity, and mature relationships with others (Baxter Magolda, 2001). According to Baxter Magdola (2001), self-authorship is the foundation of learning and evolves through (a) following external formulas (assimilation of beliefs and values from external sources), (b) crossroads (challenges to be effective contributors in conversations), and (c) self-authorship (critical thinking about beliefs, values, and assumptions). She developed the learning partnership model (LPM), which emphasizes challenging students learning by providing them academic support, freedom, and responsibility (Baxter Magdola, 2004). There is a consensus among many scholars that self-authorship contributes to the personal, academic, and professional success of college students (Baxter Magolda, 2004; King & Kitchener, 2004; Pizzolato, 2006).

METHODS

This study used an action research design (Reason & Bradbury, 2002). Action research is a qualitative research method that is used to improve practices through inquiry-based interactions between the researcher and the participants involved in the research process in order to improve practices (Reason & Bradbury, 2002; Wadsworth, 1998). According to Ross-Fisher (2008), the action research process consists of identifying and defining a problem, framing the research question (s), reviewing the related literature, collecting and analyzing data, answering the research question(s), drafting an action plan, and sharing what has been learned with colleagues. The action research approach was used because it allowed more flexibility to empower the students involved in this study as active participants in the process of inquiry (Hart & Bond, 1996). Also, the action research approach enabled instructors to use inquiry-based strategies to ask questions about a practice, develop and implement strategies for changes, evaluate the impact of such changes, improve the learning experience of the study participants, and share the findings with other professionals (Slavin, 2006).

Setting and Participants

The institutional setting of this chapter concerns a comprehensive college in the southern region of the United States. The study received approval from the institutional review board, which constitutes evidence of compliance with ethical standards in action research as suggested by Nolen and Vander Putten (2007). The instructional context involves a course titled "Race and Justice" for undergraduate students in a human service program. The class consisted of 38 adult students (ages 24 and over), including 30 females and 8 males. Although the sample size does not matter in action research (Ross-Fisher, 2008), all students in the course formally consented to collaborate in the study after they have been informed about the purpose

and the process. There have been some concerns of unequal power relations between the researcher and the participants in an action research
related to a course that applies toward a degree program (Martin, 1996).
However, as Neuman (2007) explains, "people need to know what they are
being asked to participate in so that they can become aware of their rights
and what they are getting involved in when they read and sign a statement
giving informed consent" (p. 54). Participants were given the option to opt-
out of the action research. However, no one opted-out. The racial/ethnic
composition of the participants encompassed 5 Asians (4 females and 1
male), 11 Blacks (9 females and 2 males), 7 Hispanics (5 females and 2
males), and 15 Whites (12 females and 3 males).

Procedures

According to standards set by the institution that involves the study,
students have to receive their syllabus at least one month prior to the first
class session. This policy exists partly because, for some courses, students
may have to complete a preclass assignment to submit during the first
class meeting. The only preclass assignment that the students were
required to complete in the "Race and Justice" course was to print and
bring to the first class meeting at least three course syllabi for a course
with the same title from a list of program websites provided to them.

From conversations with the students before I formally began the first
class, there was a consensus among most of them that the teacher-learner
collaborations they experienced in past classes were not authentic. This
phase of problem identification is critical in action research (Ross-Fisher,
2008). The identification of the problem led to the formulation of one
research question: What is authentic teaching-learning collaboration look
like for the students? After the usual first day of class introduction, students
were invited to take a moment to write down their expectations for the
course, their understanding of authentic teaching-learning collaboration
and share them with the group. Most of the statements were "I expect you
to…", "I hope you will….", or "I think you will…" After listening to all the
students, I asked them, "What does the 'you' in your statement stand for?"
They all confirmed that you stood for "the professor" or "the instructor."
Then, I asked them to substitute all the "you" that stood for the instructor
by "I" or "Me." Then, they had to read again their expectations and understanding of authentic teaching-learning collaboration. The key words that
they associated with authentic collaboration were mutual respect, shared
decision-making, and trust. I asked them, "How do you feel about your new
expectations and understanding of authentic collaboration in comparison

to the previous ones?" Sansan, an alias used in lieu of the actual student name, started spontaneously to speak,

> I feel like I am going to teach the course to myself. I am quite nervous about that, because you have all the power.... You are the professor, you prepare your course, you are paid to do it, you will grade me, and you want me to believe that I am in charge.... Hello!... I mean....

As a way to express their agreement with Sansan, others also protested. When I asked for additional comments, Martha (alias), a student from an Asian country, shared

> A professor fooled me before with that bluff of participation. I took her at her words, but nothing we did was good enough for her. At the end, the class barely survived her course with minimum grades. At least most of the classmates that I talked to got just the minimum grades. I want you to tell us exactly what you plan to do, how you will grade our assignments, and what you expect from us.

The class conversation went until saturation was evident. Then, I explained to them how I plan to disappoint them on their first expectations that focused on *me* as an instructor, and challenged them on the expectations that focused on *them* as learners. I acknowledged that in any given teaching assignment, the instructor-learner power relation is not necessarily balanced. However, I argued, the power relation can be relatively balanced if an authentic collaboration occurs. In that context, authentic collaboration means a collaboration that is based on mutual respect, shared decision making, and shared ownership (Cuseo, 2000). Then, the class went to lunch break. During that time, I reflected on the discussions that I had with the students on authentic collaboration. I reorganized my lecture to include a collaborative approach that combines "learning by teaching" and "research informed teaching" activities. After the lunch break, I projected a PowerPoint slide featuring the concepts of "learning by teaching" and "research informed teaching" to explain how the teaching power will be shared and the strains that will be attached to that power sharing experiment. Then, I argued that the teaching collaboration will involve (a) redesigning the course syllabus, (b) assigning teaching responsibilities to each student in the course, (c) assigning research informed teaching responsibilities to each student. A "Question and Answer" session followed. Students were divided in groups of 5-6 to compare and contrast the course syllabus with the other syllabi that they were required to print and bring to the first class meeting. Then, they provided their input, which I incorporated into what became a revised syllabus. The syllabus (including course goals, objectives, contents, assignments, definition of class participation, benchmarks, deadlines, and criteria for grading assignments) served as a learning contract between the students and me. This created a structured and stimulating basis for collaborative teaching.

The Blended Teaching Approach

As indicated in previous paragraphs, the blending teaching approach combines LBT and RIT in-class and out-of-class activities, with the assumption that such activities will foster adult-self-authorship learning. The LBT component involved (a) the learning contract (goals, objectives, contents, assignments, expectations, definition of participation, benchmarks, deadlines, and grading criteria), (b) student presentation (topic assignment to each student, 20-minute teaching on assigned topic by each student), (c) topical forums organized by groups of students, and (d) collaborative assessment (students finalization of criteria for grading assignments). The RIT component included (a) a disciplinary research-based syllabus (students compare course syllabus with other syllabi, and provide input incorporated in revised syllabus), which includes a mix of theoretical based contents and empirical data to be collected by students), (b) inquiry-based activities (basic online literature search, development of interview questionnaires, interview of community members, synthesis of findings, and presentation of research findings to class), and (c) in-class group discussions on case studies related to research findings (compare and contrast what the literature said and what interviews of community members revealed, and metacognition on class activities and assignments).

Data Collection and Analysis

During the last class session, students participated in a group interview (Fontana & Frey, 2005) about their overall experience with the course. A questionnaire was designed with students' input and feedback from two adjunct faculty members. The two faculty members helped ensure the truthfulness and consistency (Slevin & Sines, 2000) of the questionnaire by interviewing one another, listening to the recordings, and modifying the questions. The following questions guided the group interviews: (a) What were your assumptions before you started with the course? (b) Have your assumptions changed or remained the same after the course? (c) If no, why? If yes, when? At what point during the course? (d) How did you feel about your responsibility to teach a small portion of the course? (e) How did you feel about your responsibility to do some research to inform the topics that we cover in the course? (f) How did you feel about the overall approach adopted to teach the course? The group interview lasted about 2 hours and was audio recorded. The data collected from the group interview were analyzed, using the qualitative software Atlas.ti (Gibbs, 2007), to identify trends related to possible self-authorship experience (Patton, 2002). Inter- and intracomparison of student responses were used to identify and describe salient patterns or themes that emerged. The two faculty members who piloted the questionnaire double-checked to assure the codes referring to quotations were consistent and appropriate under the thematic categories (Morrow, 2005).

RESULTS: ADULT SELF-AUTHORSHIP IN LEARNING

The thematic analysis revealed that students experienced cognitive maturity (e.g., new skills acquisition), an integrated sense of personal identity (e.g., integration, and sense of worth), and developed mature relationship with others (e.g., increased awareness). The following paragraph will summarize the main themes that emerged in relation to the interaction between LBT and RIT for ASL.

Integration

The students said that they felt engaged and fully integrated in the course throughout the semester. Some students used expressions such as "inclusive process," "collaborative class environment," and "good partnership." Elie (alias), a middle age woman student, pointed out

I felt that I was part of the process. This is the first time a professor asks me to help revise the syllabus, and the inputs were included in the new version of the syllabus. Although the assignments were very challenging, you felt like you could not complain because you were part of the process.

The students constantly referred to the integration of their personal, ethnic, and racial experiences into the courses. They felt that the collaborative process enabled them to participate in the decision-making process related to the syllabus and the teaching of the course. They felt a sense of empowerment.

Sense of Empowerment

Some students confessed that they started the course with very low self-concept. Other students explained how they have been out of school for a relatively long period of time. As a result, they were not sure whether they would be able to live up to the expectations of academic courses. They felt empowered by the opportunities to assume some responsibilities by contributing to teach the course. Mark (alias), a male student, shared

> When the professor said that we are going to teach the class with him, we are going to do research, and so forth and so on, I said to myself, 'What's going on?' I was thinking about dropping the class right away.... At the end of the day, I changed my mind, because I felt that the entire class was in charge of the course until the end of the semester.

The students felt not only empowered by the collaborative approach used in the course but also experienced a sense of worth.

Sense of Worth

Problem-based learning and project-based learning strategies were used in case studies and assignments designed for the course. The students thought that such an approach helped them use their prior learning experience. They also expressed great appreciation for the fact that they had full responsibilities for the content that was assigned to them to teach. They argued that the course helped them better appreciate themselves. Susan (alias), a female student, claimed

> I had many great professors so far in the program. I can only say good things about all of them, except for one class. However, this is the first time that I felt my knowledge was taken into consideration. I don't know, but I felt like I am worth something. I had a sense that my classmates wanted to hear what I was saying...

When asked whether there was any challenge related to their collaboration in this course, the students replied by stressing how accountability was an important factor for them.

Accountability

Accountability was a recurrent theme throughout the group interview. Some students said that having specific and clearly defined responsibilities helped motivate them to not only prepare their presentation, but also to make a good impression to the class. John (alias), a male student, said "When you know that a portion of the class is your responsibility to teach, you have to make some preparation, you have to get ready; you have no excuses." Most of the students felt that they were accountable not only to the instructor, but also to their peers. Linda (alias), a Hispanic student, said "I felt like I could not let down the teacher and my classmates."

Furthermore, the students explained that the collaborative approach used in the course contributed to increase their awareness on race and justice issues in the United States, their academic self-efficacy, and their acquisition of new academic skills.

Increased Awareness

The majority of the students said that the course contributed to increase their awareness about the complexity of issues of race and justice in the United States. Some students confessed they had long held assumptions about other ethnic and racial groups. The course helped them correct these assumptions. Also, they asserted that the course helped them develop better interactions with people from different cultural backgrounds. Smith, a White male student, pointed out

> My interactions with my Black and Hispanic classmates, the people that interviewed, the discussions in the class have opened my eyes on many issues that I was not even aware of. I have a better understanding about the feelings in the immigrant communities and the minorities in America.

Increased Academic Self-Efficacy

Responding to a question asking whether any assumptions have changed after the course, the majority of the students confirmed that their experience in the course helped them believe in their ability to conduct basic research and make a substantive PowerPoint presentation. Challenged to explain at what point during the course they felt such change, some students said that the first presentations by their classmates inspired confidence. Other students said that the trust that the professor put in them contributed to boost their self-confidence. Euna (alias), a female student, noted

> I returned to school exactly 12 years after I got my GED. When I heard all the things that I had to do in that class, I automatically felt depressed. By the time the course ended, I felt a great deal of confidence about my ability to work in groups, make a Power Point presentation, and write an interview report. I never thought that I would be able to do research. I did it.

New Skills Acquisition

Students believed they acquired new skills in this course. They said that they have the ability to ask more pointed questions about a topic or an issue. Also, they cited their opportunity to incorporate their input in the course syllabus, conducting a literature search, writing an annotated bibliography, conducting a research interview, and synthesizing and presenting research findings. Mary (alias) said, "I learned to do a lot of cool things in this class. I tend to think more critically about the news on TV." Finally, the students argued that what they learned from the course was relevant and transferable to other non-academic settings.

Relevance

The students explained that the course was rooted into their individual racial and ethnic experiences. They argued that the interdisciplinary nature of the topics discussed in class helped challenge and motivate them to search for new information that did not interest them before taking this class. They perceived the course as relevant to their personal identity. Jane (alias) said, "This class taught me things that are very relevant to my personal experience as a Black woman."

Transferability

Many students repeatedly mentioned how they used strategies learned in this course to complete their assignments for other courses. Students explained how the discussions that they had in class continued at home with their family members, and in some cases, with their friends. Other students said that they used the skills learned in this course to make presentations in their community association. Mark (alias), a female student, revealed, "I learned a lot of things that I already shared with the members of my association."

DISCUSSIONS

The teaching-learning collaboration gears created mechanisms for both structural and functional collaborations that concurrently work toward better adult learning experiences. The structural collaboration refers to students' involvement in planning (revision of course syllabus by students), teaching (individual/group presentations), and assessment of the course, as well as in research informed teaching tasks (literature search, research design, data collection and analysis, and research report by students). This structural collaboration affects the overall format of the course. The functional collaboration implies the redefinition of the roles of the adult educator and adult learner in the teaching and learning process. Examples of functional collaborations included collaborations between (a) adult educator-adult learner (dialogue, metacognition), (b) adult learner and adult learner (group activities), and (c) adult learner and community (interview of community members, guest speakers invited to class by students).

As the emerging themes suggested, the blending of "learning by teaching" and "research informed teaching" approach contributed to adult self-authorship in learning. The ASL is evidenced by their perceived worthiness (acquisition of new skills) and inclusiveness of the course. Also, the course provided them a sense of empowerment, academic self-efficacy, self-worth, accountability, and the beliefs that the topics were relevant and transferable to their social and professional lives.

Furthermore, the teaching-learning collaboration gears approach, combining LBT and RIT for ASL, suggests that empowerment does not occur just by using a statement. It requires an entire conceptual framework rooted in assumptions that account for a belief in the ability of the learner to be good steward of such power sharing. When empowerment is combined with accountability, the combination creates a classroom environment that makes room for self-regulation (Beairsto & Ruohotie, 2003). There is a natural need for belonging and desire for power in almost every human being. Empowerment may tend to satisfy such need and desire, thus create a sense of community that monitors the contribution of every single member. The fact that a student has to teach a small portion of the class for about 20 minutes evokes a sense of power, belonging, responsibility, and accountability. The expectation that this 20-minute instructor comes to class prepared resides not only with the instructor, but also with every single classmate. Most adult students do not like to purposefully disappoint an instructor that they believe cares about their learning.

Empowerment is also linked to transferability and relevance. Activities, assignments, or tasks that are readily transferable to the social or professional life of the students seem motivate their active participation. Transferability, in this case, is interconnected with perceived relevance. Students tend to react positively to tasks they perceive as challenging, but relevant and doable. Although all relevant activities are not necessarily transferable, most transferable activities tend to be perceived as relevant by students (Burke, Jones, & Doherty, 2005).

With respect to the research informed teaching aspect, students conducted research after several simulations and case studies in class. Students' questionnaires were revised and customized based on the type of community member that they planned to interview. Therefore, they felt confident that they could carry the task. They were comforted by the assumption (stated by the instructor) that mistakes were considered as part of the learning process, and not an excuse to lower one's grades.

There may be a legitimate concern by some adult educators that the learners might have too much power or control over the teaching-learning gears (Tudge, 1992). First of all, this is a risk inherent to the territory called "collaboration" because collaboration involves empowering the students through a shared decision-making process. Therefore, it is obvious that students will have some power over what is being taught and how it is taught. In other words, collaboration may provide the spectacle of a confusing process in some circumstances. However, I argue that the risk of confusion in collaboration is a threat only if the process is not structured around elements such as (a) a learning contract, (b) respectful dialogue, (c) metacognition, (d) clearly written expectations, (e) definition of role and responsibilities, (f) and benchmarks for monitoring progress. Also, empowering the students implies that the instructor compiles and shares academic resources with the students as the collaboration mechanisms are unfolding.

CONCLUSION

The Blending Learning-Teaching Gears approach, based on LBT and RIT, represents a new way of practicing collaborative teaching and learning in settings that involve nontraditional adult students. This model challenges the adult educator to view teaching, learning, and research as overlapping into a holistic process that is both constructivist and transformational. The model illustrates how the collaboration contributed to facilitate student's cognitive maturity (e.g., new skills acquisition, and increased academic self-efficacy), an integrated sense of personal identity (e.g., integration, empowerment, and sense of worth), and mature relationship with others (e.g., increased awareness). In that context, the model suggests that LBT and RIT constitute examples of interactions that mediate the influence of collaboration on adult authorship in learning. However, researchers, scholars, and practitioners should appreciate the model in this chapter within the limitations of an action research. Future studies on this model may control for other factors (e.g., student characteristics, dispositions, motivation, and personal interest on the course topics) that may affect the effect of collaboration on student's learning.

REFERENCES

Baxter Magolda, M. (2001). *Making their own way: Narratives for transforming higher education to promote self-development*. Sterling, VA: Stylus.

Baxter Magolda, M. (2004). Learning partnerships model: A framework for promoting self-authorship. In M. B. Baxter Magolda & P. M. King (Eds.), *Learning partnerships: Theory and models of practice to educate for self-authorship* (pp. 37-62). Sterling, VA: Stylus.

Beairsto, B., & Ruohotie, P. (2003). Empowering professionals as lifelong learners. In B. Bearsto, M. Klein, & P. Ruhotie (Eds.). *Professional learning and leadership*. Tampere, Finland: University of Tampere.

Bierema, L. L. (2002). The Sociocultural contexts of learning in the workplace. In M. V. Alfred (Ed.). *New Directions for Adult and Continuing Education, 96*, 69-78. doi:10.1002/ace.80

Bland, S. M. (2003). Advising adults: Telling or coaching? *Adult Learning, 14*(2), 6-9.

Brown, S. M. (2002). Strategies that contribute to nontraditional/adult student development and persistence. *PAACE Journal of Lifelong Learning, 11*, 67-76.

Burke, V., Jones, I., & Doherty, M. (2005). Analyzing student perceptions of transferable skills via undergraduate degree programmes. *Active Learning in Higher Education, 6*(2), 132-144.

Cuseo, J. (2000, February). *Collaborative and cooperative learning: Pedagogy for promoting new-student retention and achievement*. Preconference workshop delivered at the 19th annual conference on The First-Year Experience, Columbia, SC.

Fontana, A., & Frey, J. H. (2005). The interview: From structured questions to negotiated text. In N. K. Denzin, & Y. S. Lincoln (Eds.), *Handbook of qualitative research* (pp. 645-672). Los Angeles, CA: SAGE.

Gibbs, G. R. (2007). Media review: ATLAS/ti software to assist in the qualitative analysis of data. *Journal of Mixed Methods Research, 1*(1), 103-104.

Gordon, S., & Fittler, K. (2004). Learning by teaching: A cultural historical perspective on a teacher's development. *Outlines, 2*, 35-46.

Griffiths, R. (2004) Knowledge production and the research-teaching nexus: The case of the built environment disciplines. *Studies in Higher Education, 29*(6), 709-726.

Hart, E., & Bond, M. (1996). Action research as a professionalizing strategy: Issues and dilemmas. *Journal of Advanced Nursing, 23*, 454-461.

Healey, M. (2005) Linking research and teaching: disciplinary spaces. In R. Barnett (Ed.), *Reshaping the university: New relationships between research, scholarship and teaching* (pp. 30-42). Maidenhead, England: McGraw-Hill/Open University Press.

Husson, W. J., & Kennedy, T. (2003). Developing and maintaining accelerated degree program within traditional institutions. In R. J. Wlodkowski & C. E. Kasworm (Eds.), *Accelerated learning for adults: The promise and practice of intensive educational formats* (pp. 51-61). San Francisco, CA: Jossey-Bass.

King, P. M., & Kitchener, K. S. (2004). Reflective judgment: Theory and research on the development of epistemic assumptions through adulthood. *Educational Psychologist, 39*(1), 5-18.

Martin, M. (1996). Issues of power in the participatory research process. In K. de Koning & M. Martin (Eds.), *Participatory research in health. Issues and experience* (pp. 82–93). London, England: Zed Books.

Morrow, S. L. (2005). Quality and trustworthiness in qualitative research in counseling psychology. *Journal of Counseling Psychology, 52*, 250-260.

National Center for Education Statistics. (2011). *The Condition of Education 2011.* (NCES 2001–071). Washington, DC: U.S. Department of Education.

Neuman, W. L. (2007). *Basic of social research: Qualitative and quantitative approaches* (2nd ed.). Boston, MA: Allyn & Bacon.

Nolen, A. L., & Vander Putten, J. (2007). Action research in education: Addressing gaps in ethical principles and practices, *Educational Researcher, 36*(7), 401-407.

Okita, S. Y., & Schwartz, D. L., (2006). When observation beats doing: Learning by teaching. *Proceedings of the 7th International Conference of the Learning Sciences* (ICLS). Bloomington, IN

Patton, M. Q. (2002). *Qualitative research and evaluation methods* (3rd ed.). Thousand Oaks, CA: SAGE.

Pizzolato, J. E. (2006). Complex partnerships: Self-authorship and provocative academic advising practices. *NACADA Journal, 26*(1), 32-46.

Pratt, D. D., & Nesbit, T. (2000). Discourses and cultures of teaching. In E. Hayes & A. Wilson (Eds.), *Handbook of Adult and Continuing Education* (pp. 117-131). San Francisco, CA: Jossey-Bass.

Reason, P., & Bradbury, H. (2002). *Handbook of action research: Participative inquiry and practice.* London, England: SAGE.

Ross-Fisher, R. L. (2008). Action research to improve teaching and learning. *Kappa Delta Pi Record, 44*(4), 160-164.

Sherin, M. G. (2002). When teaching becomes learning. *Cognition and Instruction, 20*(2), 119-150.

Slavin, R. E. (2006). *Educational psychology: Theory and practice* (8th ed.). Boston, MA: Allyn & Bacon.

Slevin, E., & Sines, D. (2000). Enhancing the truthfulness, consistency and transferability of a qualitative study utilizing a manifold of approaches. *Nurse Researcher, 1*(2), 79-93.

Tudge, J. R. H. (1992). Processes and consequences of peer collaboration: A Vygotskian analysis. *Child Development, 63*(6), 1364-1379.

Wadsworth, Y. (1998). What is participatory action research? *Action Research International, Paper 2.* Retrieved from http://www.scu.edu.au/schools/gcm/ar/ari/p-ywadsworth98.html

SECTION III

**PROGRAMMING FOR ADULTS—
REDESIGNING UNIVERSITY TO
SERVE ADULT LEARNERS**

CHAPTER 8

THE LIVED EXPERIENCE OF GRADUATES OF AN ADULT ACCELERATED DEGREE PROGRAM

Carrie Johnson, Wytress Richardson, and August Lamczyk

In 2007-2008, over 40% of students enrolled in undergraduate programs in the United States were 24 years of age and older, and approximately 65% of this group worked 35 hours a week or more while attending school (National Center for Educational Statistics, 2007). The needs of these learners are often different from the traditional 18- to 22-year old college student. A variety of options are offered by universities to accommodate the adult learner. One of these options is accelerated courses.

Accelerated courses are college-level courses delivered with less time in the classroom than a traditional course, providing less time for instruction. For example, a traditional course that meets for an entire semester might meet three times per week for an hour over a 15-week period for a total of 45 classroom instruction hours, and an accelerated course might meet for 5 or 8 weeks, one session per week, for 4 hours. In this case, the accelerated courses would provide 20 or 32 hours of in-class instruction (Johnson, 2009; Wlodkowski, 2003).

Conversations About Adult Learning in Our Complex World, pp. 109–123
Copyright © 2013 by Information Age Publishing
All rights of reproduction in any form reserved.

Accelerated programs are designed for students who cannot commit themselves to traditional-length courses due to conflicts at work and/or home. Prior to the creation of these accelerated programs and courses in the 1970s, adult students typically had to commit up to 8 years of evening classes to complete an undergraduate degree (Husson & Kennedy, 2003). By enrolling in accelerated courses, students usually attend class once a week, making their pursuit of higher education more manageable. As the adult population continues to thrive in higher education, these courses have grown in popularity. Accelerated courses and the students who enroll in them, are a significant issue in the complex world of adult higher education in the 21st century.

PURPOSE OF THE STUDY

The purpose of this qualitative study was to begin to address the gaps in the literature on adult accelerated courses by exploring the perceptions of students who have completed an accelerated degree-program. We sought to understand the participants' motivation to return to college and to discover the impact, if any, continuing their education had on the quality of their lives. We wanted to understand the learners' experiences, including their perception of the quality of their education, and any influence and/or support they received from their classmates, family, friends, mentors, faculty, and others.

LITERATURE REVIEW

In recent years, there has been an increase in accelerated courses and degree programs designed for adult students. Accelerated learning programs are one of the fastest-growing areas within higher education (Wlodkowski, 2003). This section will provide over a brief overview of the research on accelerated programs, including learning outcomes, as well as faculty and student assessments of these courses.

In 1992, Scott and Conrad completed a comprehensive analysis of the literature on accelerated courses. Comparing the learning outcomes of the students enrolled in accelerated courses to those enrolled in traditional-length courses, they reported the learning to be comparable and sometimes superior in the accelerated courses across content areas. Some design flaws were identified in the research analyzed, however. The use of final course grades as the only measure of learning was one concern. In addition, most of the studies did not utilize random assignment, and few of the studies matched control and experimental groups for homogeneity.

Wlodkowski and Westover (1999) conducted a 2-year evaluation of six undergraduate courses. Responding to several of the design flaws in previous studies that were identified by Scott and Conrad in their 1992 analysis of the literature on intensive courses, Wlodkowski and Westover utilized summative, performance-based measures of learning in an effort to more clearly assess student learning and mastery of course content. Students were evaluated on their responses to authentic case studies and problems, which required answers that reflected the general objectives of each course. Faculty experts in each subject area designed and reviewed a summative evaluation for the courses studied. These faculty experts were unaware of the student demographics or the course delivery format the students had completed. When the accelerated courses were compared to the traditional courses, no significant differences were found in learning. Looking at the work of the students enrolled in all six courses, regardless of the delivery method, traditional or accelerated, the faculty experts found that four out of five students in this study met a standard of satisfactory to excellent for course work at the college level.

Studies of faculty and students have provided support for accelerated courses. Johnson (2009) interviewed faculty who taught both accelerated and traditional-length courses. These participants cited several advantages to accelerated courses. They commented on the benefits of the longer class session of the accelerated courses and indicated that it led to better attendance, greater participation in class discussion, and an energy level that was sustained throughout the accelerated course that was not typically found in longer courses. Moreover, studies of students' perceptions indicated that most students completing an accelerated degree believe they have received a high quality education (Donaldson & Graham, 2002; Scott, 2003; Scott & Conrad, 1992; Wlodkowski, Mauldin, & Gahn, 2001; Wlodkowski & Westover, 1999).

Students in accelerated programs often described the importance of the classroom environment, instructor characteristics, and teaching methodology as contributing to their learning (Scott, 2003). Kasworm (2003) interviewed 20 students enrolled in an accelerated degree completion cohort program in applied management and found that students appreciated faculty who were practitioners, homework related to their lives, and small classes. They also mentioned the importance of a caring environment of faculty and fellow adult students, and feedback on their course work that gave them a sense of accomplishment. These students commented on the higher level of thinking they were discovering through reflection and introspection. The students also saw the accelerated degree experience as creating the setting for learning and successful degree completion. Students appreciated the predictable program structure with preset courses. They valued taking one course at a time, knowing that their meeting time would remain consistent throughout the degree program, and having a predictable time line for completion of their degree. Students appreciated the accelerated degree program for its structure that "pushed them" to completion.

METHODOLOGY

A qualitative study was completed by interviewing alumni of an accelerated degree program. Merriam and Simpson (1995) explained that qualitative methods of research are well suited to uncovering the meaning of an experience for those involved, making such methodology especially appropriate for an applied field such as adult education. In order to improve, it is important to understand the experiences of those impacted by our practice as educators. A basic assumption of qualitative research is that individuals construct their own reality based on their interaction with their social worlds. In conducting this study, we sought the perspectives of students who had completed an accelerated bachelor's degree.

Participants

Eleven graduates of an adult, accelerated degree completion program at a private, not-for-profit university in the Chicago area were interviewed. Study participants were solicited through full-time faculty and staff at the University. Two of the full-time faculty conducted the interviews. Neither of them interviewed alumni that had been in their classes while enrolled in the program. Table 8.1 provides a summary of the study participants. The demographics of the participants basically mirrors those of alumni of the program, although there has been an increase in international students in this program within the past 2 to 3 years.

Data Collection

IRB approval was secured and each study participant signed a consent form. Semistructured interviews were scheduled with each participant. The average interview lasted approximately 50 minutes. All interviews were audiotaped and transcribed by the interviewer. Although the interview guide outlined a set of potential questions, a general open-ended interview approach was utilized to provide for flexibility while covering the research questions. The two interviewers also conducted member checks to help confirm the validity of their findings. This involved asking

Table 8.1.   Summary of Study Participants

Pseudonym	Demographic Information
Alice	• Single, no children • African American female • Age: mid 40s
Melissa	• Single, children • African American female • Age: mid 30s
Kim	• Married, no children • Caucasian female • Age: late 40s
Tammy	• Single, no children • African American female • Age: mid 30s
Donna	• Married, no children • Caucasian female • Age: late 40s
Carl	• Married, children • African American male • Age: early 50s
Paige	• Married, children • Caucasian female • Age: late 40s
Shante'	• Single, children • African American female • Age: mid 30s
Mary	• Single, one child • African American female • Early 30s
Thomas	• Married, children • Caucasian male • Age: mid to late 40s
Sean	• Single, children • African American male • Late 40s early 50s

questions of the participants during the interview as well as during the data analysis process. Each participant was assigned a pseudonym to protect his or her anonymity in this publication.

Data Analysis

Data were read thoroughly to gain a general sense of understanding by the two researchers and a neutral party, who is the third author of this study. In the beginning, each of us coded the data individually. "Coding is nothing more than assigning some form of shorthand designation to various aspects of your data so that you can easily retrieve specific pieces of the data" (Merriam, 1998, p. 164). We chose hand coding because software creates a separation between the reader and the material, sometimes creating artificial categories. While software can undeniably be helpful, immersion in the material often demands hand coding.

We made notes in the margins of each transcript to identify key points and general thoughts about the data. Creswell (2003) described data analysis as a process of making sense of text and image data. This process is ongoing, requiring continual reflection on the data. This analysis moves the researcher to a deeper and deeper understanding of the data. Coding and recoding were done according to the constant comparative method. The constant comparative method involves continually comparing individual units of data with each other seeking similarities and differences (Merriam, 1998).

After each of the three authors coded the data, they organized their themes and sent them, along with the supporting data, to the lead author. There was an interrater reliability of 75% among the three authors. Each identified three themes: the motivating factors of study participants to continue their education, the impact of the cohort on them as learners, and the learning and self-awareness gained by the study participants as a result of completing their degree in this program. The third author, who did not conduct any of the interviews and did not have any connection to the study participants or this particular program, identified a fourth theme. This theme identified the stressors of returning to school. Bogdan and Biklen (2003) explained that different qualitative researchers might have different findings based on their experiences and academic training. Upon reflection, the first two authors realized that they had not focused on these findings as they were not directly related to our research questions. Also, our students had often shared such challenges with us in the classroom making this data not stand out for us. We all agreed to the addition of this theme as it added a significant element of the study participants' perceptions.

FINDINGS

The data collected identified streams that have proven very insightful, motivating, and encouraging. The participants shared information that has been valuable to us as researchers and adult educators, but the information can be very helpful for adults contemplating returning to school or are enrolled in an adult accelerated program. The findings fell into four themes. The first, the motivation of the students to return to school, is discussed in the next section.

Motivation to Return to School

Why did the study participants come back to school? There is a great deal of research in this area, some of it conflicting. Although Aslanian (2001) found that 85% of adults report their career as a key motivator in their return to higher education, other research suggests that returning students are often motivated by a need to grow and a sense of self-satisfaction and fulfillment (Scala, 1996). In her research on motives and difficulties faced by older adult returning students, Scala indicated that students seeking degrees are more likely to select a "sense of achievement/ increased self-esteem" as a positive aspect and a motivating factor in going back to school. Similar to Scala's findings, many of the participants in this study were not fulfilled by their life. Improvement in their professional work life was the least cited reason for the study participants returning to school. The theme of self-improvement overshadowed all other motivators. When discussing his reasons for continuing his education, Carl stated, "for some self-worth, and completing something that I should of done a while back." Similarly, Alice who had attended three colleges over a 10-year period explained, "I wanted to complete something ... and to be able to have an intelligent conversation."

Under the general desire to complete their undergraduate degree, students' determination to succeed was often attributed to setting an example for their families, in particular their children. Thomas was one participant motivated by this factor. He stated, "I want my children to have something and someone to look up to ... I am a first generation college graduate and I did not want that cycle to continue in my family." Coker's (2003) research found that this source of motivation is particularly true among adult African American women in higher education. In her study, Coker discovered that returning African American students were highly motivated by family development and explicitly expressed that returning to school would benefit the entire family unit. Brookfield's (1986) observations when working with adult learners were similar to those expressed by the study participants. He wrote that adults engage in educational activities due to some intrinsic desire to learn and/or improve themselves.

Kasworm (2008) stated, "Learning is an act of hope" (p. 27). This was definitely the case for the participants of this study. They looked at education as something that would fulfill them. Even the most resilient learners might find entering college challenging, however (Kasworm, 2008). As the study participants described their desires and motivations to return to school, they also explained the barriers. Their comments led to the development of the second theme which was the impact of stressors, both anticipatory and real, that were overcome by the study participants as they continued their education.

Stressors Associated With Returning to School as an Adult

Though there were several motivating reasons to return to school, some hindrances did exist. These hindrances often deterred the study participants from returning to school but were eventually over ridden by previously listed motivating reasons to return. Until this occurred, an internal tug of war ensued in the participants. Reasons of improvement were pulling the study participants towards continuing education, but this was battled strongly by reasons to remain steadfast.

The main stressor identified by the study participants was time management. The traditional student often is not restricted by outside demands that engulf a nontraditional student. Traditional students often cultivate a deeper social life on campus to socially educate themselves and prepare for life's later complexities. The nontraditional students typically do not need these additional complexities. Often their lives are filled with reasons to return to school, namely their families, but these same reasons can be a deterrent in accomplishing their goals. Prior to entering the program, study participants repeatedly worried about how they would manage work, family, and school. One of the benefits of the program was the fact that it was accelerated and more manageable for the study participants. Most of them continued to work full-time while attending school, and many of them were also parents.

The advancement in technology was another concern expressed by the study participants. The personal computer and the various software programs used in academia can be intimidating and was a common concern for the participants. Carl stated, "At the beginning (of the program) I was really skeptical. I wasn't sure because of all the electronics, the YouTube's, power points" What may appear to be common skills for traditional students may fill an adult student with fear and dread.

Society possibly produces some of the fears adults face in returning to college. College is defined by society as the domain of the young who are attending upon completion of their high school education. The reality is much different on today's college campuses. Nontraditional students are not few and far between. This might be a comfort, but sometimes a fleeting one. It is one thing to know that nontraditional students exist on campus; it is another thing to become one.

Low self-confidence and anxiety over being a nontraditional student created an initial barrier to the study participants. Kim, who was employed in the corporate world and appeared to be quite successful and confident in this arena, expressed her anxiety over being able to do well in her classes and "fit" in the academic world. This is good example of the doubt that many returning students seem to be burdened with before returning to school. It appears that they believe there is a need of improvement in their lives, but self-doubt can hinder them from moving forward. Paige expressed trepidation over returning to school at her age. "One of the things that loomed over my head was that I was going to be the oldest in the classroom with a bunch of young people. I am going to feel a lot more outdated than I already am. I was scared about my skill set." Where to begin with overcoming this stigma?

A corrective step would be reexamining the title for these students. A new name is needed for this contingent of students. New traditional student is more appropriate, life learner has a duality of meaning that of being perpetually educated and of learning from life first before attending school, or maybe something more exotic like Junto student which originates from Benjamin Franklin and his efforts to improve himself and his fellow intellects. It simply needs to be changed for the term nontraditional has a negative connotation and is false. This would be a small step in redefining what it means to be a college student.

The fears noted by the study participants seemed to basically vanish once the action of being in school occurred. Once in the program, they were too busy to have general fears and were engulfed in the realities of a demanding accelerated program. Adult learners play multiple roles in their lives, often making them more committed to their studies. It has been suggested that such students often compensate for their lack of confidence and/or skills by committing more to their academics than their traditional counterparts (Donaldson & Graham, 2002). This was definitely true of the study participants. They were willing to push past those initial anxieties and stressors to be successful students.

Fortunately, the program seemed to be designed for success. This is not to say that the program was easy or dumbed down so that individuals would easily pass. According to the participants, the program was more than challenging, but one asset given to these students was the cohort. We elaborate on this in the next section.

The Power of the Cohort

The participants in this study had taken a sequence of 12 courses together over a 13 to 14-month period. Each cohort group included approximately 15 students. The group was coordinated by a full-time faculty member who mentored the learners throughout their program, taught some of their courses, and selected the adjunct faculty who taught the remaining courses.

Several researchers have stated that the classroom is the central point of learning for adult students. Due to the limited time they spend on campus, adult students see the classroom as their main place for engagement and interaction. Unlike the traditional-aged student, whose primary support and influence comes from collegiate involvement with peers, most adult students indicate that their most significant campus experiences take place in the classroom (Donaldson & Graham, 1999; Kasworm, 2003).

In reference to the cohort, one concept that keeps recurring is that of the fasces. Fasces are basically a bundle of sticks used to represent strength through unity. One stick could be easily broken in two. The fasces fortify the individual pieces and allow this unit to endure various stresses repeatedly as long as they hold together; and, so it was with the cohort.

The cohorts developed into learning communities that impacted the participants in three major ways. First, the cohort helped the students adapt to returning to school. The students discovered that others felt the same anxiety they did and that helped them work through their own fears. Also of significance was the support the students received from classmates. Participants described meeting outside of class to work on assignments and assisting each other with things like babysitting. Finally, the cohort had a tremendous impact on the students' learning. Participants frequently mentioned new ideas they were exposed to from their classmates, as well as the ability to work with others in groups as a result of their class experience.

Reading these interviews makes one realize how easy or basic the traditional college experience is in comparison. Alice explained, "And so we actually had regular study groups that involved meeting at a restaurant, whenever and then doing our homework and eating and trying to be supportive for whatever ... your cry session, and motivating." What developed was a functioning relationship of several diverse people to accomplish one goal.

While many of the relationships within the cohort developed naturally due to the needs and personalities of the learners, there were times when intervention was needed. Participants mentioned the role of the faculty coordinator in facilitating such interventions. One participant shared that at one point during the program the group seemed to be losing focus and becoming negative. The coordinator insisted that each student share one positive thing about getting a degree. This helped them refocus on their goal.

Other participants discussed the importance of the faculty being in touch with the needs of the students. Several examples were given of the student-centered education they received. One instructor, after realizing that students were not grasping the concepts he covered in class, apologized to the students. He explained that it was obvious that he had failed in meeting their needs as learners and asked how he might better support them. Numerous similar experiences were shared by the study participants. They appreciated the role of the faculty in supporting them on their journeys. There were some negative experiences shared, but they were minimal. The participants resented faculty who did not respect them and their classmates and did not attempt to understand the needs of the group when they came into teach their courses.

Kasworm (2003) reported similar findings related to the structure of the cohort. Like these study participants, Kasworm's participants reported on the family feeling and supportive community within the cohort. In addition to the support that the cohort provided, it also enhanced the learning of the participants. Nesbit (2001) stated that although cohorts were designed for convenience, they have the potential for enhancing student learning. The next section will focus on the learning the study participants took away from their experience in the accelerated program.

Learning Beyond the Curriculum

Although the study participants' original goal was to complete their degree quickly and efficiently, at some point during the program they learned to enjoy the art of learning. Again, the cohort was mentioned when discussing the learning outcomes of the program. The participants began their program with a group dynamics course. They repeatedly mentioned how they came back to that course throughout the program. After learning things such as the phases of group development and conflict resolution, they were able to draw on this knowledge when working with their classmates. The cohort served as a laboratory for learning and practicing new knowledge, which the participants also applied to other areas of their lives such as family relationships and their work environments. Tammy explained,

> I noticed within my workplace that I grew from school. I saw that blending because in the program basically we were able to take our prior learning and enhance it … I really cherish that sense of getting more deeper into the understanding of what I learned and growing from it.

The participants were very positive about the learning from their courses. Many discussed the format of the program and how their classmates enhanced their learning. Mary shared,

> The course work offered me three forms of development that I will always appreciate; personal development, professional development and social development. Within this program and due to the course work, fellow students and professors, I have excelled in all areas.

Participants also mentioned how they learned a great deal from their classmates that enhanced their understanding of interacting with members of cultures different from their own. They commented on the honesty and respect that developed among their classmates. This was not always easy, and some conflicts did occur, but the study participants had developed knowledge from their classes that assisted them in working through issues. In addition, the faculty facilitated and intervened in a positive manner when needed.

Much of the learning went beyond course content. Participants consistently spoke of their growth as individuals, their increased self-awareness, and their growing confidence. Donna stated, "I came into the program very shy and withdrawn, but along the way I have learned to open up to others more and to communicate in a way that would make others hear and understand what I am trying to get across." Donna was not alone. Others spoke of how they felt more respected and could carry on an intelligent conversation. Some discussed the leadership skills they developed, along with solid communication skills. Describing his experience, Sean stated, "It allows students to focus on the practical application of the science of learning." Sean continued, "Working in these particular groups with teammates from a variety of backgrounds and skills level allowed me the opportunity to achieve both personal training goals as well as solutions." Sean explained how his experience in this program led him to appreciate the process of lifelong learning and inspired him to continue his education beyond a bachelor's degree.

The study participants provided numerous examples of how they shared their knowledge with colleagues and supervisors and were provided with new growth opportunities as a result. Much of the literature in adult education states the importance of adults being able to apply their new learning to various aspects of their lives (Imel, 2001; Knowles, 1980). The information provided by the participants of this study confirmed this belief. This application of their knowledge went beyond the content, however. It was about transferring such knowledge to gain confidence within them. Alice stated,

> I feel good that I have learned many things, and I am able to engage in conversations about any particular subject matter and I don't have to be a subject matter expert. I feel like I am less intimidated about being around other people.

IMPLICATIONS FOR PRACTICE

The study participants provided information that can be beneficial to staff and faculty when working with adult learners. By understanding their experiences, and what led to their success, we can put structures in place to support future students; especially those in accelerated cohorts.

The participants experienced a great deal of anxiety over returning to school. Issues such as time management and dealing with new technologies can be addressed in an orientation program. Group and individual information sessions done by recruiters can address these issues to encourage individuals to enroll. These matters should also be attended to when students enter the program. By sharing anxieties, students realize they are not alone. The perception of the study participants that they do not fit into higher education is a deeper issue. Many programs, including the one in this study, isolate the adult learners from the remainder of the student population. This might be the correct approach to providing adult students with a comfortable place to learn. However, as we continue to see diversity in higher education, it might be better to ask ourselves how to create a welcoming and supportive learning environment where no one group feels out of place.

As in Kasworm's (2003) study, participants also mentioned the significance of the cohort in their learning and persistence. The support of classmates and faculty, as well as the predictability of their course schedule, were highly valued. While the cohort might not be best for students requiring more flexibility, it did fill a significant need for these learners.

Kasworm (2011) challenged adult educators to go beyond providing new information, and encourage learners to critically reflect on their learning and apply to various contexts. The students' learning went beyond course content. They were able to see how concepts from the courses were related and how they connected to various aspects of their lives. The faculty played a key role here. Previous studies have discussed the importance of application of learning. It appeared the group work and class discussions contributed to this greatly. In addition, the faculty modeled behavior that was useful to the learners. They offered the students the challenge to address issues on their own, but provided support when necessary.

LIMITATIONS AND RECOMMENDATION FOR FURTHER RESEARCH

The authors would be remiss if they did not acknowledge the small sample size of this study, and that the study participants were limited to alumni from one program. Therefore, the findings are not generalizable. We would recommend studying more students and going beyond one institution. It would also be interesting to compare the experiences of students in a cohort program compared those who were not in a cohort to examine if students who were not placed in a formal cohort formed their own cohorts or support groups to sustain them during the program.

REFERENCES

Aslanian, C. B. (2001). *Adult students today.* Washington, DC: The College Board.

Bogdan, B. C., & Biklen, S. K. (2003). *Qualitative research and design for education: An introduction to theories and methods* (4th ed.). Boston, MA: Allyn & Bacon.

Brookfield, S. D. (1986). *Understanding and facilitating adult learning.* San Francisco, CA: Jossey-Bass.

Coker, A. D. (2003). African American female adult learners: Motivations, challenges, and coping strategies. *Journal of Black Studies, 33*(5), 654-674.

Creswell, J. W. (2003). *Research design qualitative, quantitative, and mixed method approaches* (2nd ed.). Thousand Oaks, CA: SAGE.

Donaldson, J. F., & Graham, S. W. (1999). A model of college outcomes for adults. *Adult Education Quarterly, 5,* 24-40.

Donaldson, J. F., & Graham, S. W. (2002). Accelerated degree programs: Design and policy implications. *The Journal of Continuing Higher Education, 50*(2), 2-13.

Husson, W. J., & Kennedy, T. (2003). Developing and maintaining accelerated degree programs within traditional institutions. In R. J. Wlodkowski & C. E. Kasworm (Eds.), *Accelerated learning for adults: The promise and practice of intensive educational formats* (pp. 51-61). San Francisco, CA: Jossey-Bass.

Imel, S. (2001). *Adult learners in postsecondary education.* Columbus, OH: Clearinghouse on Adult, Career, and Vocational Education. Retrieved from http://www.calpro-online.org/ERIC/docgen.asp?tbl=pab&ID=107

Johnson, C. (2009). Faculty speak on the impact of time in accelerated courses. *The Journal of Continuing Higher Education, 57*(3), 149-158.

Kasworm, C.E. (2003). From the adult student's perspective: Accelerated degree programs. In R. J. Wlodkowski & C. E. Kasworm (Eds.), *Accelerated learning for adults: The promise and practice of intensive educational formats* (pp. 17-28). San Francisco, CA: Jossey-Bass.

Kasworm, C. E. (2008). Emotional challenges of adult learners in higher education. *New Directions for Adult and Continuing Education, 120,* 27-34. doi: 10.1002/ace.313

Kasworm, C. E. (2011). The influence of the knowledge society: Trends in adult higher education. *The Journal of Continuing Higher Education, 59,* 104-107.

Knowles, M. S. (1980). *The modern practice of adult education: From pedagogy to andragogy* (2nd ed.). Chicago, IL: Follett.

Merriam, S. B. (1998). *Qualitative research and case study applications in education.* San Francisco, CA: Jossey-Bass.

Merriam, S. B., & Simpson, E. L. (1995). *A guide to research for educators and trainers of adults* (2nd ed.). Malabar, FL: Krieger Publishing Company.

National Center for Educational Statistics (2007). Table 3.3. Retrieved from http://nces.ed.gov/das/library/tables_listings/showTable2005.asp?popup=true&rt=p&tableID=6929

Nesbit, T. (2001). *Extending graduate education to non-traditional learners.* Vancouver, BC: Simon Frasier University Centre for Credit & Integrated Studies. (ERIC Document Reproduction Service No. 452 750)

Scala, M. A. (1996). Going back to school: Participation motives and experiences of older adults in an undergraduate classroom. *Educational Gerontology, 22,* 747–773.

Scott, P. A. (2003). Attributes of high quality intensive courses. In R. J. Wlodkowski & C. E. Kasworm (Eds.), *Accelerated learning for adults: The promise and practice of intensive educational formats* (pp. 29-38). San Francisco, CA: Jossey-Bass.

Scott, P. A., & Conrad, C. F. (1992). A critique of intensive courses and an agenda for research. In J. C. Smart (Ed.), *Higher education: Handbook of theory and research* (pp. 411-459). New York, NY: Agathon Press.

Wlodkowski, R. J. (2003). Accelerated learning in colleges and universities. In R. J.Wlodkowski, & C. E. Kasworm (Eds.), *Accelerated learning for adults: The promise and practice of intensive educational formats* (pp. 5-16). San Francisco, CA: Jossey-Bass.

Wlodkowski, R. J., Mauldin, J. E., & Gahn, S. W. (2001). *Learning in the fast lane: Adult learners' persistence and success in accelerated college programs.* Indianapolis, IN: Lumina Foundation for Education.

Wlodkowski, R. J., & Westover, T. N. (1999). Accelerated courses as a learning format for adults. *Canadian Journal for the Study of Adult Education, 13*(1), 11-20.

CHAPTER 9

DIFFERENCES BETWEEN COLLEGE STUDENT-PARENTS' AND NONPARENTS' FACTORS OF MOTIVATION AND PERSISTENCE

Elyse D'nn Lovell

The increasing numbers of newly identified lifelong learners (nontraditional students) leads to a dynamic environment as adult learners and their needs are being recognized (Goodman & Simms, 2005; Lloyd & Griffiths, 2008). Enrollments of nontraditional students are expected to increase more significantly than traditional students over the next 10 years (Michelau & Lane, 2010; National Center for Educational Statistics, [NCES], 2009). Students who are parents represent one group of nontraditional students. Literature suggests unique barriers occur for nontraditional students in enrollment, retention, motivation, and persistence including academic, financial, social, cultural, and personal issues (Dougherty & Woodland, 2009; Flint, 2005; Frey, 2007; Fusch, 2010; Grayson, 1996; Spellman, 2010). Nontraditional student categories (adult learners) show different views and perceptions in overcoming obstacles as they persist toward degree attainment (Brown, 2004; Chaves, 2006; Kinser & Deitchman, 2007).

Conversations About Adult Learning in Our Complex World, pp. 125–141

The focus of student-parents in the literature is primarily non-traditional or single mothers living in poverty (Burt & Nightingale, 2010; Sherr, 2010; Waring, 2010). The concentration on single mothers arises from both national demographic trends and changes in the proportion of college students who are women. Women giving birth who are single parents have risen to nearly 41% of all births in the United States (National Center for Health Statistics, 2008). Women have also become the majority of the U.S. undergraduate population at nearly 57% (National Post-Secondary Student Aid Study, 2008), and projections indicate a continued future increase in female college students (NCES, 2009).

This study examined factors that contributed to motivation and persistence among undergraduate college students who were parents compared to those who were not parents. Although the majority of parents on campus are women, little is known about the parents who are men. This study explores both women and men who are parents. Specifically, two questions were examined: (a) Is there a difference in motivation between students who are parents and students who are not parents? (b) Is there a difference in persistence between students who are parents and students who are not parents?

LITERATURE REVIEW

This literature review explored motivation and persistence factors by the indices in the survey of this study: motivation, enrollment barriers, student services, classroom services, continuing to attend college and the attainment of goals; gaps in literature concludes this review. Research is limited for student-parents, so some of this literature describes non-traditional students. Student-parents are one type of non-traditional students.

Student-parents described their motivation to degree attainment through the lens of their role as parents (Haleman, 2004). There is "no better motivation to finish college and to appreciate the marrow of the experience than a child whose future depends on your decisions" (Rizer, 2005, p. B5). Motivation to remain in school was often complicated by competing work demands, family, child care responsibilities, and school barriers (Battle, 2007). Women's perceptions about motivation have been described differently from those of men, and services responding to gender preferences can assist with academic success. For example, females reported "higher levels of overall motivation as well as intrinsic and extrinsic motivation" when compared to males in a study by Brouse, Basch, LeBland, McKnight, and Lei (2010).

As adults enroll and begin to explore the option of attending college, it is beneficial for administration to convey its understanding of diversity in students' life experiences in both their role (as a student) and existential roles (parent and employee) (Kelly & Ewell, 2009). Improved communication shows respect for the individualism of each student (Donoghue, & Stein, 2007). "Access without support is not opportunity" was a title and theme suggesting the critical nature of helping students to navigate from enrollment throughout their academic experience for improved success (Engstrom & Tinto, 2008; Tinto, 2008). Professionals and students benefit from an understanding and support of socioeconomic barriers, differing perceptions by gender, timely services, and assessment of needs (Bryan & Simmons, 2009; Frey, 2007; Satterlee, 2002).

Well-rounded student services are greatly improved with a "high-touch approach" (Hart, 2008). The "high touch approach" was described as hiring the right advisors, having pre-assessment conversations, and offering continuous rather than one-time support. Cultural awareness to accommodate needs through "cultural initiatives" can positively impact change by improving campus communication, collaboration, and ingenuity of staff (Massey, Locke, & Neuhard, 2009). Improved persistence, retention, and academic achievement have been seen when support services include technical, financial, registration, advising, and tutoring support (Dolan, Donohue, Hostrom, Pernell, & Sachdev, 2009). Inconvenient scheduling or lack of support services for financial aid was described as a hindrance to students' success (Shank, Winchell, & Myers, 2001).

When classroom experiences of adult learners' are responsive to their individual needs, recognizing students' life skills outside of the classroom and the richness of life experiences; their academic success can be improved (Barnes & Piland, 2011; Goodman & Simms, 2005; Ntiri, 1999; Stone, 2008; Wilmer, 2005). Learning environments reflective of the student's life experience and teaching with varied instruction (experiential and problem based methods) within the classroom helps to achieve stronger learning outcomes particularly for nontraditional students (Flint, 2005). Stated in the introduction of King's (2009) book, transformational learning can help the adult learner to "gain new understandings of themselves, their past and their future ... with an entirely different set of lenses" (p. xx). Adult learners benefit from metacognitive strategies and have been seen to be more competent, particularly in reading, when epistemological frameworks are considered (Ntiri, Schindler, & Henry, 2004).

Attainment goals can be related to weak relationships on campus, feeling inferior to peers, and cultural differences (Lehmann, 2007; Martinez & Munday, 1998; Purslow & Belcastro, 2006). Bean and Metzner's (1985) nontraditional student attrition model explains differences when comparing traditional and nontraditional students. First, nontraditional students are less involved in social activities on campus, but this "should have only minimal effects on retention"; and second, they spend more time with social activities and family off campus which "can play a significant role in the attrition process" (p. 530).

There are several gaps in research about student-parents including male, married, and student-parent theory. While men are a minority of student-parents on campus, they are present. This population as an individual group is unrepresented in literature. Married students seem marginalized and underrepresented in literature. The existing literature does not appear proportionate to this population. A retention theory for student-parents does not exist. The application of current feminist (Allen, Dean, & Bracken, 2008; Holland & Eisenhart, 1990), identity, cognitive, and moral development (Jewel, 2001; Svinicki, 1999; Swenson, Hiester, & Nordstrom, 2011,) cultural (Bourdieu, 1993) and retention theories (Astin, 1991; Bean & Metzner, 1985; Tinto, 1993) could provide further insight for student-parents' retention.

In this study the differences between student-parents' and nonparents' motivation and persistence (enrollment barriers, student services, classroom experiences, decision to continue attending college and attainment goals) are explored after controlling for factors which may be predictors for influencing outcomes. These factors include parental status, gender, age, marital status, and degree plan (two year/four year). When reflecting upon Bean and Metzner's (1985) nontraditional student attrition model, a hypothesis was formed that there were different factors in motivation and persistence between student-parents and nonparents.

METHODS

This study was a quantitative comparative analysis using a non-experimental approach with a quasi-experimental design. This comparison was between two populations: undergraduate student-parents and undergraduate students who are not parents. This analysis and design was selected by appropriateness for social and behavioral sciences (Gliner, Morgan, & Leech, 2009). To strengthen reliability, a published analysis and design was referenced (Myers, 2008).

Sample

The sampling design was nonprobability, which is considered appropriate for a social sciences study (Gliner, Morgan, & Leech, 2009). Four hundred twelve surveys were distributed over the last week of the spring semester to freshman English and math classes at one institution. This institution has a 2-year and 4-year campus. After eliminating incomplete surveys, a final sample was used with 356 students. Sample sizes were under thirty in degree plans: certificate, undecided, and pursuing a graduate degree. Participants in these degree plan categories were eliminated because the reduced sample size would potentially provide reduced reliability in the analysis (Gliner, Morgan, & Leech, 2009). Questions were condensed for students' ages from six selections to two: traditional and nontraditional. The institution was in a rural setting (community population 35,000) in the Rocky Mountains. Institutional data showed the 2-year population had 63% traditional students (24 and younger) and 37% nontraditional students (25 and older). The 4-year institution had 71% traditional students (24 and younger) and 29% nontraditional students (25 and older). Notably, the institution does not track students by parental status, but this study tracks students by age and parental status to increase understanding. This allows consideration of existing tracking by the institution and expanded tracking for further knowledge about parents specifically.

Instrumentation

The instrument for assessment was a survey that was designed for the purpose of this study by merging two existing surveys together (Grayson, 1996; Kinser & Deitchman 2007). The purpose of merging two surveys together was to enhance reliability. A Cronbach's alpha was run for each index to assure relationships among each group of questions (factors) to assure measurement validity. The survey was a self-report measure with comparative, associational, and descriptive approaches. The survey items were a combination of close-ended and unordered items with ordered choices. Internal consistency for reliability was established with a Likert scale with questions in six indices.

The motivation index questions asked: lack self-confidence to complete studies, do not have enough energy to complete studies, enjoy studying in general, like schools and classrooms, stress level, family motivation. There were five persistence indices with questions: (1) enrollment barriers: transportation problems, money problems, home computer with internet, friends support education, employer supports education, family supports education, courses scheduled at convenient times, staff hours adequate for enrollment, financial aid hours adequate, and too much red tape—admissions; (2) decision to continue attending college: not motivated to do the work, computer skills lacking, difficulty with time to study, difficulty with studying, too many other demands in my life affecting the classroom, good job balancing school and personal, studies rewarding, enjoy what I am learning, studies can help me make more money, feel safe in classroom, feel safe on campus; (3) classroom experiences: professors helpful, professor's effort is high in teaching, professor is interested in students' development, professor is unreasonable in demands, content is relevant, courses challenging, student participation valued, feel comfortable talking with professors; (4) student services: financial aid is adequate, tutoring adequate, counseling services adequate, on campus housing adequate; (5) degree attainment goals: eventually achieve my academic goals, earn a degree from my current college, and transfer to another college, choose to stop attending college for at least a semester, be forced to stop attending college for at least a semester. There were five control variables: gender, age, marital status, degree plan, and parental status.

Analysis

There were two sections to this analysis that were selected recommended social science methods (Gliner, Morgan, & Leech, 2009). The first section reviewed the descriptive analyses by the entire sample and the subgroups of (1) student-parent and (2) student nonparent with mean, standard deviation, and frequency (percentage) distribution. The second section reviews statistical analyses to further explore differences between sub-groups (student-parent and nonparent): t-tests, bivariate correlation. Last, linear and multiple regressions were performed for each motivation and persistence index. Each index was analyzed by Model 1 parental status to show how they differ significantly and by Model 2 with all control variables to further clarify the influence of all variables together (parental status, gender, age, marital status and degree plan). After looking at each of these results, partial correlations provide further support and explanation of significance for control variables.

RESULTS

The data were described as a whole with the entire sample and by subpopulations of student-parent and nonparent status: the entire study sample ($n = 323$), subgroup of student-parents ($n = 94$) (29%), and subgroup of non-parent students ($n = 229$) (71%).

These samples were viewed by dependent variables in Table 9.1A and were described in two categories: persistence and motivation (Lovell, 2011, p. 76). The category of persistence had five variables with higher levels of median scores for persistence for parents in the decision to continue (parents 2.87/nonparents 2.77), classroom experiences (parents 3.09/nonparents 2.98), student services (parents 2.98/nonparents 2.89), and attainment goals (parents 2.48/nonparents 2.47). Enrollment barriers had higher levels for nonparents (parents 3.09/nonparents 3.12). Motivation levels were higher for parents (2.88/nonparents 2.78).

These samples were viewed by independent variables in Table 9.1B: parental status, gender, age, marital status, and degree plan (Lovell, 2011, p. 76). Frequency distributions showed females represented a majority of both the entire sample (54%) and the student-parent sample (70%) while males represented the majority of student nonparents (53%). Traditional age students (18-24) represented a majority of both the entire sample (71%) and also student nonparents (86%) while nontraditional students (age 25+) represented a majority (74%) of student-parents. Marital status of single/separated/widowed/divorced students showed a majority for both the entire sample (71%) and student nonparents (84%). Married/living with a partner represented the majority of student-parents (65%). Degree plan of study showed a majority earning a 4-year degree (58%) for both the entire sample and the student nonparents (65%); student-parents are earning a majority of 2-year degrees (60%).

The Cronbach's alpha results showed reliability: enrollment barriers (.711) with ten questions, decision to continue attending college (.779) with 11 questions, classroom experiences (.803) with 8 questions, student services (.734) with 4 questions, attainment goals (.748) with 5 questions, and motivation (.746) with 7 questions.

**Table 9.1A.   Dependent Variable Inventory of
All Variables by the Entire Sample and Two Subpopulations
(Student-Parent and Nonparent)**

Variable	Entire Sample (n = 323)		Student-Parents (n = 94)		Nonstudent Parents (n = 229)	
	(M)	(S)	(M)	(S)	(M)	(S)
Persistence Variables	3.11	.40	3.09	.38	3.12	.42
Enrollment Barriers	2.80	.27	2.87	.28	2.77	.26
Decision to Continue	3.01	.36	3.09	.39	2.98	.34
Student Services	2.91	.49	2.98	.49	2.89	.49
Attainment Goals	2.47	.37	2.48	.37	2.47	.37
Motivation Variable						
Motivation	2.81	.48	2.88	.4	2.78	.50

Coding/Range: Parent = 0, Nonparent = 1, 1 = Strongly Disagree, 2 = Disagree, 3 = Agree, 4 = Strongly Agree

**Table 9.1B. Independent Variable Inventory of
All Variables by the Entire Sample and
Two Sub-Populations (Student-Parent and Nonparent)**

Variable	Entire Sample (n = 323)	Student-Parents (n = 94)	Nonstudent-Parents (n = 229)
Independent Variables			
Gender			
Male	46%	30%	53%
Female	54%	70%	47%
Age			
18- 24 (Traditional)	71%	26%	86%
25 + (Nontraditional	29%	74%	14%
Marital Status			
Single/separated/widowed/divorced	71%	35%	84%
Married/living with partner	29%	65%	16%
Degree			
2-year degree	42%	60%	35%
4-year degree	58%	40%	65%

Coding/Range: 0 = Male, 1 = Female, 0 = Traditional age, 1 = Nontraditional age,
0 = Single/separated/widowed/divorced, 1 = Married/living with partner, 0 = 2-year
degree, 1 = 4-year degree

Assumptions were tested by examining normal probability plots of residuals and scatter diagrams of residuals versus predicted residuals. No violations of normality, linearity, or homoscedasticity of residuals were detected, and box plots revealed no evidence of outliers (Morgan, Leech, Gloeckner, & Barrett, 2007).

In Table 9.2, the regression analysis revealed that the Set 1, Model 2 variables significantly predicted differences in enrollment barriers when controlling for all independent variables with a variance of 3% (Lovell, 2011, p. 84). In terms of individual relationship, age showed significant influence for predictions with nontraditional students showing lower levels of enrollment barriers suggesting fewer enrollment barriers.

In Table 9.3, the decision to continue attending college was significantly predicted by parental status indicating a 3% variance in the decision to continue attending college (Lovell, 2011, p. 86). Nonparents have lower survey levels on their decisions to continue attending college suggesting weaker persistence. Although this was statistically significant, this difference would be difficult to see considering Cohen's effect size. In Set 2 Model 2 when all independent variables were controlled, the difference

Table 9.2.   Regression Analysis—Enrollment Barriers

Variable	Model	B	β	t	p	R²	Partial
Enrollment Barriers Set 1, Model 1							
	(enrollment DV¹ = parent/ nonparent)	.03	.03	.54	.589	−.002	
Set 1, Model 2							
	(enrollment DV¹=parent, gender, age, marital status, degree plan)				.027*	.03	
Parent/nonparent		−.08	−.09	−1.16	.245		−.07
Gender		.09	.11	− 1.89	.059		.11
Age		−.16	−.18	−2.62	.009**		−.15
Marital status		−.04	−.05	−.77	.440		−.04
Degree plan		.04	.04	.75	.452		.04

was not significant. In terms of individual relationship, nonparents showed lower levels of response significantly influencing the decision to continue.

In Table 9.4, results indicated that classroom experiences were significantly predicted by a 2% variance for parent status which suggested nonparents reported fewer quality experiences with lower survey response rates (Lovell, 2011, p. 87).

In Table 9.5, student services differences were significantly predicted when all variables were controlled (Lovell, 2011, p. 89). In terms of individual relationships parental status significantly indicated nonparents had lower survey levels suggesting weaker experiences with student services; females had higher response levels suggesting more positive experiences.

In Table 9.6, the individual relationship of marital status was a predictor for the attainment of goals explaining that married students had lower level survey responses for their experiences in their attainment goals suggesting weaker goal attainment (Lovell, 2011, p. 90).

In Table 9.7 the regression analysis revealed no significance (Lovell, 2011, p. 91).

The discussion will provide further clarification and explanation of the results from these analyses.

**Table 9.3. Regression Analysis—
Decision to Continue Attending College**

Variable	Model	B	β	t	p	R^2	Partial
Decision to Continue Attending College Set 2, Model 1							
	(continue DV^2 = parent/ nonparent)	−.10	−.17	−3.12	.002**	.03	
Set 2, Model 2							
	(continue DV^2=parent, gender, age, marital status, degree plan)				.068	.02	
Parent/nonparent		−.11	−.19	−2.50	.013*		−.14
Gender		−.00	−.00	−.04	.969		−.00
Age		−.03	−.05	−.78	.439		−.04
Marital Status		.02	.03	.45	.654		.03
Degree Plan		−.00	−.01	−.14	.890		.01

DISCUSSION

The results for enrollment barriers, the decision to continue attending college, and student services contradicted existing research, as these results showed fewer enrollment barriers for nontraditional age students, more positive persistence by parents to continue attending, and parents' more positive experiences with student services. This striking result may suggest that the distribution of the survey during the last week of the spring semester represented nontraditional students/parents who had overcome persistence barriers, so this sample did not include those who fell out and are often described in literature with greater challenges thereby negatively affecting motivation and persistence (Brown, 2004; Chaves, 2006; Kinser & Deitchman, 2007). Notably, only one third of the sample in this study accounted for parents in these classrooms, which may suggest higher attrition for parents.

The survey results for married/partnered students suggested lower goal levels for degree attainment. The tracking of married and partnered students combined is not a traditional tracking, but it was the intent of the researcher to reduced negative stereotypes described in the literature by

Table 9.4.   Regression Analysis—Classroom Experiences

Variable	Model	B	β	t	p	R²	Partial
Classroom Experiences Set 3, Model 1							
	(class experiences DV³ = parent/nonparent)	−.11	−.14	−2.51	.013*	.02	
Set 3, Model 2							
	(class experiences DV³=parent, gender, age, marital status, degree plan)				.230	.006	
Parent/nonparent		−.08	−.11	−1.42	.158		−.08
Gender		.02	.02	.37	.711		.02
Age		.03	.03	.48	.632		.03
Marital status		.00	.00	.06	.953		.00
Degree plan		−.02	−.03	−.48	.630		−.03

Table 9.5.   Regression Analysis—Student Services

Variable	Model	B	β	t	p	R²	Partial
Student Services Set 4, Model 1							
	(student services DV4 = parent/nonparent)	−.09	−.09	−1.55	.121	.004	
Set 4, Model 2							
	(student services DV4=parent, gender, age, marital status, degree plan)				.014*	.03	
Parent/nonparent		−.17	−.15	−2.07	.040*		−.12
Gender		.16	.16	2.77	.006**		.15
Age		−.09	−.08	−1.18	.239		−.07
Marital status		−.12	−.11	−1.68	.095		−.09
Degree plan		−.01	−.01	−.09	.925		−.01

Table 9.6.   Regression Analysis—Attainment Goals

Variable	Model	B	β	t	p	R^2	Partial
Attainment Goals Set 5, Model 1							
	(attainment DV5 = parent/nonparent)	−.01	−.01	−.26	.80	−.003	
Set 5, Model 2							
	(attainment DV5=parent, gender, age, marital status, degree plan)				.161	.009	
Parent/nonparent		−.03	−.04	−.50	.616		−.03
Gender		.05	.07	1.23	.220		.07
Age		.06	.08	1.14	.255		.06
Marital status		−.11	−.13	−2.07	.040*		−.12
Degree plan		.06	.09	1.47	.142		.08

Table 9.7.   Regression Analysis—Motivation

Variable	Model	B	β	t	p	R^2	Partial
Motivation Set 6, Model 1							
	(motivation DV6 = parent/nonparent)	−.11	−.09	−1.76	.080	.006	
Set 6, Model 2							
	(motivationDV6 = parent, gender, age, marital status, degree plan)				.098	.01	
Parent/nonparent		−.03	−.03	−.38	.703		−.02
Gender		.11	.11	1.88	.062		.10
Age		.13	.12	1.76	.077		.10
Marital status		−.04	−.04	−.59	.556		−.03
Degree plan		.03	.03	.59	.553		.03

single parents living in partnered relationships. This nontraditional tracking could be considered as results are interpreted. The majority of parents (65%) in this study were married. Literature suggests the balance of family and academics is challenging (Cox & Ebbers, 2010; Devos, Biera, Diaz, & Dunn, 2007; Marklein, 2010; Quimby & O'Brien, 2006; Ricco, Sabet & Clough, 2009). Findings by Pascarella and Terenzini

(2005), showed significant numbers of students who plan on 4-year degrees fall back to 2-year degrees while attending community colleges. A majority of the parent sample (60%) was earning 2-year degrees while the majority (65%) of the nonparent sample was earning 4-year degrees. These findings support marital status as a predictor of reduced goal attainment for married students which may be a reflection of their challenges in maintaining the balance of their responsibilities potentially reducing their academic goals.

IMPLICATIONS

These findings suggest that there are differences between parents' and nonparents' (adult learners') levels of persistence; the parents in this sample have higher levels of persistence than nonparents which is different than most literature about nontraditional students. Research suggests the numbers of nontraditional student enrollments which includes the category of student-parents are increasing on college campuses and are projected to continue increasing (Applegate, 2010; Michelau, & Lane, 2010). Administration, faculty, and support staffs need to understand the differences in parents' motivation and persistence when compared to traditional students in an effort to respond to their needs and their academic success. Education can be described as a drop of water creating a ripple effect as knowledge flows to others in shared vibration (Boden, 2009). The more parents who are attaining a degree increases the likelihood that their children will too "education begets education" (Pascarella, & Terenzini, 2005, p. 440). Student-parents are conduits to their children; a familial approach within higher education could improve persistence by recognizing the inseparable roles of student and parent in degree attainment.

RECOMMENDATIONS

It is conceivable that student-parents, (adult learners) may not be enrolling at all because of the lack of adequate student services (financial aid, and/or housing) or that, once enrolled, they do not continue to the end of the academic year because of the lack of sufficient student services. Listening sessions within the community and student exit interviews could provide additional insight. Student support services including counseling, financial aid, and familial support with understanding for the unique needs of student-parents would further benefit retention.

REFERENCES

Allen, J. K., Dean, D. R., & Bracken, S. J. (2008). *Most college students are women. Women learners on campus what do we know and what have we done?* Sterling, VA: Stylus.

Applegate, J. (2010, August). *Lumina Foundation it's not all about the kids.* Paper session presented at The Governor's Forum Building a Skilled Workforce, Kalispell, MT.

Astin, A. W. (1991). *Assessment for excellence: The philosophy and practice of assessment and evaluation in higher education.* New York, NY: Macmillan.

Barnes, R. A., & Piland, W. E. (2011). Impact of learning communities in developmental English on community college student retention and persistence. *Journal of College Student Retention: Research, Theory & Practice, 12*(1), 7-24.

Battle, L.S. (2007). "I wanna have a good future": Teen mothers' rise in educational aspirations, competing demands, and limited school support. *Youth & Society, 38*, 348-371.

Bean, J.P. & Metzner, B. S. (1985). A conceptual model of nontraditional undergraduate student attrition. *Review of Educational Research, 55*(4), 485-540.

Boden, C. J. (2009). A difference of degree: A case study of Iresa Stubblefield-Jones. In M. Miller & K. P. King (Eds.), *Empowering women through literacy views from experience* (pp. 211-219). Charlotte, NC: Information Age Publishing.

Bourdieu, P. (1993). *The field of cultural production.* Cambridge, England: Polity Press.

Brouse, C. H., Basch, C. E., LeBlanc, M., & McKnight, T. L. (2010). College students' academic motivation: Differences by gender, class, and source of payment. *College Quarterly, 13*, 1-10.

Brown, J. A. (2004). Marketing and retention strategies for adult degree programs in developing and delivering adult degree programs. *New Directions for Adult and Continuing Education, Developing and Delivering Adult Programs, 103*, 51-60. doi:10.1002/ace.148

Bryan, E., & Simmons, L. A. (2009). Family involvement: Impacts on post-secondary educational success for first generation Appalachian college students. *Journal of College Student Development, 50*(4), 391-402.

Burt, M. R., & Nightengale, D. S. (2010). *Repairing the U.S. social safety net.* Washington, DC: The Urban Institute Press.

Chaves, C. (2006). Involvement, development, and retention: Theoretical foundations and potential extensions for adult community college students. *Community College Review, 34*(2), 139-152.

Cox, E. M., & Ebbers, L. H. (2010). Exploring the persistence of adult women at a midwest community college. *Community College Journal of Research and Practice, 34*(4), 337-359.

Devos, T., Biera, E., Diaz, P., & Dunn, R. (2007). Influence of motherhood on the implicit academic self-concept of female college students: Distinct effects of subtle exposure to cues and directed thinking. *European Journal of Psychology of Education, 22*(3), 371-386.

Dolan S., Donohue, C., Holstrom, L., Pernell, L., & Sachdev, A. (2009). Supporting online learners blending high-tech with high-touch. *Online Learning Exchange,190*, 90-97.

Donoghue, C., & Stein, P. J. (2007). Diversity in adult experiences and criteria for adulthood among college students. *College Student Journal, 41*(4), 1-11.

Dougherty, C. B., & Woodland, R. (2009). Understanding sources of financial support for adult learners. *The Journal of Continuing Higher Education, 57*(3), 181-186.

Engstrom, C., & Tinto, V. (2008). Access without support is not opportunity. *Change: The Magazine of Higher Learning, 40*(1), 46-50.

Flint, T. (2005). How well are we serving our adult learners? Investigating the impact of institutions on success & retention. (Research report No. ED509933). Chicago, IL: Council for Adult and Experiential Learning

Frey, R. (2007). Helping adult learners succeed: Tools for two year colleges *Catalyst (21519390), 40*(2), 21-26.

Fusch, D. (2010). Re-enrolling stop-outs: Overcoming the barriers. *Higher Ed Impact Weekly Analysis for Academic Impressions, 7*(15), 1-4.

Gliner, J. A., Morgan, G. A, & Leech, N. L. (2009). *Research methods in applied settings an integrated approach to design and analysis.* New York, NY: Taylor & Francis Group.

Goodman, P., & Simms, S. (2005). Student success through policy and practice. *Community College Journal, 76*(1), 42-43.

Grayson, J. P. (1996). The retention of first year students in Atkinson College: Institutional failure or student choice? *Institute for Social Research York University,* 1-20.

Haleman, D. L. (2004). Great expectations: Single mothers in higher education. *International Journal of Qualitative Studies in Education, 17*(6), 769-784.

Hart, P. D. (2008) *How should colleges assess and improve student learning?* Washington, DC: Peter D. Hart Research Associates. Retrieved from http://www.aacu.org/advocacy/leap/documents/2008_Business_Leader_Poll.pdf

Holland, D.C. & Eisenhart, M. A (1990). *Educated in romance.* Chicago, IL: The University of Chicago Press.

Jewell, P. D. (2001). Measuring moral development: Feeling, thinking, and doing. *The New Zealand Association of Gifted Children, 13*(1). Retrieved from http//hdl.handle.net/2328/25974

Kelly, P. J., Ewell, P. T., & National Center for Higher Education Management Systems. (2009). Colleges and universities and their stewardship of place: A guide for developing performance measures for the equity of access and student success. *National Center For Higher Education Management Systems.* Retrieved from http:/www.nchems.org/pubs/detail.php?id=118

King, K. P. (2009). *Handbook of the evolving research of transformative learning.* Charlotte, NC: Information Age .

Kinser, K., & Deitchman, J. (2007). Tenacious persisters: Returning adult students in higher education. *Journal of College Student Retention: Research, Theory & Practice, 9*(1), 75-94.

Lehmann, W. (2007). "I just didn't feel like I fit in": The role of habitus in university drop-out decisions. *Canadian Journal of Higher Education, 17*(2), 89-110.

Lloyd, M. G., & Griffiths, C. (2008). A review of the methods of delivering HE programmes in an FE college and an evaluation of the impact this will have on learning outcomes and student progression. *Journal of Further and Higher Education, 32*(1), 15–25.

Lovell, E. D. (2011). *Motivation and persistence of college students who are parents compared to non-parent college students* (Unpublished doctoral dissertation). Montana State University, Bozeman, MT.

Marklein, M. B. (2010, May). When moms in school too. *USA Today.* Retrieved from http://www.usatoday.com/LIFE/usaedition/ 2010-05-06-momgrads06_ST_U.htm

Martinez, P. & Munday, F. (1998). 9,000 voices: student persistence and drop-out in further education. *FEDA Report. 2*(7), 1-171.

Massey, R., Locke, G. M., & Neuhard, I. P. (2009). The IRSC baccalaureate transition team: leading change in a culture of communication, collaboration, and creativity. *Community College Journal of Research and Practice, 33*, 956-957.

Michelau, D. K., & Lane, P. (2010, November). *Bringing Adults Back to College: Designing and Implementing a Statewide Concierge Model.* Boulder, CO: Lumina Foundation & Western Interstate Commission for Higher Education (WICHE). Retrieved from http://wiche.edu/pub/14608

Morgan, G. A., Leech, N. L., Gloeckner, G. W., & Barrett, K. C. (2007). *SPSS for introductory statistics use and interpretation.* Mahwah, NJ: Lawrence Erlbaum Associates.

Myers, C. B. (2008). College faculty and the scholarship of teaching: Gender differences across four key activities. *Journal of Scholarship of Teaching and Learning, 8*(2), 38-51.

National Center for Health Statistics. (2008). *Single mother birth rates* [Data file]. Retrieved from http://www.cdc.gov/nchs/data/hus/hus08.pdf

Ntiri, D. W., Schindler, R. A., & Henry, S. (2004). Enhancing adult learning through interdisciplinary studies. *New Directions in Adult and Continuing Education, 103*, 41-50.

NCES National Center for Educational Statistics. (2009). *National student data base.* [Data filed]. Retrieved from http://www.nces.ed.gov/

Ntiri, D. (1999). *Pedagogy for adult learners: methods and strategies. Models for adult and lifelong learning.* (Research Report No. Vol-2).

National Post-Secondary Student Aid Study. (2008). *National student data* [Data file]. Retrieved from http://www.nces.ed.gov/surveys/npsas

Pascarella, E., & Terenzini, P. (2005). *How college affects students.* San Francisco, CA: Jossey-Bass.

Purslow, V., & Belcastro, A. (2006, November). *An integrative framework: Meeting the needs of the new-traditional student.* Chicago, IL: Faculty Work and New Academy Meeting at the Association of Colleges and Universities,.

Quimby, J. L., & O'Brien, K. M. (2006). Predictors of well-being among nontraditional female students with children. *Journal of Counseling and Development, 84*, 451-460.

Ricco, R., Sabet, S., & Clough, C. (2009). College mothers in the dual roles of student and parent implications for their children's attitudes toward school. *Merrill-Palmer Quarterly, 55*(1), 79-110.

Rizer, M. (2005). When students are parents. *Chronicle of Higher Education, 52*(17), B5.

Satterlee, A. G. (2002). Conflict resolution strategies for the adult higher education student. [Report for United States Army War College]. Washington, DC: ERIC Clearinghouse on Higher Education (ERIC Document Reproduction Service No. ED462055). Retrieved from http://www.eric.ed.gov/PDFS/ED462055.pdf

Shank, M. D., Winchell, M. H., & Myers, M. (2001). Appreciating the needs of non-traditional students: Women as a growing market for colleges and universities. *Journal of Marketing for Higher Education, 1*(1), 63-72.

Sherr, L. (2010). The second lady's first love. *More. 38.* Retrieved from http://www.more.com/news/womens-issues/second-ladys-first-love

Spellman, N. (2010). Enrollment and retention barriers adult students encounter. *Community College Enterprise, 13*(1), 63-79.

Stone, C. (2008). Listening to individual voices and stories – the mature-age student experience. *Australian Journal of Adult Learning, 48*(2), 263-290.

Svinicki, M. (1999). New directions in learning and motivation. *New Directions for Teaching and Learning, 80,* 5-27. doi: 10.1002/tl.8001

Swenson Goguen, L. M., Hiester, M. A., & Nordstrom, A. H. (2011). Associations among peer relationships, academic achievement, and persistence in college. *Journal of College Student Retention: Research, Theory & Practice, 12*(3), 319-337.

Tinto, V. (1993). *Leaving college rethinking the causes and cures of student attrition.* San Francisco, CA: Jossey-Bass.

Tinto, V. (2008). *When access is not enough.* Stanford, CA: The Carnegie Foundation for the Advancement of Teaching. Retrieved from http://www.carnegiefoundation.org/perspectives/when-access-not-enough

Waring, S. (2010, May). *Listening to adult learners and determining how to assist them.* Paper presented at The Governor's Forum Building a Skilled Workforce, Kalispell, MT.

Wilmer, E. (2005). Student support services for the underprepared student. *Inquiry, 13*(1), 5-19.

CHAPTER 10

CAN ADULT STUDENTS TRANSFORM OUR UNIVERSITIES?

Xenia Coulter and Alan Mandell

Pick up virtually any book or article about the American university, and what do you read? Here, for example, is a typical line from a recent book by the late Charles Muscatine (2009), a long-time thoughtful commentator on higher education: "Most universities and colleges [are] devoted … to providing middle class youth with a four-year transition to adulthood, away from their parents, surrounded by their peers" (p. 4). In the same vein, a *Chronicle of Higher Education* reviewer of books about colleges (Benton, n.d.) sees his audience to be, not only faculty and administrators, but also "undergraduates *and their parents* [italics added]." Similarly, the *New York Times* occasional supplement, *Education Life,* reports exclusively on issues of interest primarily to parents and their adolescent children—for example, the heavy competition for college admissions among high school seniors (Bucior, 2012).

Continuously ignored in this literature is that more than half the students attending college today are *not* recent high school graduates (Kazis et al., 2007; Purple States TV, 2010). Indeed, the addition of an ever-increasing number of mature students has been taking place almost unnoticed for almost 40 years. We developed Figure 10.1 from existing data to

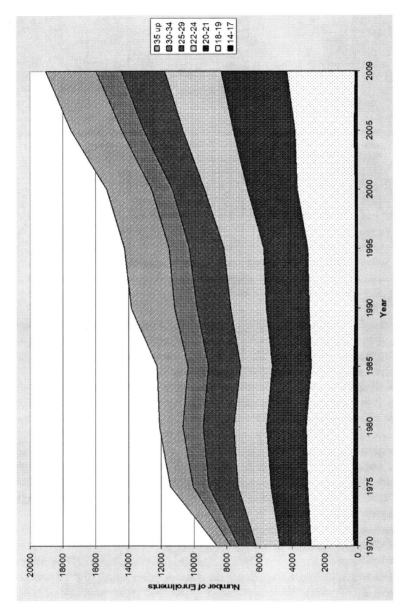

Figure 10.1. Total college enrollments by year and age. Enrollment numbers are in thousands. This is a graphical reproduction of data available from the U.S. Department of Education, National Center for Education Statistics, *Digest of Education Statistics* (2009), Table 191, retrieved from http://nces.ed.gov/programs/digest/d09

illustrate this fact. Indeed, the addition of an ever increasing number of mature students, also shown in Figure 10.1, has been taking place almost unnoticed for almost 40 years (Trow [1988/2007] dates the first serious burgeoning of adults students to 1972). Even Menand (2010), a well known historian and writer, in describing how the recent history of higher education has been marked by significant increases in many forms of diversity, omits mention of the increase in *age* diversity that is also representative of that trend. While colleges may indeed be devoted to "middle-class youth," as Muscatine (2009) claims, a growing majority of college students are, in truth, adults from all walks of life who do not live with their parents, do not compete for entrance into well-known colleges, and do not need artificial social environments in which to mature. The accepted image of college life, and its purported mission, is increasingly at odds with reality.

HIGHER EDUCATION FOR THE YOUNG

A succession of missions has marked the history of American higher education. Originally, colleges and universities focused solely upon the scholarly knowledge of the faculty (Rudolph, 1990). The principal goal was for "master" academics to nurture and acculturate "apprentice" scholars and to enlighten those bound for various professional careers. With the introduction of the public university, the mission was expanded to reflect not only faculty interests, but also increasingly diverse societal needs (Kennedy, 1997). A true democracy, it was believed, functions best with a morally responsible, well-educated public (Benson, Harkavy, & Puckett, 2007). Thus, a university education was envisioned not just to incubate scholarship, disseminate wisdom, or funnel students into professional schools, but to also provide instruction that would make responsible citizens of all students (Kennedy, 1997).

The exact nature of this last goal has varied over time—as widely, perhaps, as the mission statements in which it has been promoted (Fish, 2008). Citizenship preparation, sometimes confused with preparation for adulthood, has come to encompass whatever is currently in vogue. Thus today, we hear that to become an informed and useful member of society requires consideration of "a life worth living" (Dienst, 2011), learning experiences that debate the meaning of right and wrong (Friedman, 2011), and, often viewed as most important, the opportunity to select and prepare for a specific career. Acquiring the intellectual foundation for a chosen profession has also come to include the development of basic skills necessary for *any* career, such as numeracy, critical thinking, problem solving, and the ability to effectively communicate, work in groups, and even manage one's time (Hart Research Associates, 2010). The list is endless, exacerbated in recent years by a new obsession of government and accrediting boards with learning goals and outcomes (Brottman, 2009).

However, despite numerous debates over how exactly preparation for life relates to the scholarly pursuits ordinarily associated with college study, one assumption has remained unchallenged: the student's age. That is, even in pursuing these ever-multiplying objectives, universities have never stopped regarding their undergraduates as young and immature, and certainly less knowledgeable than their teachers. The authority of the faculty to decide what their students must learn has thus rested not only upon their scholarly credentials, but also upon their own relative maturity—presumably gained by virtue of their long educational journey and deep engagement with, as Matthew Arnold (1869) famously wrote, "the best that has been thought and known in the world current everywhere" (preface, para. 3).

HIGHER EDUCATION FOR THE ADULT

It is easy to see how awkwardly an adult student might fit within such a setting. Although adults have traditionally been defined by age alone, the trend today, as described in a 2002 report, *Nontraditional Undergraduates* (as cited in Kazis et al., 2007, pp. 7-8) is to identify an adult by one or more of the following characteristics:

- Delayed enrollment in college
- No high school diploma
- Part-time attendance in college
- Financial independence
- Full-time work employment elsewhere
- Having dependents with or without a spouse

For individuals with such attributes (strikingly referred to by Kazis et al., p. 8, as "risk factors"), a focus upon preparation for life, or even citizenship, seems misplaced. More importantly, the belief that faculty, and by extension the college, knows in advance what is best for these students appears unwarranted. Many of these students have had not only as much life experience as many faculty, but collectively they bring to the academy a much broader range of interests and social competencies than is ordinarily seen there. Indeed, some adult students are actually more knowledgeable and have greater insights about life and citizen responsibilities than their teachers, particularly in such areas as social service, organizational management, cutting-edge technology, political advocacy, public schools, health issues, and the day-to-day realities of ethnic diversity and social class divisions. Herman and Mandell (2004a) offer particularly cogent examples of adult student competencies, as do Smith (2010) and the recent documentary series by Purple States TV (2010). Does it make sense to welcome such students with a preset list of required courses designed explicitly to introduce them to life, as if their life experiences had no significance at all? How can we comfortably tell them what to learn, as if their own questions, concerns, and interests are not worth exploring?

Adults are, in fact, not empty vessels into which knowledge is poured (Freire, 1972, pp. 57-64). As a group, they enter university study already embedded in complex lives, touched by experiences that offer both opportunities for and impediments to academic work. Consider the following illustrative cases: A single mother of an autistic child, deeply involved in advocacy and support programs for the developmentally disabled, works at night as a waitress while she pursues a degree in psychology; a 50-year old man at the height of a successful sales career, with children now graduating from prestigious colleges, suddenly feels compelled to quit his job and return to school to seek a teacher's certificate in order to "give back" to his community; a long-time administrator in a social agency that has lost its funding wonders if she might be able to pursue an old dream of earning a degree in philosophy; a self-taught computer whiz who has helped automate the machines in a local manufacturing company sees himself being supplanted by young college graduates and realizes that to keep his job, he must acquire a broader education and a degree.

While adults as a group share qualities that distinguish them from students fresh out of high school (see, e.g., Bjorklund, 2011, or such classics on adult learning as Brookfield, 1986; Cross, 1992; Merriam, Caffarella, & Baumgartner, 2007; and Mezirow, 1991), their combined backgrounds, dispositions, and educational needs, reflect, much more strikingly, their many differences. Compare the case of a successful 45-year old business professional, high in the ranks of his corporation, who is paralyzed with fear about writing a 10-page paper to the case of a professional dancer who has toured the world and communicates easily in three languages and who now wants to change careers. Or contrast a woman, an effective community organizer who has given talks in living rooms and at major rallies, who has never even seen the inside of an academic library, with another woman, having taken a job at 18 in a factory to support her young family avidly reads literature at night and has written hundreds of poems that she has never shared with anyone. Clearly, a simple single curricular plan does not begin to do justice to their diverse educational needs.

DE FACTO SEGREGATION

So what happens to these individuals, with their unique combination of competencies and limitations, when they move into the college community? Only a few—those with flexible schedules or the wherewithal to immerse themselves full-time in a world of schooling—are able to attend traditional four-year colleges or universities. When they do, they adapt themselves, usually with good humor, to the classroom rules, regulations, and requirements designed to keep unruly youngsters on the road to maturity. The vast majority of adult students, however, are either relegated to special night classes, or various weekend or online programs, or they find their ways to an array of colleges, many for-profit, designed explicitly for working adult learners (Smith, 2010). The one venue where they are not ignored is the 2-year college, which, originally called a "junior" college, is now considered a "community" college, which better reflects its broader orientation. Typically with smaller classes rather than large lectures, staffed by faculty dedicated to teaching, these colleges welcome students of all ages. As Kasworm (2005) describes it, the intergenerational experience adds value in itself. Community colleges are also routinely responsive to public and business needs, offering, along with traditional liberal arts courses, a continually expanding variety of topical studies, certificates, and associate-level degree programs. However, in the world of higher education, community colleges (despite the recent focus upon them at the national level) are considered the lowest echelon—quite literally a world apart. As such, these institutions, along with the adult students they welcome, still remain effectively segregated from the research universities and elite colleges, the home of "real" scholarship where knowledge is discovered and disseminated (Cole, 2009).

In the minds of many academics, this *de facto* segregation is fully justified. No matter how complex their priorities, adults are seen as too instrumental, too focused upon results, too concerned with the practical. An individual unable to devote her life full-time to scholarship, at least for the requisite four years, is regarded as unsuited to the demands of the fabled ivory tower. Adults with other priorities, it is believed, will be distracted from the intellectual life that defines the university; they will not have time to engage in basic research or pursue the wandering path of discovery. Despite the popularity of the GI bill, even at its inception academics grumbled that the complex personal situations adults carry with them would only serve to dilute the disciplined atmosphere and, as expressed by Robert Hutchins, convert universities into "educational hobo-jungles" (Nassaw, 1979, p. 178). With the adult learner thus perceived as an indifferent scholar, it is easy to see why a second-class education for such students could be both justified and appropriate.

By a second-class education most educators mean one that lacks sufficient exposure to the liberal arts, a category of study sharply differentiated by the higher education establishment from the professional or vocational (Brint, Riddle, Turk-Bicakci, & Levy, 2005; Roos & Eefsting, 2007). Even though it is not as easy to distinguish these categories as it might seem, the literature is filled with philosophical odes to the value of the liberal arts (e.g., Nussbaum, 1997) particularly the humanities that are presumably missing from practical or applied programs. This distinction is one of a number of such educational "oppositions" critically scrutinized by John Dewey (1916, p. 306). To the opposing categories, liberal versus practical, he also added cognitive versus experiential, theory versus practice, and learning for leisure rather than learning to labor. The finer sides of these oppositions, those that ostensibly speak to the cultivation of the mind, have been identified, no doubt since the time of Plato's *Republic*, as crucial in properly shaping the character and disposition of the young. By default, then, the apparently coarser sides of these educational oppositions have come to be closely associated with adult students whose characters and dispositions are already fully formed.

We would argue, as did Dewey in 1916, that such educational dichotomies are wrong-headed. They have no place in a democratic society that values diversity, and they also inhibit us from thinking more clearly about what a truly human education should be. In fact, it is a gross caricature, a reductionist ploy, to personify the adult student as a wholly instrumental individual who only wants to learn what is useful, and the traditional student who rightfully belongs in our better universities, as one who enjoys delving into subjects simply for their own intrinsic value. The so-called instrumental adult business student is also deeply interested in the nature of evil, the limits of power, and how globalization, and all it represents, will change the world for his children. The so-called idealistic traditional student is also greatly concerned about whether she should get married, how she can reconcile her urge to become a writer with her poor grades, and what job she will be able to find that might cover her mounting college debts. Neither one necessarily dislikes the college subjects they are required to study—for example, sociology for the traditional student, human resource management for the adult. But in our experience, knowledge defined as either liberal or professional is really not sufficient for *either* student.

Unfortunately, the obvious solution—to eschew these divisions and focus instead upon more broadly conceptualized areas of study—runs counter to the long-standing, and administratively effective, disciplinary structure of the university (Graff, 1988). Indeed, seemingly bent upon strengthening these divisions, recent writers now urge that the separation of traditional-aged students from adult learners be institutionalized. Smith

(2010), a progressive educator and a long-time advocate for adult students, explicitly espouses the creation of special colleges, many for-profit, designed specifically for busy adults. Christensen and Eyring (2011), while promoting a proliferation of uniquely configured postsecondary schools, reinforce Smith's dualistic views by highlighting the differences between Harvard University, which, for them, illustrates "sustaining innovation" with its strong liberal arts education for young students, and Brigham Young University-Idaho, which illustrates "disruptive innovation" with its adult-friendly pragmatic community involvement. It is not an accident that these two colleges also differ in their methods of instruction: whereas Harvard emphasizes face-to-face classes that are very difficult for adults to attend, BYU-Idaho offers classes that are almost exclusively online, and thus very convenient for them. When adult learners are eliminated from the higher echelons of university education that stress content and complexity and relegated to schools that stress convenience and efficiency, their apparent nonexistence in higher education becomes a reality. As we argue elsewhere (Coulter & Mandell, 2012), this exclusion represents segregation by age that is as educationally undesirable as any other form of segregation.

AN IDEAL EDUCATION FOR ALL

Our personal experience with adult learners suggests that they are more deeply engaged if instead of focusing first and foremost on a particular discipline or category of knowledge, they are allowed, whether in a given course or for an entire curriculum, to explore from any perspective, questions of their own. Such open explorations are not ordinarily possible when the institution decides in advance what students must know. Many pressures and practices clearly encourage faculty to design courses that emerge out of their own disciplinary concerns. Yet, what academic goal justifies the obstacles we place in front of adult students that separate them from their own purposes and require them to address only those issues that seem important to faculty? The final outcome, it seems to us, is not the highly educated citizens we intend our requirements to produce, but students who learn that, given their time and money constraints, the best policy is simply to go along with the system.

Without question, faculty craft their studies around issues they believe are of interest to the average undergraduate. And, it is easy with young students to assume we know their common concerns. As one faculty member once remarked thoughtlessly (yet revealingly) to us—"all they think about are sex, money, and cars." But when we step out from behind our podiums to actually talk with these students, we find that even 18-year-olds, no matter how immature we believe they are, have their own highly diverse interests, concerns, and questions. With older learners, such an assumption of commonality is obviously untenable from the start. Even if we could read our students' minds and design in advance what we take to be perfectly relevant courses, second-guessing student interest or need is not really an appropriate way to teach, particularly at the undergraduate level. Is not one of the key goals of higher education to help students no matter what their age learn to recognize, articulate, and refine their own questions? Don't we deprive both young and adult students of the very education we claim they need when we try to ask their own questions for them (Finkel, 2000; Freire & Faundez, 1989; Herman & Mandell, 2004b)?

We are certainly not the first to suggest that our educational methods in college need improvement. (Recent critiques include: Arum & Roksa, 2011; Grafton, 2011; Lustig, 2011; and Piereson, 2011.) There is no shortage of books, many written by faculty, that advocate new ways of improving the quality of undergraduate learning (Anderson, 1993, Bok, 2006, Muscatine, 2009, Taylor, 2010, Zemsky, 2009). As these critics of higher education point out, graduate programs do not include even the rudiments of teacher training (Berrett, 2012). Most new faculty have had little serious exposure to theories of learning, cognitive processes, motivation—those aspects of teaching that are central to helping students understand and retain new information. But what future college teachers *do* learn in graduate school in their own disciplines is the nature of inquiry. They understand the driving force of questions and how to craft them so they can be productively addressed. They know how to search for relevant information to create an appropriate context for such questions, and they are masters at the methods of inquiry used in their particular disciplines. What better background could we ask of faculty if the university were designed, not to deliver information, but to help undergraduates recognize and express their own questions, guide them in seeking responsible answers, and provide them with criteria by which to judge the limits of the answers they uncover?

With young students, a change in pedagogy and all that might imply never seems particularly urgent. As Collins and Halverson (2009, p. 48) argue, traditional educators operate in a "just in case" mode expecting that the knowledge students acquire in school will remain available whenever they need it later. They assume that the mind is a ready repository of knowledge, referred to by Bereiter (2002, pp. 7-8) as the "mind-as-container metaphor," despite considerable evidence for a more complex and interactive model (Ambrose et al., 2010; Bransford, Brown, & Cocking, 2000; Knowlton & Sharp, 2003). But when we add a significant number of adult students to the mix, buttressed by older progressive (Dewey, 1916; Freire, 1972) and newer technology-based (Kamenetz, 2010) arguments, deferring their concerns to some future date seems much harder to jus- tify. After all, these learners are already grown up, and unlike young stu- dents, as workers, parents, volunteers, and voters, they are forced daily to make important and consequential decisions. For them, a "just in time" approach to teaching (Collins & Halverson, 2009, pp. 14-15) is not only more in tune with contemporary models of learning, but for active partic- ipants in an increasingly complex society, it is a more far more effective way of addressing their personal, academic, and professional needs.

COMPONENTS OF AN IDEAL UNIVERSITY

What if we took this call for change seriously? What if institutions wel- come young and old students alike? Moreover, what if all learners are assumed to have questions of their own? And what if faculty orient them- selves to individual students as seriously as they embrace their disciplines? What if their instructional priorities are to understand student personal histories, evaluate their particular academic strengths and limitations, accept their professional needs, and explore with them their other varie- gated concerns? Will such a change in focus encourage institutions to relax their prescriptive grip, and even more interestingly, to recognize the diverse circumstances of their learners as a legitimate source of curricular development? If so, what impact will these changes have upon many of our long-held academic traditions? How will our institutions, no doubt also impacted by the current revolution in technology, be redefined? What areas in particular will need attention?

Access

Given the multiple responsibilities of most adult students, and increas- ingly all students, universities must find ways of making classes and other educational activities more flexibly accessible. The rigidity of college terms and schedules are academically unnecessary; more than anything else, they serve as serious obstacles for busy learners (Arthur & Tate, 2004). Similarly, the location in which students learn also has little bear- ing upon the quality of their instruction. In this age of the Internet, why should learners be penned into specific classrooms when virtual class- rooms allow them access whenever they have free time (Allen & Seaman, 2011)? Why should they crowd into lecture halls when podcasts of lectures can be easily posted online to be seen and heard at any hour of the day or night—and as many times as needed (Bergmann, Overmyer, & Wilie, 2011)? Why can they not have class discussions on the Internet through blogs or twitter that allow asynchronous conversations and, incidentally, leave a complete written record for subsequent review and analysis? We rely upon schedules, physical locations, and synchronous communications because that is the way things have already been done. The fact is that what we really need is to engage in serious research to determine under what circumstances a face-to-face, place-bound instruction truly assists learning and when it does not. Then, when a busy human service administrator takes time to leave her office, drive to campus, find a place to park, and make her way to an office tucked away in a building a mile from her car, it will truly be worth her while to be there.

Learning Sources

Similarly, faculty must recognize with greater clarity that students can learn effectively from multiple sources besides their own lectures and classroom activities. Aside from books, libraries, and the array of open-education resources available on the Internet (Cormier & Siemens, 2010), students can learn from public meetings, community workshops, museum presentations, television and radio broadcasts, sponsored talks, and, certainly, from their own experiences (Andersson & Harris, 2006). Another major resource is the university itself and the extensive expertise found on any campus. An important challenge is to find ways of making that expertise better known among the students and faculty, perhaps through open lectures, websites, or the availability of informal consultations, so that for relevant information or guidance, students are not limited to any one person or particular course. Courses, too, must become more flexible and open-end—characterized, for example, by varied entry points, individualized outcomes, and frequent revisions.

Student Guidance

Students cannot learn effectively in multiple locations and from multiple sources without a concrete plan. Thus, faculty must be willing to serve as guides, working collaboratively with their students to make concrete the questions being asked and the kind of knowledge needed in order to address them (Cohen, 1995; Daloz, 1999). Such mentors must be expert enough, certainly in their own fields, to be able to easily identify content areas relevant to the student's question that are important in the field and yet accessible for a novice. They should also know enough about the structure of knowledge in general to at least point the student toward other relevant areas of study, courses, written texts, or sources of information, or individuals who might offer them new insights. Over time, these mentors will help students learn to track down these resources on their own. Of course, faculty will also know how best to assess the quality of what a student learns. Whether the student's quest is a project that is part of a larger class or whether it is an independent study, the nature of what students ultimately must do should be put in writing in order to keep them on track. A standard protocol for such documents would no doubt facilitate this process (Knowles, 1986).

Faculty Skills

When students seek knowledge for their own reasons, they do not need classroom teachers who know how to entertain them or make the subject matter appear practically relevant or inherently interesting. Thus, the kinds of special skills faculty need to thrive in a university that focuses upon students' queries are not that different from those associated with faculty scholarly activities. Faculty must be intellectually curious, appreciate not only what they know, but what they do not know, and should be open to new ideas and explorations. Above all, they must be able to recognize the inherent value of their students' concerns even in their most nascent form. They must know, not always how to lecture effectively, but, above all, how to listen and ask the right questions. In the end, faculty need to be willing, on the one hand, to stay abreast of what is happening in various fields of inquiry, and at the same time, to comprehend the nature of student questions and the level at which they can be successfully pursued (Schneider, Klemp, & Kastendiek, 1981; Taylor, Marineau, & Fiddler, 2000).

Curricular Requirements

Properly guided, students do not need specific course requirements. With knowledge accumulating at accelerated rates, it is shortsighted to believe that what every person should know can be confined to one small list. There are more "great books" and "essential" areas of study than any single person could come close to mastering in a lifetime. An 18th century polyglot is not an appropriate model for a 21st century undergraduate. Thus, faculty should not spend time agonizing about what content areas an increasingly diverse body of students should all know in common (Hall & Kelves, 1982). By all means, a university can require "breadth" (for example, an appreciation of "historical perspectives" or a glimpse at unfamiliar cultures or some facility in science and mathematics), but let the student, with the help of a faculty guide, decide how best to integrate these expectations into his or her particular program of study (Herman, 2004).

Self-Directed Lifelong Learning

A response to the presence of adult learners must be more than just a particular set of conditions and methods. The ways we have suggested to better meet their educational needs promote, not necessarily citizenship or character, but a goal consistent with faculty expertise: competent self-directed and lifelong learning skills. Who would not want a college graduate, when confronted with a political or moral or social dilemma, to be capable of asking probing questions and locating appropriate information before making a decision? Yet, whatever our graduates today know about decision making, it is unlikely that it came from their university experience. From the minute they arrive, they are told what courses to take, what books to read, what information to seek, what papers to write, and even in what order topics should be addressed. The other lesson they learn from the test-obsessed schooling they've been prepped for since the third grade is that for every question there is one correct answer. Thus, our better graduates leave us believing that the key to success in life is to find the right authorities and to seek the right answers. Despite the good intentions of those who fervently believe they know best what students should learn, such an approach does not produce the kind of graduates our society needs. If we turn over the task of setting the agenda to the students, if we help them take increasing responsibility for the content and direction of their studies, if we allow them to be animated by their own concerns and questions, they will necessarily acquire the highly valued skills of life-long learners. Perhaps even more importantly, they will be far better prepared to respond to the unknown personal and public challenges they, indeed, all of us, will inevitably face.

CONCLUSION

Up until now, a vision of an education built around student concerns has remained largely out of sight and absent from most serious discussions about the state of higher education today. Nonetheless, we believe that once colleges are prepared to welcome adults as legitimate learners, the educational potential of student concerns—whether personal, academic, or professional—will become much more obvious. In truth, institutions of higher learning *must* step forward to offer these students the kind of accessible education they deserve, not only for the students, but as a way of revitalizing the institutions themselves. Otherwise, these students will indeed flock to colleges whose only lure is the flexible schedules upon which they depend. Unfortunately, many of these colleges cater primarily to student career needs, leaving largely unexplored all the other questions adults have about the complex world in which they live and work. Their segregation because of age and life responsibilities not only denies them a rich education, but also deprives traditional colleges of the new perspectives their unique knowledge can bring to the academy (Coulter, 2002). While our proposal does not tell the student how to live the good life or be a good citizen, it seems self-evident that when students acquire self-directed life-long learning skills and learn to link existing scholarship to their own inquiries, they will come to address these questions themselves. To expect more, as Fish (2008) has argued, confuses "a hoped-for effect with what can actually be taught" (p. 12).

The greatest contributions universities can offer are the debates, discussions, and discoveries that have accumulated since humans learned to write. All university students, no matter what their age, deserve equal access to this repository of wisdom. What we are suggesting here is simply that this access should be motivated by student concern rather than faculty conviction. The true object of adult education, the andragogical ideal, is to teach students, not what to know, but how to explore the already vast and still increasing realm of knowledge in order to pursue questions meaningful to them. This change in focus seems eminently sensible for adult students. We also believe that an institution that takes seriously the diverse needs of adult students will come to realize that younger students as well can readily flourish in such a context (Bauerline, 2009, p. 165). Ultimately, age should not define the nature of higher education or further fragment the academy. It is our conviction that if adults were truly integrated into all colleges and universities, their impact would inevitably improve our institutions and transform the educational experience for all.

REFERENCES

Allen, I., & Seaman, J. (2011). *Going the distance: Online education in the United States 2011*. Retrieved from http://www.babson.edu/Academics/centers/blank-center/global-research/Documents/going-the-distance.pdf

Ambrose, S. A., Bridges, M. W., DiPietro, M., Lovett, M. C, Norman, M. K., & Mayer, R. E. (2010). *How learning works: 7 research-based principles for smart teaching*. San Francisco, CA: Jossey-Bass.

Anderson, C. W. (1993). *Prescribing the life of the mind: An essay on the purpose of the university, the aims of liberal education, the competence of citizens, and the cultivation of practical reason*. Madison, WI: University of Wisconsin Press.

Andersson, P.. & Harris, J. (Eds.) (2004). *Re-theorising the recognition of prior learning*. Leicester, England: National Institution of Adult Continuing Education.

Arnold, M. (1869). *Culture & anarchy* [Gutenberg Adobe Editions]. Retrieved from http://www.gutenberg.org/cache/epub/4212/pg4212.html

Arthur, L., & Tate, A. (2004). Time: The new commodity in life-long learning. *All About Mentoring, 27,* 14-18.

Arum, R. & Roksa, J. (2011). *Academically adrift: Limited learning on college campuses*. Chicago, IL: University of Chicago Press.

Bauerline, M. (2009). *The dumbest generation: How the digital age stupefies young Americans and jeopardizes our future*. New York, NY: Jeremy P. Tarcher/Penguin.

Benson, L., Harkavy, I., & Puckett, J. (2007). *Dewey's dream*. Philadelphia, PA: Temple University Press.

Benton, T. H. (n.d.). Chronicle of Higher Education book review. [Review of the book *How the university works,* by M. Bousquet & C. Nelson]. Retrieved from http://www.amazon.com/How-University-Works-Education-Low-Wage/dp/0814799752/ref=sr_1_1?ie=UTF8&s=books&qid=1274875344&sr=1-1

Bereiter, C. (2002). *Education and mind in the knowledge age*. Mahwah, NJ: Lawrence Erlbaum Associates.

Bergmann, J., Overmyer, U., & Wilie, B. (2011, November). The flipped class: Myth v. reality. *The Daily Riff*. Retrieved from http://www.thedailyriff.com/articles/the-flipped-class-conversation-689.php

Berrett, D. (2012, February 28). Harvard conference to jolt university training. *Chronicle of Higher Education*. Retrieved from http://www.chronicle.com/article/Harvard-Seeks-to-Jolt/130683

Bjorklund, B. R. (2011). *The journey of adulthood* (7th ed.). Upper Saddle River, NJ: Pearson/Prentice Hall.

Bok, D. (2006). *Our underachieving colleges: A candid look at how much students learn and why they should be learning more*. Princeton, NJ: Princeton University Press.

Bransford, J. D., Brown, A. L., & Cocking, R. R. (Eds.). (2000). *How people learn*. Washington, DC: National Academy Press

Brint, S., Riddle, M., Turk-Bicakci, L., & Levy, C. S. (2005). From the liberal to the practical arts in American colleges and universities: Organizational analysis and curricular change. *The Journal of Higher Education, 76*(2), 151-180.

Brookfield, S. D. (1986). *Understanding and facilitating adult learning*. San Francisco, CA: Jossey-Bass.

Brottman, M. (2009, December 13). Learning to hate learning objectives. *Chronicle of Higher Education*. Retrieved from http://www.chronicle/article/Learning-To-Hate-Learning/49399

Bucior, C. (2012, July 22). Extreme campus touring [Education Life Supplement]. *New York Times*, p. ED 4.

Christensen, C. M., & Eyring, H. J. (2011). *The innovative university: Changing the DNA of higher education from the inside out*. San Francisco, CA: Jossey-Bass.

Cohen N. H. (1995). *Mentoring adult learners: A guide for educators and trainers*. Malabar, FL: Krieger.

Cole, J. R. (2009). *The great American university: Its rise to preeminence: Its indispensable national role; Why it must be protected*. New York, NY: Public Affairs.

Collins, A., & Halverson, R. (2009). *Rethinking education in the age of technology: The digital revolution and schooling in America*. New York, NY: Teachers College Press.

Cormier, D., & Siemens, G. (2010). Through the open door: Open courses as research, learning, and engagement. *EDUCAUSE Review, 45*(4), 30-39.

Coulter, X. (2002). The role of conscious reflection in experiential learning. *All About Mentoring, 24*, 8-13.

Coulter, X., & Mandell, M. (2012). Adult higher education: Are we moving in the wrong direction? *The Journal of Continuing Higher Education, 60*(1), 1-3.

Cross, K. P. (1992). *Adults as learners: Increasing participation and facilitating learning*. San Francisco, CA: Jossey-Bass.

Daloz, L. A. (1999). *Mentor*. San Francisco, CA: Jossey-Bass.

Dewey, J. (1916). *Democracy and education*. New York, NY: The Free Press.

Dienst, K. (2011, November 14). Examining ideas of a life worth living. *Princeton University Bulletin, 101*(3), 1, 7.

Finkel, D. L. (2000). *Teaching with your mouth shut*. Portsmouth, NY: Boynton/Cook.

Fish, S. (2008). *Save the world on your own time*. New York, NY: Oxford University Press.

Freire, P. (1972). *Pedagogy of the oppressed*. New York, NY: Herder & Herder.

Freire, P., & Faundez, A. (1989). *Learning to question: A pedagogy of liberation*. New York, NY: Continuum.

Friedman, T. (2011, June 15). Justice goes global. *The New York Times*, p. A27.

Graff, G. (1988). *Professing literature: An institutional history*. Chicago, IL: University of Chicago Press.

Grafton, A. (2011, November 24). Our universities: Why are they failing? *The New York Review of Books*. Retrieved from http://www.nybooks.com/articles/2011/nov/24/our-universties-why-are-they-failing

Hall, J., & Kelves, B. (Eds.). (1982). *In opposition to core curriculum: Alternative models for undergraduate education*. Westport, CT: Greenwood Press.

Hart Research Associates (2010). *Raising the bar: Employers' views on college learning in the wake of the economic downturn*. Retrieved from http://www.aacu.org/leap/documents/2009_EmployerSurvey.pdf

Herman, L. (2004). Love talk: Educational planning at Empire State College, State University of New York. In E. Michelson & A. Mandell (Eds.), *Portfolio development and the assessment of prior learning* (2nd ed., pp. 100-120). Sterling, VA: Stylus.

Herman, L., & Mandell, A. (2004a). *From teaching to mentoring: Principle and practice, dialogue and life in adult education*. New York, NY: Routledge-Farmer.

Herman, L., & Mandell, A. (2004b). Asking questions. In L. Herman, & A. Mandell (Eds.), *From teaching to mentoring: Principle and practice, dialogue and life in adult education*. (pp. 44-69). New York, NY: Routledge-Farmer,

Kamenetz, A. (2010). *DIY U*. White River Junction, VT: Chelsea Green.

Kasworm, C. (2005). Adult student identity in an intergenerational community college classroom. *Adult Education Quarterly, 56*(1), 3-20.

Kazis, R., Callahan, A., Davidson, C., McLeod, A., Bosworth, B., Choitz, V., & Hoops, J. (2007). *Adult learners in higher education: Barriers to success and strate-*

gies to improve results (Occasional Paper 2007-03). Washington, DC: US Department of Labor Employment and Training Administration.

Kennedy, D. (1997). *Academic duty.* Cambridge, MA: Harvard University Press.

Knowles, M. (1986). *Understanding learning contracts.* San Francisco, CA: Jossey-Bass.

Knowlton, D. S., & Sharp, D. C. (Eds.). (2003). Problem-based learning in the information age. *New Directions for Teaching and Learning, 75.*

Lustig, J. (2011). The university besieged. *Thought & Action, 27,* 7-22.

Menand, L. (2010). *The marketplace of ideas: Reform and resistance in the American university.* New York, NY: W. W. Norton.

Merriam, S. B., Caffarella, R. S., & Baumgartner, L. M. (2007). *Learning in adulthood* (3rd ed.). San Francisco, CA: Jossey-Bass.

Mezirow, J. (1991). *Transformative dimensions of adult learning.* San Francisco, CA: Jossey-Bass.

Muscatine, C. (2009). *Fixing college education: A new curriculum for the twenty-first century.* Charlottesville, VA: University of Virginia Press.

Nassaw, D. (1979). *Schooled to order.* Cambridge, England: Oxford University Press.

National Center for Educational Statistics (2009). *Digest of Education Statistics,* Table 191. Retrieved from http://nces.ed.gov/programs/digest/d09.

Nussbaum, M.C. (1997). *Cultivating humanity: A classical defense of reform in liberal education.* Cambridge, MA: Harvard University Press.

Piereson, J. (2011). What's wrong with our universities? *The New Criterion, 30*(1), 17-25.

Purple States TV (Producer). (2010, week of May 26). *Degrees of difficulty* [Video series]. Retrieved from http://www.usatoday.com/news/education/degrees-of-difficulty.htm

Rudolph, F. (1990). *The American college & university: A history.* Athens, GA: University of Georgia Press.

Smith, P. (2010). *Harnessing America's wasted talent: A new ecology of learning.* San Francisco, CA: Jossey-Bass.

Roos, B., & Eefsting, G. (Co-Producers/Directors). (2007). *The conversation continues: Liberal & professional education* [DVD]. Retrieved from http://faculty.gvsu.edu/roosb

Schneider, C., Klemp, Jr., G., & Kastendiek S. (1981). *The balancing act: Competencies of effective teachers and mentors in degree programs for adults.* Boston, MA: McBer & Co.

Taylor, M. C. (2010). *Crisis on campus: A bold plan for reforming our colleges and universities.* New York, NY: Knopf.

Taylor, K., Marienau, C., & Fiddler, M. (2000). *Developing adult learners: Strategies for teachers and trainers.* San Francisco, CA: Jossey-Bass.

Trow, M. (2007). American higher education: Past, present, and future. In L. Goodchild & H. Wechsler (Eds.), *ASCHE reader on the history of higher education* (3rd ed., pp 582-596). Needham Heights, MA: Ginn Press. (Original work published 1988)

Zemsky, R. (2009). *Making reform work: The case for transforming American higher education.* New Brunswick, NJ: Rutgers University Press.

CHAPTER 11

REDEFINING SUCCESS

The Postcollege Career Experiences of First-Generation Adult College Graduates

Joann S. Olson

It seems that the path to, through, and beyond college was once more straightforward. The young adult, often a product of some sort of privileged background or benefactor, "went off to college" and emerged four years later to work in a career, equipped with an education that would suffice until retirement. This nostalgic view of the past is almost certainly an illusion, a function of collective forgetfulness or academic myopia. Regardless, this vision stands in stark contrast to the current landscape of higher education and career trajectories. A broadened understanding of the college experience (Pascarella & Terenzini, 2005), a recognition that adult and nontraditional learners make up an increasing proportion of almost every student body (Chao, DeRocco, & Flynn, 2007), and a rapidly changing employment landscape (Dresang, 2008; Hanneman & Gardner, 2010) suggest that neither the college experience nor college outcomes should be discussed in one-size-fits-all terms.

The research described in this chapter brings together three streams of literature that are increasingly relevant to higher education and adult learning in the 21st century: first-generation college students, adult learners,

Conversations About Adult Learning in Our Complex World, pp. 161–176

and the college-to-work transition. The purpose of this study was to explore the college-to-work transition for adult students whose parents had not earned a college degree. The research question driving the project was: How does the first-generation college graduate understand the idea of "career," specifically for the graduate who completed his or her degree as a returning adult learner who also returned to higher education in the hopes of changing careers, in a time of economic uncertainty?

REVIEW OF THE LITERATURE

The research related to first-generation college students and that related to adult learners has run along parallel tracks but with little overlap. According to Chen and Carrol (2005), first-generation college (FGC) students graduate at much lower rates than those students whose parents attended college: 24% of FGC students who enroll in college complete a bachelor's degree, compared to 68% of non-FGC students. They are often less academically prepared for college level work (Choy, 2001; Warburton, Bugarin, Nuñez, & Carroll, 2001) and earn lower grade point averages and fewer credits (Chen & Carrol, 2005) than non-FGC students. These findings hold, even after controlling for background characteristics such as race/ethnicity and academic preparation (Ishitani, 2006; Pascarella, Pierson, Wolniak, & Terenzini, 2004).

Likewise, adult students seem to struggle with persisting to the completion of a degree. The challenges facing adult learners are varied and increasingly well-documented (e.g., Aslanian, 2001; Berker, Horn, & Carrol, 2003; Choy, 2002), to the extent that Liebowitz and Taylor (2004) described many working adult learners as "one step away from a crisis" (p. 9) that would result in a delay or derailment of their educational pursuits. Many first-time community college students (78%) do not complete a 2-year program within 3 years (Chao, DeRocco, & Flynn, 2007), and it may take a low-skilled, part-time adult student an average of 5 to 6 years to complete an associate degree (Liebowitz & Taylor, 2004).

The influence of family and other support systems has been identified as a significant factor in the first-generation college student's experience (Horwedel, 2008; London, 1989; Orbe, 2008; Van T. Bui, 2002). At times, the *perception* of support has been shown as more influential than the *presence* of support for the first-generation student (Dennis, Phinney, & Chauteco, 2005; McCarron & Inkelas, 2006). For the adult learner, this support is also essential to his or her success (Bamber & Tett, 1999; Bauman et al., 2004; Edwards, 1993; Reay, 2003; Sorey & Duggan, 2008). Steele, Lauder, Caperchione, and Anastasi (2005) reported the critical nature of this support: their participants indicated that "I couldn't have done it, there's no way I could have done it" (p. 577) without support of spouses or parents.

Research related to the college-to-work transition has highlighted that college graduates feel unprepared for the transition (Banerji, 2007; Coulon, 2002; Martin, Matham, Case, & Fraser, 2005) and those in the midst of this transition describe it as a time of tension (Holden & Hamblett, 2007; Perrone & Vickers, 2003). With few exceptions (Choy, 2001; Nuñez & Cuccaro-Alamin, 1998), there is no mention made of the ways that the FGC graduate's background (in terms of social or cultural capital; Bourdieu, 1986; London, 1992; Putnam, 2000) might impact his or her transition from college to work. Likewise, this literature has also ignored the experience of adult learners who are transitioning to postcollege employment.

The project described in this chapter adds to the sparse literature related to first-generation college students who also happen to be adult learners (as in Giancola, Munz, & Trares, 2008; St. Clair-Christman, 2009). It also seeks to explore the college-to-work transition. At the same time, a more fully developed understanding of the postcollege experiences of adult learners can inform our current student services to adult learners and promote student success.

METHOD

This exploration of the post-college work experiences of FGC graduates who completed a bachelor's degree as an adult learner was conducted using a phenomenological approach. Spiegelberg (1975) suggested phenomenology "may at least be a help in facing the data of our world squarely and honestly, without deflation or inflation, without the impoverishment of a reductionist positivism" (p. 79). My goal was to bring depth to the discussion of the postcollege work-related experiences of the FGC adult learner. More specifically, I approached the study using the assumptions of hermeneutic phenomenology, aligning with van Manen's (1997a) suggestion that "phenomenology merely shows us what various ranges of human experience are possible, what worlds people inhabit. How these experiences may be described and how language ... has powers to disclose the worlds in which we dwell" (p. 52).

Researcher Identity

In a practice known as bracketing, I began by exploring my own assumptions related to the phenomenon under investigation (van Manen, 1997a), considering the extent to which my own experience could influence my exploration of this topic. I am a first-generation college student. Although I attended college as a traditional-aged college student, I am only now beginning to understand the extent to which my FGC status shaped my experience—not only as a college student, but also as I began my first postcollege job. The transition to work was exceptionally challenging for me, filled with experiences that no one in my family of origin could understand. At the same time, I found it challenging to explain my angst to friends whose parents had attended college. As this study progressed, I discovered that other aspects of my life history mirrored elements of my participants' experiences (e.g., returning to school after a significant gap in my pursuit of formal education, changing careers). Therefore, the bracketing of my own experiences and presuppositions continued throughout the research process.

Participants

After the study was approved by the college's institutional review board, I began my recruiting efforts following the norms of purposeful sampling (Lincoln & Guba, 1985). Participants were recruited from a list of recent graduates (between 1 and 6 years prior to the beginning of the study) who had completed a bachelor's degree at a small, faith-based college in the Upper Midwest. These participants had completed their degrees while enrolled in the "adult and graduate studies" division of the institution, where I currently serve in an administrative (faculty development) role. Using a list of recent adult graduates provided by the college's assistant registrar, I began recruiting participants who had experienced the phenomenon (i.e., first-generation student, adult learner, recent graduate), in the pursuit of "information-rich cases" (Patton, 2002, p. 242) related to the research question.

Participants had graduated at least 1 year before I arrived at the college. The institution currently maintains very limited contact with alumni, and I found that many of the records contained outdated contact information. Therefore, I relied heavily on the input of coworkers who helped me identify potential participants.

A total of four individuals were interviewed, two men and two women. Participant ages ranged from 33-46; Troy, Jim, and LeeAnna (all names are pseudonyms) were married, while Mary was single at the time of the interviews. LeeAnna and Mary had earned degrees in psychology/counseling; Troy and Jim had each completed a management and ethics degree. Although the division offers both face-to-face and online programs, these four participants had all completed their degrees in a face-to-face setting. Troy, Jim, and LeeAnna had taken classes at the college's main campus; Mary had completed her degree at one of the institution's extension sites. LeeAnna and Mary had both pursued graduate degrees in psychology at other institutions; Troy indicated a strong desire to begin an MBA program as soon as he was eligible for tuition reimbursement from his employer. Jim, who began a year-long military deployment two days after our interview, did not express any plans to pursue any post-baccalaureate credential.

DATA COLLECTION AND ANALYSIS

After discussing and obtaining informed consent with each participant, I conducted semistructured interviews, in keeping with phenomenological goals of "[focusing] on specific situations and action sequences that are instances of the theme under investigation" (Polkinghorne, 1989, p. 49) and following Seidman's (1998) three-phase approach to phenomenological interviewing: obtaining a focused life history, exploring the details of the experience, and reflecting on the meaning of the experience. I conducted two interviews with each participant, with the exception of Jim (whose deployment did not allow for a follow-up interview); total interview time ranged from 1:25 to 2:24 hours. Interviews were conducted in person or using Skype, digitally recorded, and transcribed.

Data analysis began as I transcribed the data, and the process of listening and typing the words of the participants did, at times, trigger initial reactions to their statements. I recorded my thoughts using the comment feature of Word. In keeping with Moustakas (1994), the analysis of data continued using a process of horizonalizing—breaking the text into statements where "each horizon of the research interview adds meaning and provides an increasingly clear portrayal [of the phenomenon]" (p. 125). As Polkinghorne (1989) suggested, these statements (horizons) are, at times, "concrete, vague, intricate, and overlapping expressions" (p. 52), but this process proved helpful in fragmenting the data to allow for more detailed and precise coding.

The horizonalized transcripts were imported into nVivo 8.0. I then examined each horizon of data and created a "free node" (code) with the intention that these free nodes would be "more precisely descriptive" (Polkinghorne, 1989, p. 52) of the statement, its meaning, and its contribution to my understanding of the phenomenon. This process resulted in 700 free nodes, which I then began to group into subthemes. The thematizing process involved grouping free nodes together and assigning a descriptive label. I worked through each free node, assigning it to an existing subtheme or adding a subtheme as appropriate. After each free node had been assigned to a subtheme, I examined each subtheme, to insure that the nodes that had been assigned both fit the sub-theme and added depth of understanding to that theme. Quite often, this resulted in reassigning, rearranging, and renaming; throughout this process, I also began to consider the ways in which subthemes could be grouped into themes (constituents) that best expressed the "essential themes" and "essential relationships" (van Manen, 1997b, p. 107) of the phenomenon. This process continued in an iterative manner until I was satisfied that the three identified themes represented the subthemes and participants' descriptions of the experience.

I sought to establish trustworthiness and credibility throughout the study by using several of the key principles suggested by Creswell (2007). The process of transcription, horizonalizing, and thematizing resulted in prolonged engagement with the data. As mentioned earlier, my process of bracketing my assumptions also served to help clarify my own bias before and throughout the study. Conducting multiple interviews with all participants (except Jim) allowed me to clarify and further explore issues and events described by participants in their initial interviews. This follow-up served as a manner of member-checking. In addition, I have presented preliminary results of this study to others who work with adult learners and first-generation college students, and I have received feedback that my description "rings true," resulting in a "phenomenological nod" (van Manen, 1997b, p. 27), where my phenomenological description resonates with the experience and observation of others.

RESULTS

On the surface, aside from their pursuit of college as adult learners, there was very little commonality among the participants' experiences. Their career paths, marriage and family stories, and educational histories varied widely. However, in seeking to answer the question "How does the first-generation college graduate understand the idea of "career," specifically for the graduate who completed his or her degree as a returning adult learner who also returned to higher education in the hopes of changing careers, in a time of economic uncertainty?", I identified three themes in the data: changing direction, seeing possibility, and finding success.

Changing Direction

For each of the participants, there was a sense that pursuing a bachelor's degree was important to career and future, which I identified as a theme of "changing direction." Subthemes included overcoming educational history, facing the family (both family of origin and the responsibilities of current family), and knowing self. Jim had started college as a traditional-aged student, and he jokingly referred to the "sabbatical" he had taken from his studies—right before his academic standing would have resulted in his dismissal from the college. He eventually returned to complete his degree in the adult-focused program offered by the same institution that he attended right out of high school. Troy had dropped out of high school at 15 to help care for his mother. He eventually earned a GED but had no initial plans to go to college; those plans developed as he evaluated the types of jobs he had access to without furthering his education. LeeAnna indicated that even though she was technically skilled at her job, she had found the interpersonal aspects of cosmetology to be the most fulfilling—a realization that later fueled her interest in counseling and psychology.

A fourth subtheme was the participants' sense that a bachelor's degree would lead to "something better." As Troy indicated: "I started thinking about college, um, working, you know-, the jobs were, basically you're just a number. They told you to jump; you said how high. I just figured I didn't have any input."

Immediately following high school, LeeAnna trained as a cosmetologist, and she did this work for 20 years. Her pursuit of further education began when the physical nature of the work became debilitating. At the point where she said "it's time to be done" doing hair, she pursued and completed a 2-year degree in histology but did not find work in that field. When I asked her what she was hoping for, in returning to college to complete a bachelor's degree, she said:

> I don't really know. I don't know. Um, just a better life. So maybe a better job.... At the time, I think I was getting $12/hour at the social service agency, so I think I was hoping for more like $14, with benefits ... I just want to do better for my kids and be able to do more with them ... I'm not talking about, you know, trips to Hawaii or anything like that ... but [when] you're going to the food shelf, you're going to wherever it is that you have to get birthday presents for your kid because you can't afford them—you think to yourself, "God, I want to be- ... I don't want to keep going like this. This is not someplace I want to be." ... The main thing—was just wanting to do something better.

Jim also expressed a vague sense that college would "[help] me with my [military] promotions" and potentially open doors to "government jobs with better pay." Returning to college represented a conscious decision to shape the trajectory of life and career.

Seeing Possibility

As these recent graduates reflected on their pursuit of college, they spoke in terms of possibilities, rather than specific plans. Therefore "seeing possibility" became a second theme. Subthemes were college as "a means to an uncertain end," "a direction that emerges," and "the ties that bind" (referring to decisions related to school, career, and work that were made within the context of outside and sometimes conflicting constraints). As Jim described it:

> I wasn't really looking at careers, as in changing careers, because I went from being a waiter to working at a little factory ... making bubble bath, to working at Goodyear, to customer service.... It was just more, I guess, to actually finish my degree. Um, so, I mean I hope someday, I can actually use my degree for something, ah, but if I find something in the military, then-, I guess like, I guess I can say I am using my-, for my military career, because it's helping me advance in my promotions.

LeeAnna recalled: "I wasn't really thinking specifically about career or that kind of thing, until-, actually until I was done with my bachelor's, and then I was like 'Now what?' you know, 'What do I do now? What do I do with this?'"

As I spoke with participants, I began to notice a sense of the tension between the possibilities presented by continuing education and the limitation imposed of everyday life. For example, LeeAnna had begun doctoral coursework, excelling academically. However, at the time of our first interview, she indicated that two of her children were facing significant transitions, and she was reevaluating the time and emotional commitment that her studies required. By the time of our second interview, she had put her studies on hold and was quite satisfied with the decision. Troy and his wife had both completed degrees as adult learners, and they were now making combined student loan payments of nearly $1,100 each month. When I asked Troy if he had thought college would automatically lead to a better life, he said:

> Well. I've heard that several times, before. Um, and I probably thought it. But I think here's-, here's the key. Um, we-, you know, we have situations that arise whether we have a college degree or we don't have a college degree.... I think life can be more challenging without the degree, because you don't have as many options. Does the degree give you the right? I don't think so. But does it open up more doors? I would say yes it does. It does open up more doors. But should it entitle you? No. You should still have to work hard to get that job and put your best effort.... I don't think it's a rite of passage. It's one of those things where I do think it does help, versus hinder. Of course, the "hinder part" is paying student loans back.

With each participant, the postcollege choices they described to me seemed to strike a balance between possibilities and constraints. The possibilities were shaped by the degree they had pursued. Troy had specifically chosen a degree in management and ethics because he had wide-ranging interests and the breadth of the degree was attractive to him. As he said:

> So, and I decided, well, everyone is going into these specialized fields. What can I go into that, I don't want to, kind of just, get too specialized, so I can have a really broad, you know ... [a] bachelor's degree in management and ethics, or business, would be the best that I could go into, basically, anything.

Likewise, LeeAnna had found that the 20 years she had spent listening to her cosmetology clients had helped her develop a relational style that fit well with a psychology/counseling career path. She described her work as a counselor as deeply satisfying, and she said "I really want to be doing this for a long time." However, she enjoys the setting and clients, but her current position is only budgeted for 2 days a week, which creates financial challenges. At the time of our conversations, she was finishing up the last of her supervised hours required for licensing and was content to stay at her current location. However, she did describe several other thoughts she had related to the work she might pursue, once her licensing requirements were completed. Even as she described these possibilities, though, she talked about how her part-time schedule gives her the flexibility to meet the needs of her family.

Early in our conversation, Mary had described her realization—during her last bachelor's-level class—that:

> It suddenly dawned on me that I am a short-term kind of person. If I ended up [counseling] the same person for years, and they did not do anything to help themselves, I would have a very hard time not telling them to pull their heads out and look around. And as a therapist you can't do that.... Yup. It would be-, it would be very difficult for me. I'm a fairly blunt, to-the-point kind of person.

At the same time, she knew that she would have a difficult time finding work related to psychology with just a bachelor's degree, so she enrolled in a graduate program. She was nearing the completion of a master's degree in forensic psychology at the time of our conversations, spoke of postcollege options with a deep sense of ambivalence. When I asked her to describe her "perfect job," she said:

> That's a really good question. If I could answer that, my life would be wonderful. ... the government thing would be really cool ... opening a

[women's] shelter ... transitional housing kind of thing [for] kids in the foster system ... something with FEMA ... I just don't know which one "it" is.

Throughout our interviews, she had repeatedly returned to the idea of working with FEMA (the Federal Emergency Management Agency) in some sort of disaster relief and recovery role. She was drawn by the opportunity to provide tangible assistance to people in need, and the necessarily short-term nature of the assignments fit well with her personality. At the same time, she is a single mother, and she indicated that the extent of travel and time away from home that a FEMA-type job would require makes it an impossible option right now, even though she referred to this type of job as "right up my alley."

Finding Success

The third theme identified, "finding success," came from the various ways that these participants talked about success. The subtheme "studying perseverance" highlights the pride these men and women found in their academic accomplishments, especially in light of previous educational challenges. Within the "learning the work" subtheme, participants talked about precollege experiences and self-knowledge, along with a willingness to explore boundaries. As Troy said:

> I tested the waters to see ... how far will they let me lead, and I really want to be a leader. And it's-, you know, it's not about ... making all the right decisions, but it's also—being a leader—it's also about making the bad decisions, too, and sticking with, "hey, you know, I messed up" and you move [on].

For LeeAnna, learning the work of a counselor began with a realization that "I'm dealing with someone's life," and she expressed comfort in knowing that as a novice/intern counselor, she was required seek input from her supervisor.

I also identified a subtheme of "being the worker," in which participants spoke about their identity as employees. Mary referred to how "our work is more abstract than our parents' work," and perhaps a bit more challenging to evaluate. Jim described a relationship with a former supervisor:

> He knows what kind of worker I am.... Like I said, anything I do-, and every job I've had, I try to excel at it. And it got to the point that I was out doing jobs that he was supposed to do, to make sure things got done right. I was doing that on my own. So he was-, he trusted me to do, you know, with my own judgments on, you know, to make sure certain [they] were done right.

In following up on themes identified in previous research with first-generation college graduates (Olson, 2010), I asked participants to talk about the idea of "work ethic." These responses also spoke to this sub-theme of identity as a worker. LeeAnna noted:

> My kids don't see me work as hard as my parents did. My mom's parents were, um, pretty German and Lutheran. And so there was this major work ethic.... I mean, like, you don't sit down. You just work from morning until night, work-, pretty much your fingers to the bone.... And, um, and they worked hard.... And so they saw their parents working and working really hard. And now we have these ... everything is a modern convenience ... I can spend one day and get all my laundry done. You know, and that's, and then I can sit around. And I can sit around in between while it's washing.... My kids don't see me work, probably-, probably as hard as what [my parents did].

As Lubrano (2004) indicated, this well-developed, blue-collar work ethic is "the kind that gets you up early and keeps you locked in until the job is done, regardless of how odious or personally distasteful the task" (p. 17). Mary described a good work ethic as a "taking care of business kind of thing" and equated having a good work ethic with being a good employee.

Further exploring this idea of worker identity, I identified a fourth sub-theme: "framing success." These adult learners are not (currently) in work settings that might typically be seen as college success stories, the rags-to-riches tales propagated by higher education policymakers and university marketing specialists: LeeAnna was working 2 days a week; Troy was in an administrative support, entry-level role; Mary lost her job in the interim between the first and second interviews; Jim was about to be deployed overseas, fulfilling a military commitment that was not at all contingent on his status as a college graduate.

At times, this idea of "success" was treated with humor, as when Jim said, "They say I graduated with a bachelor's, but I don't know—I guess 10 years, I would think I'd be a doctor, you know." Mary, however, was less upbeat. At the time of our second interview, her part-time employment had ended unexpectedly. Although she was on the verge of completing her master's degree, she had described a recent struggle to remain motivated to complete her coursework, referring to it as self-sabotage. Mary expressed deep concern regarding her future, saying:

> I'm scared I'm going to make the wrong decision, so I don't do anything at all. And I was talking to a friend about it ... and she said, "How do you think you'd end up failing?" And I said, "I'll end up back in the hotel business." You know, which I love. I love working in the hotels, but that's not what I

went to school for. Why did I just pay $60,000 to get all these degrees and not use them? And that scares me.

Jim had also spoken of the hope of being able to "use my degree for something," but not with the sense of resignation found in Mary's statement.

I did not ask my participants directly about their definitions or experiences of success. However, I did ask them to describe both "good day" and "good job." Jim said that a good day was "getting work done, um, not having to, you know, rely on somebody else, you know, to do your work for you, because, you know, you're doing, you know what you're supposed to." Troy talked about wanting to eventually move into a role where he could lead, train, and direct others; Mary indicated that a good job was "knowing that I'm helping.... Somewhere. Somehow." LeeAnna described a good day at work by saying:

> I think the common thread is knowing that God has used me.... We'll be sitting in session and we'll get to the root of some problem, or I'll ask some question or something, and the person will be like, "Oh." You know, you can see that light bulb go on. And so those are really humbling moments, where it's like "wow," you know, like I can't believe God used me to bring that to that person.... And I have a lot of those.

These are responses describe an individually mediated experience and definition of success, rather than one that is contingent on external factors.

DISCUSSION AND FUTURE DIRECTION

At the outset of this project, I hoped to gain a better understanding of how the experience of being both a first-generation college student and an adult learner intersected with the college-to-work transition. What emerged was a sense that the complexity of life may well trump all other considerations. Not only is the 21st century world-at-large a complex place, the world of an adult learner is complex. While completing a college degree certainly opens doors to new possibilities, the competing demands of life may serve to constrain these possibilities, as seen in Mary's desire to pursue a particular career path and her simultaneous acknowledgment that the demands of a disaster relief job will not "work" with her current family situation.

In an era marked by economic uncertainty and rapidly shifting workplaces, what does it mean to be successful? The themes expressed by these men and women speak to an emerging understanding of success that has very little to do with prestige, title, or salary. As adult learners and first-generation students, they pursued education and persevered in college—in spite of challenging life, family, and educational histories. As they move beyond their bachelor's degrees, the habits of changing direction, seeing possibility, and defining (and redefining) success will become the skills they need in a complex and fast-paced world.

REFERENCES

Aslanian, C. B. (2001). *Adult students today.* New York, NY: The College Board.

Bamber, J., & Tett, L. (1999). Opening the doors of higher education to working class adults: A case study. *International Journal of Lifelong Education, 18*(6), 465-475.

Banerji, S. (2007, February 8). Report: Employers say college graduates lack essential skills to succeed in today's global economy. *Diverse: Issues in Higher Education, 23*(26), 18. Retrieved from http://diverseeducation.com/article/6979/

Bauman, S. S. M., Wang, N., DeLeon, C. W., Kafentzis, J., Zavala-Lopez, M., & Lindsey, M. S. (2004). Nontraditional students' service needs and social support resources: A pilot study. *Journal of College Counseling, 7*(1), 13-17. doi:10.1002/j.2161-1882.2004.tb00254.x

Berker, A., Horn, L., & Carrol, C. D. (2003). *Work first, study second: Adult undergraduates who combine employment and postsecondary enrollment.* Washington, DC: U.S. Department of Education, National Center for Education Statistics.

Bourdieu, P. (1986). The forms of capital. In J. G. Richardson (Ed.), *Handbook of theory and research for the sociology of education* (pp. 241-258). Santa Barbara, CA: Greenwood.

Chao, E. L., DeRocco, E. S., & Flynn, M. K. (2007). *Adult learners in higher education: Barriers to success and strategies to improve results.* Washington, DC: U.S. Department of Labor, Employment and Training Administration. Retrieved from http://www.jff.org/publications/education/adult-learners-higher-education-barriers/157

Chen, X., & Carroll, C. D. (2005). *First-generation students in postsecondary education: A look at their college transcripts (NCES 2005-171).* Washington, DC: U.S. Department of Education, National Center for Education Statistics, U.S. Government Printing Office. Retrieved from http://nces.ed.gov/pubs2005/2005171.pdf

Choy, S. (2001). *Students whose parents did not go to college: Postsecondary access, persistence, and attainment* (NCES 2001–126). U.S. Department of Education, National Center for Education Statistics. Washington, DC: U.S. Government Printing Office. Retrieved from http://nces.ed.gov/pubs2001/2001126.pdf

Choy, S. (2002). *Nontraditional Undergraduates.* Washington, DC: U.S. Department of Education, National Center for Education Statistics.

174 J. S. OLSON

Coulon, A. (2002). Underemployment amongst New Zealand graduates: Reflections from the lived experience. *New Zealand Journal of Industrial Relations, 27*(3), 283-297.

Creswell, J. W. (2007). *Qualitative inquiry and research design: Choosing among five approaches* (2nd ed.). Thousand Oaks, CA: SAGE.

Dennis, J. M., Phinney, J. S., & Chauteco, L. I. (2005). The role of motivation, parental support, and peer support in the academic success of ethnic minority first-generation college students. *Journal of College Student Development, 46*(3), 223-236.

Dresang, J. (19 February, 2008). New grads in demand: Employers seeing change in generations. *McClatchy-Tribune Business News*. Retrieved from ABI/INFORM Dateline. (Document ID: 1431135621).

Edwards, R. (1993). *Mature women students: Separating or connecting family and education*. London, England: Taylor & Francis.

Giancola, J. K., Munz, D. C., & Trares, S. (2008). First- versus continuing-generation adult students on college perceptions: Are differences actually because of demographic variance? *Adult Education Quarterly, 58*(3), 214-228. doi:10.1177/0741713608314088

Hanneman, L., & Gardner, P. (2010). *Under the economic turmoil a skills gap simmers*. CERI Research Brief 1-2010. East Lansing, MI: Collegiate Employment Research Institute. Retrieved from http://www.ceri.msu.edu/wp-content/uploads/2009/10/skillsabrief1-2010.pdf

Holden, R., & Hamblett, J. (2007). The transition from higher education into work: Tales of cohesion and fragmentation. *Education & Training, 49*(7), 516-585. doi:10.1108/00400910710832014

Horwedel, D. M. (2008). Putting first-generation students first. *Diverse: Issues in Higher Education, 25*, 10-12. Retrieved from http://diverseeducation.com/

Ishitani, T. T. (2006). Studying attrition and degree completion behavior among first-generation college students in the United States. *The Journal of Higher Education, 77*(5), 861-885. doi:10.1353/jhe.2006.0042.

Liebowitz, M., & Taylor, J. C. (2004). *Breaking through: Helping low-skilled adults enter and succeed in college and careers*. Boston, MA: Jobs for the Future. Retrieved from http://www.breakingthroughcc.org/sites/default/files/BreakingThrough.pdf

Lincoln, Y. S., & Guba, E. G. (1985). *Naturalistic inquiry*. Newbury Park, CA: SAGE.

London, H. B. (1989). Breaking away: A study of first-generation college students and their families. *American Journal of Education, 97*(2), 144-170.

London, H. B. (1992). Transformations: Cultural challenges faced by first-generation students. *New Directions for Community Colleges, 80*, 5-11. doi:10.1002/cc.36819928003

Lubrano, A. (2004). *Limbo: Blue-collar roots, white-collar dreams*. Hoboken, NJ: John Wiley.

Martin, R., Matham, B., Case, J., & Fraser, D. (2005). Engineering graduates' perceptions of how well they were prepared for work in industry. *European Journal of Engineering Education, 30*(2), 167-180.

McCarron, G. P., & Inkelas, K. K. (2006). The gap between educational aspirations and attainment for first-generation college students and the role of parental involvement. *Journal of College Student Development, 47*(5), 534-549.

Moustakas, C. (1994). *Phenomenological research methods.* Thousand Oaks, CA: SAGE.

Nuñez, A.-M., & Cuccaro-Alamin, S. (1998). *First-generation students: Undergraduates whose parents never enrolled in postsecondary education* (NCES 98-082). U.S. Department of Education, National Center for Education Statistics. Washington, DC: U.S. Government Printing Office. Retrieved from http://nces.ed.gov/pubs98/98082.pdf

Olson, J. S. (2010). *Chasing a passion: The early-career lived experience of first-generation college graduates* (Doctoral dissertation). Retrieved from *ProQuest.* (AAT 3436090)

Orbe, M. P. (2008). Theorizing multidimensional identity negotiation: Reflections on the lived experiences of first-generation college students. In M. Azmitia, M. Syed, & K. Radmacher (Eds.), *New Directions for Child and Adolescent Development, 120,* 81-95, doi:10.1002/cd.217

Pascarella, E. T., Pierson, C. T., Wolniak, G. C., & Terenzini, P. T. (2004). First-generation college students: Additional evidence on college experiences and outcomes. *The Journal of Higher Education, 75*(3), 249-284. Retrieved from http://muse.jhu.edu/journals/journal_of_higher_education/toc/jhe75.3.html

Pascarella, E., & Terenzini, P. (2005). *How college affects students: A third decade of research* (Vol. 2). San Francisco, CA: Jossey-Bass.

Patton, M. Q. (2002). *Qualitative evaluation and research methods* (3rd ed.). Thousand Oaks, CA: SAGE.

Perrone, L., & Vickers, M. H. (2003). Life after graduation as a 'very uncomfortable world': An Australian case study. *Education & Training, 45*(2), 69-78.

Polkinghorne, D. E. (1989). Phenomenological research methods. In R. S. Valle & S. Halling (Eds.), *Existential-phenomenological perspectives in psychology: Exploring the breadth of human experience* (pp. 41-60). New York, NY: Plenum Press.

Putnam, R. D. (2000). *Bowling alone: The collapse and revival of American community.* New York, NY: Touchstone.

Reay, D. (2003). A risky business? Mature working-class women students and access to higher education. *Gender and Education, 15*(3), 301-317. doi:10.1080/0954025032000103213

Seidman, I. (1998). *Interviewing as qualitative research: A guide for researchers in education and social sciences.* New York, NY: Teachers College Press.

Sorey, K. C., & Duggan, M. H. (2008). Differential predictors of persistence between community college adult and traditional-aged students. *Community College Journal of Research and Practice, 32*(2), 75-100. doi:10.1080/10668920701380967

Spiegelberg, H. (1975). *Doing phenomenology: Essays on and in phenomenology.* The Hague, Netherlands: Martinus Nijhoff.

St. Clair-Christman, J. (2009, May). *Recruitment and retention of low income, first generation students: What administrators, faculty, and staff need to know.* Paper presented at the Hendrick Best Practices for Adult Learners Conference, University Park, PA.

Steele, R., Lauder, W., Caperchione, C., & Anastasi, J. (2005). An exploratory study of the concerns of mature access to nursing students and the coping strategies used to manage these adverse experiences. *Nurse Education Today*, *25*(7), 573-581. Retrieved from http://www.nurseeducationtoday.com/article/S0260-6917(05)00095-X/fulltext

van Manen, M. (1997a). Phenomenological pedagogy and the question of meaning. In D. Vandenberg (Ed.), *Phenomenology and educational discourse* (pp. 41-68). Johannesburg, South Africa: Heinemann Higher & Further Education.

van Manen, M. (1997b). *Researching lived experience: Human science for an action sensitive pedagogy*. London, Ontario: The Althouse Press.

Van T. Bui, K. (2002). First-generation college students at a four-year university: Background characteristics, reasons for pursuing higher education and first-year experiences. *College Student Journal*, *36*(3). Retrieved from http://www.freepatentsonline.com/article/College-Student-Journal/85007762.html

Warburton, E. C., Bugarin, R., Nuñez, A.-M., & Carroll, C. D. (2001). *Bridging the gap: Academic preparation and postsecondary success of first-generation students* (NCES 2001-153). Washington, DC: U.S. Department of Education, National Center for Education Statistics, U.S. Government Printing Office. Retrieved from http://nces.ed.gov/pubs2001/2001153.pdf

CHAPTER 12

FORCING A SQUARE PEG INTO A ROUND HOLE

Asynchronous Online Education Credit Hours Based on Seat Time

Frederick Carl Prashun

Distance education has been and continues to be an instructional modality found in the U.S. education system. Historically, distance education has not been completely accepted by the academy as a format that could be used in providing learning opportunities for adult learners. Today's common form of distance education is online learning and is used by many adults gaining education. Regulations and expectations within the field of education were created based on instructional formats occurring within a classroom setting. The credit hour is one such standard and is defined by time in a classroom. Nontraditional instructional formats, such as asynchronous online education, are being forced into traditional policy and standards. This practice is, using an analogy, forcing a square peg into a round hole. Online learning is not the same as classroom learning. Using a time metric on instruction is forcing instruction to meet the metric criteria instead of developing an appropriate and just measurement. Educational formats have changed significantly over the last century.

Conversations About Adult Learning in Our Complex World, pp. 177–193
Copyright © 2013 by Information Age Publishing
All rights of reproduction in any form reserved.

177

However, the credit hour metric has not transformed or been replaced to adequately measure evolving instructional formats and learning. This study addressed this issue by examining current regulations for determining credit hour values for asynchronous online education.

THEORETICAL BACKGROUND

Asynchronous Online Education

Education has been an important element within American history. Providing learning opportunities for adults took instruction beyond the confines of a classroom and an institution. Distance education, learning that was not assigned to a classroom at a designated institution, took form within the U.S. through offerings such as the Lyceum movement, Chautauqua College, and Correspondence University (Larreamendy-Joerns & Leinhardt, 2006; Meyer, 1975; Shaw, 1993; Watkins, 1991). Other examples of learning beyond the academy were found in correspondence courses and extension programs. Advancements in technology and society have challenged traditional education for the past century. One outcome of this evolution is found in asynchronous online education (Feasley, 1991; Pittman, 1991; Watkins, 1991).

As a result of technological advancements over the past years, educators used radio, videoconferencing, and more recently, computers and Internet to provide possible learning opportunities. Education is no longer bound to a classroom and an institution with a designated instructor and established meeting times. Lim, Morris, and Kupritz (2007) and Shale (2002) discussed how asynchronous online education, with the instructor and learner separated by time and distance, removes the classroom setting and the need for a designated meeting time. Instead of teacher and student being face-to-face, instruction and interaction may occur asynchronously by use of the Internet and computers making asynchronous online education significantly different than traditional classroom learning.

Adult Education

A growing trend in higher education is for those over the traditional college age of 18-22 years of age to enroll in courses. These adult learners are outnumbering traditionally college aged students. Hussar and Bailey (2008) and Poley (2008) discussed how higher education overall enrollments are dominated by persons 25 years of age and older. Annetta and

Shymansky (2006) projected that online education students will be comprised of more learners over the age of 35 than traditionally aged students (18 to 22 years old). The Web-Based Education Commission (2000) provided information showing that due to a developing global society, adult learners' needs are evolving. Adult learners continue needing new knowledge and skills due to job demands and a changing global society. According to Poley (2008), employers desire more education and that expectations exist for employees' continually learning. These points are also discussed by Hrastinski (2006), who emphasizes that adults require greater amounts of lifelong learning. These changes, according to Abel (2005) and Poley (2008), are forcing higher education institutions to offer more online courses, adjust scheduling, and change policies and practices. Allen and Seaman (2010), reporting for the Sloan Consortium, also indicated that due to economic impact, higher education institutions reported increased demands for new courses and degrees in addition to the demand for greater number of existing online course offerings.

A shift in higher education is needed to better meet the demand of busy schedules. Learners may not always be able to get to campuses and may not have the luxury of attending many weeks of classes. Today's adult learners are consumers looking for education that meets their needs and schedules, and are compatible with lifestyle (Jones, Voorhees, & Paulson, 2002; Shale, 2002). The challenge for higher education, according to Bishop and White (2007), Shale (2002), and the Web-Based Education Commission (2000), is to make a paradigm shift away from traditional learning based on classroom, time, and place. New policies and practices are required to meet adult learning needs.

Credit Hours

Beginning over a century ago, the U.S. education system adopted a metric that became known as the credit hour (Heffernan, 1973; Shedd, 2003a). Since the introduction of credit hours, little has changed with how it is defined, used, and applied to courses. The credit hour metric was implemented for quality control and transferability of learning between institutions, especially, between secondary and postsecondary education schools (Shedd, 2003a, 2003b). The credit hour design measures the amount of learning time, or class time, that students participate in instruction, which is also known as seat time. Traditionally, one credit hour equates to 1 learning hour (50 minutes) with an instructor per week for the duration of a semester (Maeroff, 1994; Shaw, 1993). A commonly accepted practice in higher education is for every learning hour, a student would spend 2 additional hours in preparation and study (U.S. Network for Education Information, 2008b, 2008c). The total would be three learning hours per 1 credit hour for each week of the term.

Assessment and Significant Issue of Virtual Seat Time

Based on time, the credit hour provides a measurement of student time with an instructor involved in learning. Asynchronous online education, however, does not have a set class time and often limited direct instructor interaction. Thus, online education cannot be measured by credit hour standards. Adams and Morgan (2007), DiMartino and Castaneda (2007), and Eaton (2002) argued that online education, and distance education in general, are not built on classroom time and cannot be measured by traditional standards. With education no longer bound by time and classroom, a new metric is needed. Educational formats have changed, but the application and use of the credit hour and the credit hour's meaning have not evolved with instructional modalities and learning needs.

Data and current trends indicated that online education would become a dominant form of education. Saba (2005), SchWeber (2008), and Zhang Niu, and Jiang (2002) discussed how statistics continually show an increase in organizations providing web-based learning and an increase in student enrollments for web-based courses. Another study indicated an annual rate of approximately 1.5% growth of students taking online courses, which was a greater growth than overall higher education enrollment figures (Allen & Seaman, 2007a, 2007b). According to Web-Based Education Commission (2000), that the fastest growing segment enrolling in higher education are adults over the age of 25. These older nontraditional students are working to stay current on knowledge and skills in a constantly changing and developing global society. The Web-Based Education Commission further indicated that taking learning to the student was now a needed practice of education. Education on all levels could no longer depend on students coming to "the learning." The Internet, as a tool, could empower educators and institutions to take the learning to students. Martyn (2003) furthered the discussion by noting how nontraditional learners require flexible access to education. Cerone (2008), Hickman (1999), and Jones, Voorhees, and Paulson (2002) developed this thought further by discussing how today's learners were educational consumers whom search for learning that meets their specific needs of life, schedule, work, and/or personal interests.

The purpose of this study was finding and examining policies of how asynchronous online education "class time" was translated into credit hours. The specific question guiding this research: "What methods do policies set forth for determining the translation of online class time into credit hours?" This document is a general report presenting the summative findings from a study that reviewed policies and documents from the U.S. Department of Education, regional accrediting commissions, and public higher education systems.

RESEARCH DESIGN AND ANALYSIS OF STUDY

Design of the Study

The design of this study was based on policy analysis allowing for constant data comparison by holding one document against other documents and their meanings (Rose, 2002). Musick (1998) defined policy analysis as a formal discipline within the field of education that is an analysis and evaluation in a method, program, or policy relational to its effectiveness and successful outcomes or results as the content of policies. For purposes of this study, polices are regulations, rules, and procedures that are in place to guide present and future actions and decisions for the organization. Documents that interpret and guide application of policies are included in this study to more fully understand the application and use of credit hours (Musick, 1998; Rose, 2002; Smith, 2002). Policies and related documents were gathered and reviewed from the United Stated Department of Education, the six regional accrediting agencies that oversee and credential educational institutions within America, and the top 10 public higher education systems as based on total enrollment (National Center for Education Statistics, 2010a, 2010b, 2010c). Semistructured interviews were conducted with persons representing accrediting commissions and public higher education systems. These discussions were used to validate policies and documentation data, and to add another layer of comparison. Participants' transcripts were assigned the letter "P" followed by a randomly assigned two-digit number in order to protect confidentiality. Citations within this report will follow the same identification.

Data Analysis

Analysis used for this study may be described as a spiral method (Hesse-Biber & Leavy, 2006) of the policies and documentation collected from the organizations. In this type of review, a researcher is able to start from a large view and incrementally get more detailed. The constant comparison nonlinear process permits comparisons between policies and documents for the duration of the study (Krippendorff, 2004; McCulloch, 2004) The advantage of this form of analysis, according to Bogdan and

Biklen (2007), "is a research designed for multi-data sources, which is like analytic induction and that the formal analysis begins early in the study and is nearly completed by the end of the data collection" (p. 73).

Bogdan and Biklen (2007), Hesse-Biber and Leavy (2006), and Rose (2002) explained that constant comparison is an important aspect of policy analysis and allows for discovery of themes and for elements of distinction. Reviewing and comparing data allows for better understanding of the information (Cooper, Fusarelli, & Randall, 2004; McCulloch, 2004). Data was also analyzed beyond the "normal reading and viewing habits" (Jones, 1961, p. 122) looking for common thematic characteristics. Finding themes were beneficial in learning from data with a deeply rich understanding (Bogdan & Biklen, 2007; Kelle, 2004) of the policies and documents collected.

Checklists were completed and compared during the project to assure complete data were collected systematically from all sources. The final outcome resulted in a systematic analysis (Merriam & Simpson, 2000) of how educational governing agencies' policies regulate asynchronous online education credit hour determination and practices. All organizational data were reviewed to respond to the research question by organizing findings with two guiding questions: (1) What is the agency's published definition of the credit hour? (2) What published guidelines does the agency have for calculating credit hour value to traditional and online education courses?

National review. Data gathered and analyzed from United States Department of Education provided a credit hour definition and how the credit hour system is unique to American education (U.S. Network for Education Information, 2007, 2008a, 2008b, 2008c, 2008d). Also, data were reviewed looking for answers to how the credit hour should be calculated and used for traditional and online educational settings.

Regional review. The second phase of data analysis was conducted on the information gathered from the six regional accrediting agencies. As discussed, these governing bodies are responsible to administer and provide accreditation to institutions providing education to all levels of learning from K-12 through higher education. Data gathered was reviewed in similar fashion as the national and system data for credit hour definition and information on using the credit hour. Interviews of persons representing accrediting agencies were conducted. These participants had responsibilities for academic oversight and accreditation of respective commission's membership.

With participant approval, interviews were recorded. Transcripts were made from the recordings and used for analysis. The purpose of interviews was to validate policy and document findings. Therefore, using the spiral method described previously, each transcript was reviewed for themes and compared against the commission's policies, documents, and other transcripts. Data from each commission was analyzed for credit hour definition and calculation details for credit hour determination of traditional instruction and asynchronous online education. Comparative analysis of transcripts against policies and documents confirmed the tatter findings. Interviews also provided elaboration on data through examples and further detailed discussion. Once individual transcripts were reviewed against respective policies and documents, comparison between commissions, U.S. Department of Education, and public systems commenced. Comparative examination continued with the focus on answering the research question: "What methods do policies set forth for determining the translation of online class time into credit hours?"

Public higher education review. Based on The Integrated Postsecondary Education Data System (IPEDS) the top 10 public systems based on 2008 total enrollments were used for this project. Data collections for each of the systems focused on answering the research question. Information was organized by defining the credit hour and how the system translates asynchronous online education into credit hours. Data were gathered following the process discussed for the regional commissions. Participants with responsibility in academic affairs representing respective systems were interviewed allowing for another layer of comparison validating findings and more detailed understanding of data and practices. Interviews were recorded as permitted and transcribed for analysis. Discussion with participants corroborated data found in each system's policies and documents. Data from a system was then compared against other systems, regional, and U.S. Department of Education information. Organization of system data were organized by credit hour meaning and how asynchronous online education credit hours were determined.

RESULTS

There was no data found that conclusively answered the research question: What methods do policies set forth for determining the translation of online class time into credit hours? Found in the data, however, were three primary themes. First, credit hours as a metric are based on time. Second, determination of credit hours for asynchronous online education is the same process as traditional course work. Application of and use of credit hours are based on judgments by two groups: (a) faculty and administration, and (b) regulatory agencies. Third, the possibility of a new metric measuring outcomes and competencies was discussed. These three elements are discussed in the sections following.

Credit Hour Definition

The credit hour was originally introduced in the late 1800s for providing a measurement for institutions to track and quantify instruction. The design was based on one credit hour representing a subject's instruction in a classroom for one week, or five class hours over 5 days (U.S. Network for Education Information, 2008c). A more recent definition found for a credit hour was "how much time a typical student is expected to devote to learning in one week of full time undergraduate study" (New England Association of Schools and Colleges Commission on Institutions of Higher Education, 2005, p. 2). Nearly all of the regional accrediting commissions provided a documented credit hour definition. The general consensus and praxis of a credit hour was 1 instructional hour plus 1 student preparation hours (Middle States Commission on Higher Education, 2009c, 2009d; New England Association of Schools and Colleges Commission on Institutions of Higher Education, 2005, 2011; North Central Association of Colleges and Schools—The Higher Learning Commission, 2000, 2003; Northwest Commission on Colleges and Universities, 2003, 2010; Western Association of Schools and Colleges Accrediting Commission for Senior Colleges and Universities, 2010a, 2010b). One agency, Commission on Colleges, did not provide a documented definition of the credit hour. Although the definition and application of credit hours varied slightly by organization, all were based on an instructional hour (50 minutes) with 2 hours of student preparation time outside of class.

During the course of this study, the Department of Education issued the *Program Integrity Issues* (2010) regulation. In the ruling, the commonly accepted understanding of credit hours was placed into federal rule: one credit hour is "equivalent to" the amount of learning that would occur during 1 hour of instruction and 2 hours of student preparation or study for the course of a semester (Program Integrity Issues, 2010). The meaning of the "new credit" hour does not appear different than what was already defined and practiced in existing policies and documents. Shown in Table 1 are the amounts of learning time involved for one credit hour. Time expected to be involved in traditional classroom learning to receive one credit hour is nearly identical to the post-Program Integrity ruling "equivalent to" definition. The only significant difference is that a definition is now part of federal rule with compliance expectations and defined accountability for fulfillment of regulations.

When considering time involved in learning, the credit hour holds different values depending on the type of activity (see Table 12.1). Originally, the credit hour, known as the Carnegie Unit, was based on five instructional hours per week for a term. This resulted in 75 hours of learning time per term.

Table 12.1.   Learning Time Per Credit Hour

Credit Hour Type	Class(es)/Week	Time/Class[a]	Extra Time[b]	Total Time
Original	5	1 hr	0	75 hrs
Commonly Practiced w/ Instructor	1	1 hr	2 hrs	45 hrs
Commonly Practiced w/o Instructor	1	1 hr	2 hrs + X hrs	45 hrs + X hrs
Equivalent To[d]	1	1 hr	2 hrs	45 hrs

Note: Table 12.1 is a synthesis of findings.
[a]Time per class is based on one instructional hour. This is equivalent to 50 minutes of clock time.
[b]Extra time was described as student preparation and study time that occurred outside of regularly scheduled class time.
[c]Total time is based on one instructional hour per credit.
[d]Created from *Program Integrity Issues: Final Rule,* 75 Fed. Reg. U.S. Department of Education, 34 C.F.R. §600.2, §602.24, §603.24, and §668.8. pp. 66832-66975. (2010). Retrieved from http://www2.ed.gov/legislation/FedRegister/finrule/2010-4/102910a.html; and Ochoa, E. M. (2011). *Dear Colleague Letter.* (GEN-11-06). Washington, DC: U.S. Department of Education. Retrieved from http://ifap.ed.gov/dpcletters/attachments/GEN1106.pdf

The commonly practiced credit hour was based on direct interaction with an instructor in a classroom. This equated to one instructional hour plus two student study hours per week per credit; the result is 45 learning hours per credit hour. Courses that did not include direct instructor interaction had extra time added as determined to the normative 45 hours. These type of courses would include laboratory, practicums, studio, and independent study courses. The total learning time would result in 45 hours plus an amount of extra time as determined per week per credit. With the definition provided in the *Program Integrity Issues* (2010) ruling, all learning, regardless of format, is "equivalent to" the learning that occurs in one instructional hour plus two student study hours (a common credit hour). The ruling did not change the credit hour meaning. The ruling provides a common documented definition for all U.S. education and maintains existing practices.

Determination of Credit Hours

The Department of Education, the commissions, or the state systems did not provide credit hour translation for online education. Instead, the common practice was to make online courses similar to traditional on campus courses. Therefore, credit determination for online learning followed the same practice as assigning credit hours to traditional courses. In other words, all credit hour values and associated learning are based on judgments with varying criteria.

The introduction of the *Program Integrity Issues* (2010) ruling provided a clearly defined credit hour definition. Comparison of the "new" definition to prior meaning and practice did not show any significant difference between the pre- and postruling descriptions. Interview participants 10, 12, and 25 also voiced how the ruling only reinforced the traditional credit hour practice and understanding. All learning, by the new definition, is now equated to the learning that occurs in 1 instructional hour plus 2 student study hours, as was commonly practiced prior the ruling. Since there were no policies for translating online course work into credit hours, and the common praxis continues to equate online courses to traditional classes, the determination of credit hours was found the same before and after the ruling regardless of modality. Therefore, credit hour decisions continue to be made based on judgments of how much learning occurs within a time allotment. These decisions are made by persons at the local institutional level and expected to be within the constructs of commonly held praxis and understanding of higher education credit hours.

The *Program Integrity Issues* (2010) ruling now mandates that accrediting commissions provide standards for institutions in how they make decisions about credit hours and their use. Institutions are also required to document how they determine credit hours for course work. Ultimately, the persons responsible for credit hour decisions are faculty and administrative persons on the local level. These people judge course work, content, design, and number of credits. State systems and regional commissions then assess local decisions for compliance. There is no significant difference between pre- and post-*Program Integrity Issues* credit hour meaning and use.

A New Metric

Discussed in some detail during the interviews was a new metric measuring and tracking learning outcomes and competencies. Participant 13 indicated that the region was adding criteria to standards that aligned the commission's desire to place emphasis on learning. Also discussed was how measurable outcomes would provide freedom for the instructional modality while assuring the same quality of learning. Participant 19 referred to the Middle States Commission on Higher Education documentation. One such document (Middle States Commission on Higher Education, 2009d) discussed that learning associated with credit hours should be based on stated outcomes and measured by assessment evidence. Other data from Middle States Commission on Higher Education (2009a, 2009b, 2011) reiterated similar thoughts and related the practices to quality higher education. Ochoa (2011), the U.S. Department of Education, discussed how learning was the focus of education and the *Program Integrity Ruling*. Ochoa also emphasized that learning outcomes and assessment were necessary to ensure quality education.

Participants 13 and 17 discussed at length the importance of learning outcomes and assessments. Both persons stressed that the commissions placed great amount of attention and energy on placing learning as a priority over number of credit hours. From the system perspective, P10, P12, P14, and P25 discussed at length how learning was central. According to these participants, the measurement of learning outcomes was more important than determination of credit hours. P10 elaborated more on this theme by discussing how learning benchmarks are needed regardless of maintaining the credit hour or instituting a new metric. P12 argued that change was needed and that new standards should come from the institutional level instead of the Department of Education and accrediting commissions. However, the Department of Education and accreditation commissions could organize such activities and assist in developing a new metric. P12 provided examples of how the represented system incorporated discussion and input of representatives from all the local institutions.

DISCUSSION AND CONCLUSION

The purpose of this study was to determine if policies provided guidance for the translation of online courses into credit hours. To accomplish this task, comparative policy and document analyses were conducted on Department of Education, regional accrediting commissions, and state public higher education system documentation. Even though credit hours were defined and associated to 1 instructional hour plus 2 student preparation hours, no policy addressed the translation of asynchronous online courses into credits.

Concern about credit hours has existed for many years. Data showed that application of credit hours to asynchronous online education was reported as an issue and that change was needed (Lew, 2003; Office of Postsecondary Education, 2001). However, no change to credit hours was found in data. Also reported by Paige, Stroup, and Andrade (2003), Riley, Fritschler, and McLaughlin (2001), and Spellings and Stroup (2005) was that online education provides an alternative to traditional education, but the current way of measuring and tracking education was needed. Reports continued to indicate that higher education organizations wanted an alternative to credit hours. The design of the *Program Integrity Issues* (2010) was to address the concern of credit hours. However, as shown in Table 12.1, the ruling did not significantly change credit hour meaning or use.

Findings indicated that faculty and administrative persons on the local system level maintain the most influence in deciding credit hour values. Additionally, the *Program Integrity Issues* (2010) regulation was designed to address issues related to credit hours, especially so for nontraditional learning and accelerated calendars. The ruling continued the same standard as before the "new" credit hour definition. The only significant difference was making all learning modalities equivalent to the learning that occurs in one instructional hour plus two student study hours totaling three learning hours per week per credit hour. Such determinations will continue to be made at local levels while commissions and the Department of Education will assess the judgments of faculty and administration.

Findings indicated that the credit hour system does not properly represent learning and the need for a new metric existed for many years. Interview participants presented how creation of a new metric as a way to support evolution within the field of education was needed. Findings support further investigation of using learning outcomes, competencies, and assessments as metric instead of a time-based credit system. The support for common benchmarks across all institutions would provide a more sound foundation for education within the United States.

The outstanding issue, then, is that the *Program Integrity Issues* ruling or any of the policies and documents examined did not provide information or guidance to associate the equivalent amount of learning to three learning hours. The same was found true of the regional and system data. In other words, there was no indication of how much learning should occur per credit hour. Further research is needed to address the amount of learning "equivalent to" 1 instructional hour plus 2 student study hours if using credit hours continues.

REFERENCES

Abel, R. (2005). Implementing best practices in online learning: A recent study reveals common denominators for success in Internet-supported learning. *Educause Quarterly, 28*(3), 75-77.

Adams, J., & Morgan, G. (2007). "Second generation" e-learning: Characteristics and design principles for supporting management soft-skills development. *International Journal on E-Learning, 6*(2), 157-185.

Allen, I. E., & Seaman, J. (2007a). *Making the grade: Online education in the United States, 2006* (Southern Edition). Needham, MA: The Sloan Consortium.

Allen, I. E., & Seaman, J. (2007b). Online nation: Five years of growth in online learning. Retrieved from https://www.sloanconsortium.org/publications/survey/pdf/online_nation.pdf

Allen, I. E., & Seaman, J. (2010). Learning on demand: Online education in the United States, 2009 report. Retrieved from http://www.sloan-c.org/publications/survey/pdf/learningondemand.pdf

Annetta, L. A., & Shymansky, J. A. (2006). Investigating science learning for rural elementary school teachers in a professional-development project through three distance-education strategies. *Journal of Research in Science Teaching, 43*(10), 1019-1039.

Bishop, M. J., & White, S. A. (2007). The clipper project: Discovering what online courses offer residential universities. *EDUCAUSE Quarterly, 30*(1), 14-20.

Bogdan, R. C., & Biklen, S. K. (2007). *Qualitative research for education: An introduction to theories and methods* (5th ed.). Boston, MA: Allyn & Bacon.

Cerone, K. (2008). Characteristics of adult learners with implications for online learning design. *AACE Journal, 16*(2), 137-159.

Cooper, B. S., Fusarelli, L. D., & Randall, E. V. (2004). *Better policies, better schools: Theories and applications*. Boston, MA: Pearson.

DiMartino, J., & Castaneda, A. (2007, April). Assessing applied skills: The Carnegie Unit, awarding course credit for seat time, is working against efforts to teach and test 21st century workforce skills. *Educational Leadership*, 38-42.

Eaton, J. S. (2002). Maintaining the delicate balance: Distance learning, higher education accreditation, and the politics of self-regulation *Distributed Education: Challenges, Choices, and a New Environment*. Washington, DC: Center for Policy Analysis, American Council on Education.

Feasley, C. E. (1991). The research, evaluation, and documentation of independent study. In B. L. Watkins & S. J. Wright (Eds.), *The foundations of American distance education: A century of collegiate correspondence study* (pp. 231-253). Dubuque, IA: Kendall/Hunt.

Heffernan, J. M. (1973). The credibility of the credit hour: The history, use, and shortcomings of the credit system. *The Journal of Higher Education, 44*(1), 61-72.

Hesse-Biber, S. H., & Leavy, P. (2006). *The practice of qualitative research*. Thousand Oaks, CA: SAGE.

Hickman, C. J. (1999). Public policy implications associated with technology assisted distance learning. *Adult Learning, 10*(3), 17-20.

Hrastinski, S. (2006). The relationship between adopting a synchronous medium and participation in online group work: An explorative study. *Interactive Learning Environments, 14*(2), 137-152.

Hussar, W. J., & Bailey, T. M. (2008). *Projection of educational statistics to 2017*. Washington, DC: National Center for Education Statistics.

Jones, E. A., Voorhees, R. A., & Paulson, K. (2002). *Defining and assessing learning: Exploring competency-based initiatives*. Washington, DC: National Center for Education Statistics.

Jones, R. A. (1961). *Research methods in the social and behavioral sciences*. Sunderland, MA: Sinauer Associates.

Kelle, U. (2004). Computer-assisted qualitative data analysis. In C. Seale, G. Gobo, J. F. Gubrium & D. Silverman (Eds.), *Qualitative Research Practice* (pp. 443-459). Thousand Oaks, CA: SAGE.

Krippendorff, K. (2004). *Content analysis: An introduction to its methodology* (2nd ed.). Thousand Oaks, CA: SAGE.

Larreamendy-Joerns, J., & Leinhardt, G. (2006). Going the distance with online education. *Review of Educational Research, 76*(4), 567-605.

Lew, H. (2003). *Memorandum: Final audit report.* (ED-OIG/A09-COOI4). Washington, DC: Department of Education. Retrieved from www2.ed.gov/about/offices/list/oig/auditreports/a09c0014.pdf

Lim, D. H., Morris, M. L., & Kupritz, V. W. (2007). Online vs. blended learning: Differences in instructional outcomes and learner satisfaction. *Journal for Asynchronous Learning Networks, 11*(2), 27-42.

Maeroff, G. I. (1994). The assault on the carnegie unit. *NCA Quarterly, 68*(3), 408-411.

Martyn, M. (2003). The hybrid online model: Good practice. *Educause Quarterly, 26*(1), 18-23.

McCulloch, G. (2004). *Documentary research in education, history, and the social sciences.* New York, NY: Routledge-Falmer.

Merriam, S. B., & Simpson, E. L. (2000). *A guide to research for educators and trainers of adults* (2nd ed.). Malabar, FL: Krieger.

Meyer, P. (1975). *Awarding college credit for non-college learning: A guide to current practice.* San Francisco, CA: Jossey-Bass.

Middle States Commission on Higher Education. (2009a). *ALO newsletter: Fall 2009.* Philadelphia, PA: Author. Retrieved from http://www.msche.org/newsletters/Fall-2009-ALO-Newsletter090911094756.doc

Middle States Commission on Higher Education. (2009b). *Characteristics of excellence in higher educaton: Requirements of affiliation and standards for accreditation* (12th ed.). Philidelphia, PA: Author.

Middle States Commission on Higher Education. (2009c). *Definitions of higher education and accreditation terms.* Philadelphia, PA: Author. Retrieved from http://www.msche.org/documents/Glossary.doc

Middle States Commission on Higher Education. (2009d). *Guidelines: Degree and credits.* Philadelphia, PA: Author. Retrieved from http://www.msche.org/documents/Degree-and-Credit-Guidelines-062209-FINAL%5B1%5DDec09.pdf

Middle States Commission on Higher Education. (2011). *Distance education programs: Interregional guidelines for the evaluation of distance education (online learning).* Philidelphia, PA: Author. Retrieved from http://www.msche.org/publications/Guidelines-for-the-Evaluation-of-Distance-Education-Programs.pdf

Musick, D. W. (1998). Policy analysis in medical education: A structured approach. *Med Educ Online, 3*(2).

National Center for Education Statistics. (2010a). *Compare individual institutions 2008 data* [Data search criteria]. Available from Author within U.S. Department of Education Institute of Education Sciences, The Integrated

Postsecondary Education Data System (IPEDS) http://nces.ed.gov/ipeds/datacenter/Default.aspx

National Center for Education Statistics. (2010b). Integrated postsecondary education data system. Retrieved from http://www.nces.ed.gov/ipeds/about/

National Center for Education Statistics. (2010c). Integrated postsecondary education data system glossary: 2010-11 survey materials. Retrieved from https://surveys.nces.ed.gov/ipeds/Downloads/Forms/IPEDSGlossary.pdf

New England Association of Schools and Colleges Commission on Institutions of Higher Education. (2005). *Statement on credits and degrees*. Beford, MA: Author. Retrieved from http://cihe.neasc.org/downloads/POLICIES/Pp111_PolicyOnCreditsAndDegrees.pdf

New England Association of Schools and Colleges Commission on Institutions of Higher Education. (2011). *Policy on credits and degrees*. Bedford, MA: Author.

North Central Association of Colleges and Schools—The Higher Learning Commission. (2000). *Commission policy and good practices on transfer of credit*. Chicago, IL: Author. Retrieved from https://content.springcm.com/content/DownloadDocuments.ashx?Selection=Document%2C17981973%3B&accountId=5968

North Central Association of Colleges and Schools—The Higher Learning Commission. (2003). *Handbook of accreditation* (3rd ed.). Chicago, IL: Author.

Northwest Commission on Colleges and Universities. (2003). *Accreditation handbook* (2003 ed.). Redmond, WA: Author.

Northwest Commission on Colleges and Universities. (2010). Northwest Commission on Colleges and Universities search results: Credit hour. Retrieved from http://www.nwccu.org/Search/search.htm

Ochoa, E. M. (2011). *Dear colleague letter*. (GEN-11-06). Washington, DC: U.S. Department of Education. Retrieved from http://ifap.ed.gov/dpcletters/attachments/GEN1106.pdf

Office of Postsecondary Education. (2001). *Student financial assistance and nontraditional educational programs (including the "12-hour rule"): A report to Congress*. Washington, DC: U. S. Department of Education. Retrieved from www2.ed.gov/policy/highered/guid/12hourrulereport.doc

Paige, R., Stroup, S., & Andrade, J. R. (2003). *Second report to congress on the distance education demonstration programs*. Washington, DC: U.S. Department of Education.

Pittman, V. (1991). Academic credibility and the "image problem": The Quality issue in collegiate independent study. In B. L. Watkins & S. J. Wright (Eds.), *The foundations of American distance education: A century of collegiate correspondence study* (pp. 109-134). Dubuque, IA: Kendall/Hunt.

Poley, J. (2008). Asynchronous learning networks: Policy implications for minority serving institutions and for leaders addressing needs of minority learners. *Journal for Asynchronous Learning Networks, 12*(2), 73-82.

Riley, R. W., Fritschler, A. L., & McLaughlin, M. A. (2001). Report to congress on the distance education demonstration programs. Washington, DC: U.S. Department of Education.

Rose, R. (2002). Policy analysis as an academic vocation. In S. Nagel (Ed.), *Policy evaluation: Beyond the cutting edge* (pp. 9-23). New York, NY: Nova Science.

Saba, F. (2005). Critical issues in distance education: A report from the United States. *Distance Education, 26*(2), 255-272. doi:10.1080/01587910500168892

SchWeber, C. (2008). Student learning and student services: Policy issues. *Journal of Asynchronous Learning Networks, 12*(2), 67-72.

Shale, D. (2002). The hybridisation of higher education in Canada. *International Review of Open and Distance Learning, 2*(2), 1-11.

Shaw, R. (1993). A backward glance: To a time before there was accreditation. *North Central Association Quarterly, 68*(2), 323-335.

Shedd, J. M. (2003a). The history of the student credit hour. *New Directions for Higher Education, 122*, 5-12.

Shedd, J. M. (2003b, Summer). Policies and practices in enforcing the credit hour. *New Directions for Higher Education, 122*, 13-30.

Smith, N. (2002). Policy evaluation and analysis: A response. In S. Nagel (Ed.), *Policy evaluation: Beyond the cutting edge* (pp. 39-41). New York, NY: Nova Science.

Spellings, M., & Stroup, S. (2005). *Third report to congress on the distance education demonstration programs.* Washington, DC: U.S. Department of Education. Retrieved from http://www2.ed.gov/programs/disted/DEDP-thirdreport.pdf

Program Integrity Issues: Final Rule, 75 Fed. Reg. U.S. Department of Education, 34 C.F.R. §600.2, §602.24, §603.24, and §668.8. pp. 66832-66975. (2010.). Retrieved from http://www2.ed.gov/legislation/FedRegister/finrule/2010-4/102910a.html

U.S. Network for Education Information. (2007). *Accreditation and quality assurance: Postsecondary accreditation.* Washington, DC: U.S. Department of Education. Retrieved from www2.ed.gov/about/offices/list/ous/international/usnei/us/accred-postsec.doc

U.S. Network for Education Information. (2008a). Recognition of foreign qualifications. Retrieved from http://www2.ed.gov/about/offices/list/ous/international/usnei/us/edlite-visitus-forrecog.html

U.S. Network for Education Information. (2008b). *Structure of the U.S. education system: Comparing U.S. and other credit systems.* Washington, DC: U.S. Department of Education. Retrieved from http://www.ed.gov/international/usnei/us/comparecredit.doc

U.S. Network for Education Information. (2008c). *Structure of the U.S. education system: Credit systems.* Washington, DC: U.S. Department of Education. Retrieved from http://www2.ed.gov/about/offices/list/ous/international/usnei/us/credits.doc

U.S. Network for Education Information. (2008d). *Structure of the U.S. education system: Experiential credit conversion.* Washington, DC: U.S. Department of Education. Retrieved from http://www.ed.gov/international/usnei/us/expcredit.doc.

Watkins, B. L. (1991). A quite radical idea: The intervention and elaboration of collegiate correspondence study. In B. L. Watkins & S. J. Wright (Eds.), *The foundations of American distance education: A century of collegiate correspondence study* (pp. 1-36). Dubuque, IA: Kendall/Hunt.

Web-Based Education Commission. (2000). *The power of the Internet for learning: Moving from promise to practice*. Washington, DC: U. S. Department of Education.

Western Association of Schools and Colleges Accrediting Commission for Senior Colleges and Universities. (2010a). *How to become accredited: Procedures manual for eligibility, candidacy, and initial accreditation*. Alameda, CA: Author. Retrieved from http://www.wascsenior.org/findit/files/forms/ How_to_Become_Accredited__Jan_10.pdf

Western Association of Schools and Colleges Accrediting Commission for Senior Colleges and Universities. (2010b). *Policies manual*. Alameda, CA: Author. Retrieved from http://www.wascsenior.org/findit/files/forms/ Policy_Manual_current.pdf

Zhang, W., Niu, J., & Jiang, G. (2002). Web-based education at conventional universities in China: A case study. *International Review of Open and Distance Learning, 2*(2), 1-24.

CHAPTER 13

MENTORING DOCTORAL STUDENTS

Challenges and Models for Success

Catherine A. Hansman

As a faculty member at a public university, I recently attended a faculty development workshop focused on mentoring junior faculty members. The workshop facilitator, from a neighboring private research university, discussed mentoring programs on her campus that assist junior faculty members' progress to tenure and promotion in a timely fashion. She described several programs that involve both formal and informal one-on-one mentoring relationships, with senior faculty mentoring junior faculty members, as well as some peer and group mentoring programs. Since the university at which I teach has no universal mentoring program for faculty members or university supported programs for faculty members to engage in mentoring doctoral students, I listened with much interest, as seemingly did the rest of audience. At the end of the session, however, I was surprised by the questions asked by some of the members of the audience. Many of their questions focused on what could go wrong in mentoring relationships, how mentors may or may not be recognized for mentoring other faculty members or students, and whether mentors are legally liable for advice they gave to junior faculty members that resulted

Conversations About Adult Learning in Our Complex World, pp. 195–207
Copyright © 2013 by Information Age Publishing
All rights of reproduction in any form reserved.

in them being denied tenure. In all, instead of embracing the concepts of mentoring and developing empowering mentoring programs on their campus, many participants in the workshop seemed resistant to the idea of serving as mentors to others.

The reaction of the faculty members in attendance at the workshop described above underscores the difficulties that may exist for junior faculty members and doctoral students seeking to engage in both formal and informal mentoring relationships in higher education institutions. Mullen (2003) suggests that many faculty members never experienced mentoring themselves in their own lives as they became members of academe, so they may be reluctant or uncomfortable serving as mentors to junior faculty or doctoral students. Despite this reluctance, however, "mentoring is an educational tool of empowerment" (Fresko & Wertheim, 2006, p. 149), and good mentoring relationships may be key to doctoral students and junior faculty members learning the cultures of academe (Hansman, 2002; Hansman & Garofolo, 1995) in order to be successful.

Learning to successfully negotiate academic culture is made even more difficult and multifaceted by the larger complex political and economic world in which higher education institutions function. As state budgets are reduced and institutions of higher education experience significant funding cuts, universities are not always replacing retiring faculty members and hiring new tenure-track faculty (Berdahl, Gumport, & Altbach, 2011; Cohen & Kisker, 2010), The result is that faculty members are faced with increased workloads, including amplified teaching loads (Forest & Kinser, 2002; Newman, Couturier, & Scurry, 2004), while also supporting numerous doctoral and graduate students through assisting with dissertations, advising, and mentoring. In addition, due to tight budgets, universities may have little interest in investing funds to support formal or university sanctioned mentoring programs (Hansman, 2012; Mullen, Fish, & Hutinger 2010).

Many graduate students may desire mentoring relationships with faculty members to prepare them for their future roles in higher education or other professions. But in these challenging times, how can these mentoring relationships develop? The question this chapter explores is how mentoring programs prepare those new to or unfamiliar with higher education to learn the institutional culture and skills necessary to become successful faculty members. The purpose of this chapter is to explore models and research regarding supportive mentoring relationships that can empower this learning. The chapter will conclude with a new model for peer mentoring, summarizing the ideas presented and suggesting directions for future research and practice in mentoring in higher educational institutions.

DEFINING MENTORING

There are many multifaceted definitions, models, and descriptions of the complex relationships between mentors and protégés. Fletcher (2007) describes mentors as empowering their protégés to imagine and realize their future possible selves. Daloz (1999) describes the role of mentors as "interpreters of the environment" and mentors as having "the magic that allows us to enter the darkness: a talisman to protect us from evil, a gem of wise advice, a map, and sometimes simply courage" (p. 18). In higher education, Daloz's description may translate into mentors who take the time to help their doctoral student protégés understand the landscape of higher education, including assisting them with the writing and teaching skills necessary to persist and eventually achieve tenure. To facilitate this, faculty mentors and doctoral student protégés may engage in "reciprocal and collaborative learning between two or more individuals who share mutual responsibility and accountability for helping a mentee work toward achievement of clear and mutually defined learning goals" (Zachary, 2005, p. 3).

Mentoring relationships are viewed as integral to learning in the workplace, for career help, and for developmental and psychosocial support (Hansman, 2000, 2002). The success of mentoring relationships is highly dependent on the quality of the relationship developed by mentors and their protégés. Classifications of mentoring relationships typically include informal, formal, career-related, psychosocial, and peer mentoring (Kram, 1983; Kram & Isabella, 1985). All of these mentoring types may be helpful to doctoral students whose future career plans focus on becoming tenure-track faculty members. Informal mentoring relationships usually form through the mutual interests between mentors and protégés. In higher education, a faculty mentor may choose with whom to work, which is a typical arrangement for dissertation/thesis advisement. However, an obstacle to informal mentoring for doctoral students may be the unavailability of faculty members to serve as mentors due to their already overwhelming course and advising load and the economic reality of institutions of higher education not replacing vacant faculty positions with tenure track faculty members. Potential faculty mentors may have little knowledge of mentoring because they themselves never had mentors (Mullen, 2003), and therefore, they may not understand the "entrenched power dynamics" that are present in all mentoring relationships and the power they have as mentors (Hansman, 2005). Faculty mentors may make assumptions about their protégés and the cultures and contexts from which they come, which may impede the advice and support they give (Searby, 2009). For example, when I was a doctoral student, many of the male professors who mentored me knew that I was a married mother of young children and made the assumption that I would not be interested in a career in academics which may require my family to change locations. Because of their suppositions of my "role" in life, I was given little advice on publishing my work in peer-reviewed journals, presenting at conferences, or preparing an academic vita, but it was apparent that my male student colleagues were given assistance with their future careers. Fortuitously, I found other mentors, male and female, who guided me into academic culture. Mentors may hurt their protégés through omission when they do not assist their graduate student protégés to navigate the organizational politics and contexts of academe that may assist them with their future careers.

Some universities have adopted formal mentoring relationship models, in which senior faculty members are selected and trained to be mentors to junior faculty (Bilimoria, 2011) or doctoral students. These types of formal mentoring programs may also be designed to help those who "because of race, class, gender, or sexual orientation, may have limited opportunities for advancement" (Hansman, 2000, p. 496). Bilimoria (2011) describes formal mentoring programs at her private research university as including centrally administered programs that have clearly stated goals, defined process for matching protégés to mentors, clearly outlined time commitments for both mentors and protégés, rewards for faculty members who serve as mentors, written feedback to protégés, and program evaluations that measure goals and outcomes. The formal mentoring programs at this institution have been successful in helping junior faculty members achieve tenure (Bilimoria, 2011). However, not all formal mentoring programs in higher education are as comprehensive and include the extent of administrative support as the programs she described.

Whether mentoring relationships are the result of informal collaboration or formally arranged partnerships, good mentoring relationships are a two-way street, including give and take between mentors and protégés (Hansman, 2000, 2002; Kram, 1983). Committed mentors share knowledge, advice, insight, and evaluations of their protégés' work with them, allowing for mutual discourse and reflection on actions and information. Through building a climate of respect and trust, protégés may be encouraged to be self-reflective about both their successes and failures. Mentors can also engage in self-reflection concerning their own careers and the paths they took to achieve success, which allows them to also learn through their engage in learning in mentoring relationships.

PEER MENTORING: EMERGING MODELS

Due to a variety of circumstances, informal mentoring relationships between faculty members and students and formal mentoring programs may not always be available to doctoral students in institutions of higher education. Bilimoria (2011) lists other types of mentoring than individual one-on-one mentoring dyads, including committee mentoring, zone mentoring (by area of expertise), e-mentoring (with university support for protégés to meet with their disciplinary mentors outside of the university), long and short-term professional academic coaching, and peer mentoring. Several researchers (Mullen, 2003; Mullen & Hutinger, 2008; Mullen, Fish, & Hutinger, 2010; O'Neil & Marsick, 2009) propose models for peer mentoring and coaching among doctoral students that can inform the types of mentoring that universities can offer their doctoral students.

O'Neil and Marsick (2009) describe action learning conversations as critically reflective practice and peer mentoring engagement that enables participants to change. Incorporating the concepts of transformational learning (Mezirow, Taylor, & Associates, 2009), their model encourages peer cohorts composed of seven or fewer members to identify underlying values, beliefs, and assumptions about a particular issue or problem so that they can change and move forward in their personal and professional lives. These researchers identify critical reflection as a process in which the members of the peer cohort engage to "identify underlying values, beliefs, and assumptions" (O'Neil & Marsick, 2009, p. 19) concerning situations or problems. Reframing their understandings can lead peer members to potentially take new actions that might transform themselves or others through their actions. O'Neil and Marsick's model consists of three phrases: Framing and engaging, advancing, and disengaging. In Phase 1, framing and engaging, a member of the group introduces a problem or issue to the other group members. The peer group members then individually reflect in writing about their understandings and reactions to the issue introduced to them. Next, they ask questions and engage in discourse to clarify the problem and its context. At the end of Phase 1, the peer group member who brought this problem articulates the support she or he needs to confront it. During Phase 2, advancing, peer group members are encouraged to expand their consideration and assumptions about the problem through four kinds of questions: objective, reflective, interpretative, and decisional. Peer group members articulate in writing assumptions that the problem holder may have or issues they themselves might face if they were in a situation similar to the problem holder. These questions are shared with each other and the problem holder. In Phase 3, Disengagement, peer members review the questions written in Phase 2 and discuss decisions and ideas to address the problem or issue. The group's critical discourse on these concepts encourages reflection concerning what was gained through this process, which allows group members to choose if to act, and if so, choose the type of action they might take. *Action Learning Conversations* may encourage transformational learning.

The concepts of *action learning conversation* have much potential to provide a model for peer mentoring within doctoral programs. With a faculty members serving as an advisor to the action learning conversation doctoral student peer cohort, a student member could propose a question or issue concerning the skills needed to become a tenure-track faculty member. These questions could focus on concerns about developing research and writing skills. Cohort members could then dialogue about the types of skills needed, framing their discussion as questions, and providing support to the problem poser to further explore this issue. Finally, group members could support each other through providing peer review to the problem poser's writing and research assignments, as well as peer reviewing each other's writing. The faculty member who serves as the advisor to the group can deepen the conversation through sharing her or his experiences and knowledge concerning researching and writing in academe. Through discourse, the peer group doctoral cohort can learn skills to gain better understandings of academic culture and expectations, which will assist them as they move forward in their academic careers.

Mullen (2003) proposes another model that will assist doctoral students to engage in peer mentoring. Through her research, she developed the mentoring cohort model, which she describes as "collaborative faculty-student support group that brings together doctoral students and their academic mentors" (p. 412) to engage in discussions and practice of the skills necessary for them to advance as scholars and teachers in academe. In conducting research with her own doctoral advisees, Mullen and her students developed the goal of building relationships within the mentoring cohort while also providing a safe place for cohort members to review and critique each other's dissertation research and writing. Through their work, the cohort group developed connections beyond that of one-to-one student/faculty mentoring relationships and provided support for members to pursue and attain their dreams. The mentoring cohort model allowed faculty member Mullen and the doctoral student cohort members to experience mutual support of shared goals. The cohort group members discussed the dynamics of power at play within the cohort, but also were empowered by mutually critiquing each other's writing while reflecting about their further scholarly development. Mullen's research shows that a strong and supportive mentoring network was built and sustained that enabled the doctoral cohort students to complete their dissertations while moving forward in their academic career paths.

Another peer mentoring model, mentoring mosaics (Mullen, Fish, & Hutinger, 2010), emphasizes the developing mentoring relationship among student group members with less faculty member involvement. As an informal peer group for mentoring students, mentoring mosaics "functions as a network, a community, or simply a resource" (p. 421). The goal of the group is to provide nonhierarchical and reciprocal mentoring interactions that can address scholarly writing, presentation skills, and graduate student life. Mentoring mosaics can enhance a one-on-one mentoring relationship in which a student may already be involved, or it can be the only mentoring relationship in which a student is involved. The point of mentoring mosaics is to provide opportunities for students to be engaged in mutual processes of learning and development while acting as critical friends to each other. Members may respectfully challenge long-held beliefs another member may hold, while encouraging the member to engage in critical self-reflection concerning these beliefs, utilizing the concepts of transformational learning (Mezirow, Taylor, & Associates, 2009). Through participating in mentoring mosaics, group members increase their abilities to nurture, advise, and instruct, and be critically supportive of each other.

COMMUNITIES OF PRACTICE IN MENTORING

It is clear from the descriptions of the mentoring concepts and models above that peer group mentoring may diffuse the power dynamic of a typical one-to-one mentoring relationship, in which mentors have more experience and power. The models described doctoral student peers engaged in the important learning strategies of power sharing, turn taking, co-leading, dialogue, and providing and accepting constructive feedback, which promotes transparency and authenticity in peer mentoring relationships. Peer mentoring group members promote self-directed learning among their peer protégés, which may be helpful to doctoral students who desire a mentoring relationship but have been unable to find a faculty mentor.

Wenger's (1998) concepts of communities of practice (CoPs) may advance new ideas for developing models for doctoral student peer mentoring groups. In describing CoP's, Wenger stresses that they form to address issues that matter to people, reflecting members' understandings of what is important to them. As Hansman (2008) states, "CoPs form around common interests, ideas, passions and goals—in other words, the things that matter to people" (p. 299). Group members, not people or conditions external to the CoP, set the goals and the "practice" in which the group engages. Members of CoPs develop a "shared repertoire of communal resources" (Kimble & Hildreth, 2006, p. 329) and common activities. In CoPs, there are no hierarchical relationships; group leadership is decided within the group through negotiations concerning the purpose for the group (Hansman, 2008). The group members decide the life cycle of their CoP; it is not set by outside members or institutional edicts.

> The life cycle of CoPs can include what Wenger (1998) describes as the stages of development: potential, in which people face similar problems but are not connected; coalescing, in which members meet and recognize the potential of group interaction; active, where members are actively engaged in developing the group and their practice; dispersed, where the community members no longer interact as much or as intensely, but the community still provides a centre (sic) of knowledge, and finally, memorable, where the community is no longer functioning but participants still remember it and the part it played in their identities. (Hansman, 2008, p. 300)

CoPs in Practice

Henrich and Attebury (2010), in describing their experiences concerning a community of practice formed by junior library faculty at the University of Idaho, discuss the characteristics of the library CoP for its members as having common goals or interests and "willingness to share and/or create knowledge in a safe environment. The voluntary nature of membership is key as well" (p. 162). In describing the process the library peer group adopted to create and sustain their CoP, the library peer faculty members suggested that:

> The primary goals of the group should be to help each individual find their own path towards promotion and tenure. The group agreed that the largest benefit to the group would be the focus on goals such as collaboration, publication, research, and fostering relationships between faculty members. However, all present agreed that the group would be more beneficial to all involved if the focus was shifted away from support in achieving promotion and tenure in particular and more towards research and collaboration in general. (Henrich & Attebury, 2010, p. 163)

This shift from individual goals to collaboration between and among faculty members during their work in the library peer mentoring CoP allowed members to receive feedback on research presentations and articles; in addition, discussions at the meetings resulted in research collaborations among junior and more senior faculty members. The CoP also served to "strengthen relationships across departmental lines and foster a feeling of collaboration and support among members ... participation was fairly evenly distributed among new faculty and more experienced faculty" (p. 163). Thus, Wenger's CoP concepts framed the work accomplished by this library peer faculty group mentoring experience.

A NEW MODEL: COMMUNITY OF PEER MENTORS

Drawing from the peer mentoring models and concepts of O'Neil and Marsick (2007), Mullen (2003), Mullen, Fish, and Hutinger (2010), and Henrich and Attebury (2010), as well as Wenger's (1998) notions of communities of practice, I propose community of peer mentors as a new model for doctoral student peer mentoring. This mentoring model is similar to yet different from the CoP life-cycle described earlier in this chapter and consists of five points: forming, connecting, engaging, concluding and new beginnings, and enduring networks.

At the first point, forming, doctoral students in all stages of their programs are invited to an organizing meeting by faculty members charged with overseeing the peer mentoring community. In this meeting, students learn about the overall purpose for the community of peer mentors, which is to foster learning and development for their future careers in academe. Once students have decided to join the group, the second point of connecting begins with active dialogue among members to engender shared learning processes. During the connecting point, with the oversight of faculty members, community members engage in activities and discourse aimed at furthering knowledge and understandings of each other and their places in the doctoral program. In the third point, engaging, mutually defined goals

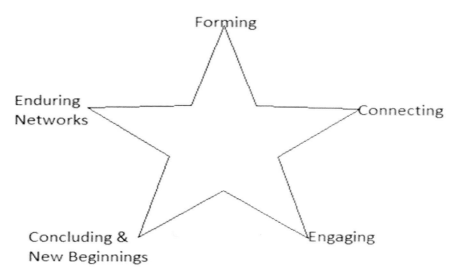

Figure 13.1.   Star-shaped model illustrates the paths between the points of the community of peer mentors model. Membes may travel between and among the points to facilitate their connections with and support for others in the community. Copyright 2012 by Catherine A. Hansman.

are collaboratively decided through problem posing and questions concerning the nature of academe and the skills and knowledge perceived as needed by peers to further their careers in higher education. After the problems are exposed, community of peer mentors members engage in activities and discourse to further their perceptions of the questions/problems, develop understandings of how to change their perceptions and actions related to these problems, and further, cultivate the knowledge and skills required to address them. Group members collaboratively decide on which activities to focus; for example, group members may decide that presenting their research and then receiving supportive critical reviews from community members may help them individually improve their writing and presentation skills while furthering research collaborations among peers. The engaging point is continual; as more experienced doctoral students move onto concluding and new beginnings, less experienced doctoral students will move into engaging and seek to employ discourse and activities around their own collaboratively defined problems and goals.

Throughout the fourth point, concluding and new beginnings, some community members may move further away from their peers in the community of peer mentors group as they complete their dissertations and graduate from their doctoral programs. Community members engaged in the work of concluding and new beginnings may design activities such as mock interviews and role play with other group members to engender support as they apply for academic or other types of positions. Community members, who when they joined the peer mentoring program were in the early stages of their doctoral programs, may now become more senior members of community of peer mentors, taking on and sharing responsibility with faculty members for recruiting newer doctoral students to the community of peer mentors. Thus, the final point, enduring networks, is not so much an ending phase as a continuation of the mentoring process, in which communities of peer mentors members are connected with each other, perhaps electronically via e-mail or social media sites, to provide support and critical friendships to members throughout their careers. Participants in the enduring networks point may also continue to provide their support and critical friendships to doctoral students in earlier points of the community of peer mentoring.

CONCLUSION

I began this chapter with a story that illustrated some perceptions of problems faculty members may envision as they contemplate mentoring junior faculty member and doctoral students. Some of the resistance faculty members may have towards serving as mentors may have to do with their own lack of experience in mentoring relationships, as they may not have had mentors themselves when they were doctoral students or junior faculty members. The increasingly complex world of higher education, including the pressure faculty members experience while working towards tenure, and the ever increasing teaching course loads due to economic constraints, may affect whether faculty members are willing to mentor others. Models discussed in this chapter, such as community of peer mentors, respond to these issues through engaging participants in a process of peer mentoring. Community of peer mentors can not only provide doctoral students with some much needed mentoring throughout their doctoral programs, but through its points, the model trains and empowers future faculty members to become supportive mentors to others.

Empowered mentoring relationships involve equal partnerships, collaboration through dynamic dialogue, active learning, mutually constructed goals, and continuing development for both mentors and protégés. Through supportive one-to-one and peer mentoring relationships, protégés can gain insider knowledge and perspectives of organizational culture, critically reflecting upon skills they need to develop and refine (Hansman, 2012). Learning through mentoring relationships is future-directed, and mentors assist their protégés in developing the knowledge and abilities to achieve their goals. Mentoring practices should encompass principles of empowerment for all involved.

Many issues confound establishing mentoring relationships, chief among them how faculty members and graduate students can engage in mentoring in these challenging times of limited funding for new programs in higher education. Further, what creative and innovative models can assist the formation of and maintenance of one-to-one and peer mentoring relationships in academe? In addition, how can mentoring models and research guide higher education faculty and administrators in planning for successful mentoring experiences for students and faculty members? Future research and development should focus on mentoring models that can address these questions and empower protégés and their mentors while developing a new generation of mentors.

REFERENCES

Berdahl, R. O., Gumport, P. J, & Altbach, P. G. (2011). The contexts of American higher education. In P. Altbach, P. Gumport, & R. Berdahl (Eds.), *American higher in the twenty-first century: Social, political and economic challenges* (3rd ed, pp. 1-14). Baltimore, MD: John Hopkins University Press.

Bilimoria, D. (2001, November). *Best practices in faculty mentoring.* Paper presented at Cleveland State University Faculty Development Workshop, Cleveland, OH.

Cohen. A., & Kisker, C. (2010). *The shaping of American higher education: Emergence and growth of the contemporary system.* San Francisco, CA: Jossey-Bass.

Daloz, L. A. (1999). *Mentor: Guiding the journey of adult learners.* San Francisco, CA: Jossey-Bass.

Fletcher, S. (2007). Mentoring adult learners: Realizing possible selves. In M. Rossiter (Ed.), *New Directions for Adult and Continuing Education, 114,* 75–86. doi:10.1002/ace.258

Forest, J., & Kinser, K. (Eds.). (2002) *Higher education in the United States: An encyclopedia.*   Retrieved   from   http://ebooks.ohiolink.edu/xtf-ebc/view?docId=tei/abc/hred/hred.xml;chunk.id=HRED.2;toc.depth=1;toc.id=;brand=default

Fresko, B., & Wertheim, C. (2006). Learning by mentoring: Prospective teachers as mentors to children at-risk. *Mentoring & tutoring: Partnership in learning, 14*(2), 149–161.

Hansman, C. & Garofolo, P. (1995) Toward a level playing field: The roles of mentors and critical friendships in the lives of doctoral students. *Proceedings of the 36th Annual Adult Education Research Conference,* University of Alberta, Edmonton, AB, Canada.

Hansman, C. A. (2000). Formal mentoring programs. In A. Wilson & E. Hayes (Eds.), *Handbook of adult and continuing education* (pp. 493-507). San Francisco, CA: Jossey-Bass.

Hansman, C. A. (2002). Diversity and power in mentoring relationships. In C. A. Hansman (Ed.), *Critical perspectives on mentoring: Trends and issues* (pp. 39-48). Information series no. 388. Columbus, OH: ERIC Clearinghouse on Adult, Career, and Vocational Education (ED99CO0013).

Hansman, C. A. (2005). Reluctant mentors & resistant protégées. *Adult Learning, 14*(1), 14-16.

Hansman, C. A. (2008). Adult learning in communities of practice: Situating theory in practice. In C. Kimble, P. Hildreth, & I. Bourdon (Eds.), *Communities of practice: Creating learning environments for educators* (Vol 1, pp. 279-292). Charlotte, NC: Information Age.

Hansman, C. A. (2012). Empowerment in the faculty-student mentoring relationship. In C. Mullen & S. Fletcher (Eds.), *Handbook of mentoring and coaching in education* (pp. 368-381). Thousand Oaks, CA: SAGE.

Henrich, K. J, & Attebury, R. (2010). Communities of practice at an academic library: A new approach to mentoring at the University of Idaho. *The Journal of Academic Librarianship, 36*(2), 158-165.

Kimble, C., & Hildreth, P. (2006). The limits of communities of practice. In E. Coakes & S. Clarke (Eds.), *Encyclopedia of communities of practice in information and knowledge management* (pp. 327-333). Hershey, PA: Idea Group Reference.

Kram, K. E. (1983). Phases of the mentor relationship. *Academy of Management Journal, 26,* 608-625.

Kram K. E., & Isabella, L. A. (1985). Mentoring alternatives: The role of peer relationships in career development. *Academy of Management Journal, 28*(1), 110-128.

Mezirow, J., Taylor, E., & Associates (2009). *Transformative learning in practice: Insights from community, workplace and higher education*. San Francisco, CA: Jossey-Bass.

Mullen, C. A. (2003). The WIT Cohort: A case study of informal doctoral mentoring. *Journal of Further and Higher Education, 27*(4), 411-425.

Mullen, C. A. & Hutinger, J. L. (2008). At the tipping point? Role of formal faculty mentoring in changing university cultures. *Journal of In-Service Education, 34*(2), 181-204.

Mullen, C. A., Fish, V. L., & Hutinger, J. L. (2010). Mentoring doctoral students through scholastic engagement: Adult learning principles in action. *Journal of Further and Higher Education, 34*(2), 179-197.

Newman, F., & Couturier, L, & Scurry, J. (2004). *The future of higher education: Rhetoric, reality, and risks of the market*. San Francisco, CA: Jossey-Bass.

O'Neil, J., & Marsick, V. (2009). Peer mentoring and action learning. *Adult Learning, 20*(1/2), 19-24.

Searby, L. (2009). "But I thought...." An examination of assumptions in the mentoring relationship. *Adult Learning, 20*(1/2), 10–13.

Wenger, E. (1998). *Communities of practice: Learning, meaning & identity*. Cambridge, England: Cambridge University Press.

Zachary, L. J. (2005). *Creating a mentoring culture: The organization's guide*. San Francisco, CA: Jossey-Bass.

SECTION IV

PROFESSIONAL DEVELOPMENT, TEACHER TRAINING, AND LEADERSHIP DEVELOPMENT

CHAPTER 14

THE JOURNEY FROM NOVICE TO EXPERT

Toward a Model of Purposeful Ongoing Mentoring

Kathy Peno and Elaine M. Silva Mangiante

The world of work continues to change at an ever-increasing pace (Parker, 2008). Innovation cycles, especially in technology, have been reduced significantly often making preservice education insufficient for new workers (Bransford, 2007). Whether one is entering a new job or field or is challenged to respond to ever-changing workplace performance expectations (i.e., technology, standards of practice, etc.), there is a need for purposeful ongoing professional development (Schmidt, Mott, & Lanoux, 2009).

We propose a model for improvement of professional practice that is both purposeful and ongoing. The model is founded on the premise that in order to navigate new or ever-changing performance expectations, workers need professional development that is sustained and meaningful. This chapter seeks to provide education practitioners and learners with an understanding of the process of moving from a novice practitioner toward expertise. Our aim is to connect several of the view-

Conversations About Adult Learning in Our Complex World, pp. 211–221

points that exist in the literature into a clear expression of action that can be used by individuals and organizations that desire high levels of professional performance and autonomy in practice. Although we propose this model for use in any field of practice, the authors are engaged in teacher preparation from kindergarten through adulthood; therefore, we draw from experience with teachers and their development along the continuum for examples.

THEORETICAL FRAMEWORK

The proposed model is grounded in the Dreyfus and Dreyfus (1980, 1986) novice to expert continuum (the continuum) and Vygotsky's (1978) zone of proximal development (ZPD). The continuum provides a frame for examining the possible growth that can occur in professional practice as well as goals for moving to higher levels of performance. According to Dreyfus and Dreyfus (1980), movement to higher levels on the continuum can occur through experience and/or instructional guidance. We concur that experience is a necessary component, but argue that professional development in the form of ongoing mentoring is vital to the growth process as mentees make sense of their experiences. Daloz (1986) details the mentoring process as a transformational journey with the help of someone who has "been there before" (p. 27). We posit that movement toward higher levels of performance requires a goal-oriented (purposeful) approach to mentoring. A lack of goal-orientation in the mentoring process can leave learning of important concepts and practices to chance. Therefore, purposeful, ongoing mentoring is proposed as the vehicle by which effective movement along the continuum can occur. We illustrate how the scaffolding process embedded in Vygotsky's (1978) ZDP can play a major role in the mentoring process. We further examine the role of experience and reflection in the meaning making process as mentees progress along the continuum.

PURPOSEFUL ONGOING MENTORING MODEL

The model, as we propose it, consists of three sections: The characteristics of mentees at each of the five stages of the novice to expert continuum as proposed by Dreyfus and Dreyfus (1980, 1986), goals for mentee performance to reach the next level on the continuum, and actions the mentor can take to scaffold the mentee to reach the next level of performance.

Novice to Expert Continuum

Dreyfus and Dreyfus (1980, 1986) developed the continuum as a result of work with chess players, pilots, and second language learners. The continuum was later applied to the field of nursing by Benner (1984) and used with teachers by Berliner (2004). The continuum elucidates adult skill acquisition at five levels: "novice, advanced beginner, competent, proficient, and expert" (Dreyfus & Dreyfus, 1986, p. 21). Each level contains characteristics that represent performance at that level. The continuum begins with a person acting on their rules-based knowledge without flexibility and progressing toward intuition-based actions (see Table 14.1).

Table 14.1.   Purposeful Ongoing Mentoring Model (Characteristics Section Adapted From Dreyfus and Dreyfus, 1980)

	Novice	*Advanced Beginner*	*Competent*	*Proficient*	*Expert*
Characteristics	*Applies rules learned in training to guide his/her actions without flexibility.	*Recognizes the context of situations.	*Develops own plans recognizing which situations are important and which can be ignored.	*Replaces rules with situational intuition.	*Reacts flexibly with intuitive practiced, understanding from thousands of hours of reflective performance.
	*No regard for context.	*Generates guiding maxims to deal with specific situations	*Develops own rigid, inflexible rule-making, if averse to taking risks, if lacks confidence, or if fearful of losing control.	*Still deliberates when making decisions.	*Aware of the context and the needs of those they serve.
		*Has difficulty sensing what is important and/or handling challenging situations.			*Possesses domain specific knowledge.

(Table continues on next page)

Table 14.1.   (Continued)

	Novice	Advanced Beginner	Competent	Proficient	Expert
Goals	*To increase awareness of context of situations. Examine rules as applied.	*To increase awareness of the relative importance of different situations.	*To increase efficacy in ability to handle difficult, threatening, or uncertain situations.	*To increase analysis of and reflection while in situations.	*To increase intuitive thinking to guide practice in new situations.
Mentor actions (with learner/ mentee)	*Assist the learner in reflecting on current practice.	*Assist learner to reflect on practice as applied in different situations.	*Model strategies for continuous reflection-on-practice in typical and challenging situations.	*Model strategies for continuous reflection-in-practice.	*Assist learner to consider how they can transfer their experience to new domains.
	*Model an effective strategy for using a rule in a given context.	*Model alternative approaches.	*Model self-regulation in challenging situations.	*Assist learner to become self-directed in their reflection in situations.	*Provide on-going opportunities for discourse regarding practice.
	*Provide feedback on the learner's construction of a new approach.	*Provide feedback on the learner's construction of practice in a variety of situations.	*Help learner develop options with the purpose of expanding possible responses.	*Provide regular feedback to support reflective thinking.	

Goals and Mentor Actions

According to Dreyfus and Dreyfus (1980), movement along the continuum occurs as a result of experience and knowledge acquisition. What is less clear is how the interaction of knowledge and experience leads to movement to the next level. Of concern is that, left alone to navigate new circumstances and experiences, the mentee may be unable to make sense of their experiences and act accordingly. This is especially an issue for novices who are rules-oriented; operating without flexibility and regard for context. Therefore, we propose the ongoing assistance of a mentor whose role is to provide purposeful guidance to the learner when navigating the levels of the continuum. This purposeful guidance is founded in the goals we delineate in the model that need to be attained in order to move to the next level along the continuum.

Zone of Proximal Development

Vygotsky (1978) defines the zone of proximal development as "the distance between the actual development level as determined by independent problem solving and the level of potential development as determined through problem solving under adult guidance or in collaboration with a more capable peer" (p. 86). Therefore, the ZPD represents the difference between the learner's current level of development and the level that can be attained through effective collaboration with a more capable person. This collaboration consists of scaffolding on the part of the more capable person; a combination of challenge with support. The more capable peer provides a model for a higher level of practice through demonstration and/or explanation (challenge) while supporting (coaching/feedback) the learner's attempts to make sense of and emulate what is being taught. During the mentor/mentee collaboration, it may be the mentor, at first, who initiates the teaching/learning activities because the mentee may not yet be aware of what they do not know (Daley, 1999) or contexts they may face. As the mentee gains experience; however, they may be more likely to initiate the collaborative learning process with questions and concerns about situations that arose. It is important to note here that it is not sufficient for the more capable person or mentor to only possess a higher level of knowledge; that person must exhibit the capability to scaffold effectively in order for maximum mentee learning to occur.

Novice. To begin, a novice receives instruction from a teacher or mentor of rules to guide his/her actions during recognizable situations free of context, "just like a computer following a program" (S. Dreyfus, 2004, p. 177). A novice relies heavily on rules learned because of their lack of experience with different contexts and applications.

Moving from novice to advanced beginner. The goal for movement from novice to advanced beginner is to increase the mentee's awareness of the context of situations that may arise. They must examine rules they applied to a situation and examine the result to see what they might have done differently if they were unsuccessful. In this early stage, Dreyfus and Dreyfus and Dreyfus (1986) explain that learners use an analytical, detached approach to tasks. Novices judge their performance based on how well they follow the rules. However, the novice learner needs an understanding of the context, in addition to rules, in order to perform successfully in real situations. For example, a novice teacher is armed with all sorts of knowledge about child and/or adult learning and development, content and pedagogy or andragogy, but may not possess the tools to deal with a myriad of behavioral or other issues they will face in the classroom. Berliner (2004) found that novice teachers were taught educational terms (i.e., reinforcement, learning disabled) and given rules such as "'give praise for right answers,' 'wait 3 seconds after asking a higher order question,' and 'never personally criticize a student'" (p. 206) to begin teaching. The teaching novices, who could not always make sense of situations, tended to follow the rules they had been taught with inflexibility. Here is where working closely with a purposeful mentor, a more capable peer (Vygotsky, 1978), can help the novice navigate their experiences with an eye toward flexibility of action.

Mentor actions. The mentor can be instrumental in assisting the mentee to reflect on what occurred as a result of a rule(s) being applied in a certain situation. This focused attention on the experience is then a place for the mentor to assist the mentee in reflection and revised action. The importance of reflection after action was promoted by Dewey (1910) and later, Schön (1983, 1987), as a means for learning and professional growth. For example, a novice who was taught to praise correct answers may not have a sense of what to do when incorrect answers are given and may, instead, choose to do nothing. The mentor can ask probing questions of the mentee such as, "What occurred? How did it occur? When and to whom did it occur as a result of a rule being applied?" Once the mentor and mentee unpack the situation, the mentor can then scaffold an effective strategy for dealing with the situation that may not necessarily fit within the rules orientation of the novice. The mentor can then ask the mentee to consider an approach to dealing with another, similar situation and provide feedback to the novice on their new conception. This process may occur repeatedly while the novice moves through a myriad of new experiences and situations.

Advanced beginner. The move from novice to advanced beginner is highlighted by the development of knowledge about different contexts that require different actions. The advanced beginner is capable of generating guiding maxims that are used in specific situations, however, they are still unable to handle challenging circumstances that fall outside of their comfort zone.

Moving from advanced beginner to competent. With experience, the advanced beginner gains insight into the context of situations. The learner notices or the mentor points out examples of "situational" aspects that are distinguishable from context-free elements (Dreyfus & Dreyfus, 1986, p. 23). From viewing several examples, a learner can begin to recognize situational aspects and generate guiding maxims that are situation specific (S. Dreyfus, 2004). Yet, the advanced beginner still approaches the task in an analytical, detached manner by following both the context-free rules and the situational maxims. Thus, a second or third year teacher is in the advanced beginner stage attempting to recognize similarities in situations to build their own case knowledge (Berliner, 2004). For example, both novice and advanced beginner teachers often have difficulty knowing what to do in challenging situations (i.e., classroom management) (Lin, 1999). During the advanced beginner stage, the teacher begins to learn from different types of incidents in order to build his/her practical knowledge for teaching. A teacher's practical knowledge grows from situation specific experiences that are action-oriented and influenced by the teacher's knowledge and personal beliefs (van Driel, Beijaard, & Verloop, 2001). However, though a teacher is learning "to label and describe events, follow rules, and recognize and classify contexts," the advanced beginner "may still have no sense of what is important" (Berliner, 2004, p. 206).

Mentor actions. To cope with uncertainty and move toward competence, the mentor can help the mentee develop a plan or perspective to determine which elements in a situation are important and which can be ignored. This approach allows the learner to "simplify and improve his performance" by organizing the situation and focusing on the most important elements (Dreyfus & Dreyfus, 1986, p. 24). The mentor will then be able to effectively model alternative approaches for action in different contexts while coaching the mentee through reflection and development of expanded guiding maxims.

Competent. The next stage, competent, is pivotal in skill acquisition. The nature of this stage presents a metaphorical fork in the road for the developing person. Through experience, as a learner recognizes more potential elements and procedures of a task, the learner may become frustrated, overwhelmed, or exhausted. H. Dreyfus (2004) presented that the learner seeks rules to deal with all these relevant elements; however, there are too many different situations to address. Thus, learners at the competent stage must choose a plan or perspective without knowing if the choice is appropriate. S. Dreyfus (2004) described the pivotal nature of the competent stage through the results of Benner's research on skill acquisition for nurses. Benner (2004) found that slavishly adhering to one's plans and preconceived notions can interfere with a person's ability to perceive and react in a situation. Yet, in contrast, Benner proposed that those adult learners who continue to gain a greater experience base with reading situations eventually feel the confining limits of formal training and rigid planning.

Moving from competent to proficient. A person can advance to the proficient stage if rules and principles are replaced by situational "intuition" and "know-how" from seeing similar situations from previous experiences (Dreyfus & Dreyfus, 1986, p. 28). Yet, despite using intuition in a new situation, the proficient person will still turn to analytic thinking to evaluate what to do. S. Dreyfus (2004) explained that at this stage the involved learner can perceive important aspects of a situation, but may not know how to react.

Mentor actions. To advance to the stage of proficiency requires a major shift in performance (Benner, 2004). S. Dreyfus (2004) explained that, "if one seeks the safety of rules, one will not get beyond competence.... Experiencing deeply felt rewards and remorse seems to be necessary" (p. 179). In education, Berliner (2004) reported that after approximately five years of experience a relatively small number of teachers progressed beyond competence into the proficient stage. To enable the mentee to move beyond their comfort zone, the goal is to increase the mentee's efficacy in their ability to handle difficult, threatening, or uncertain situations. The mentor can model strategies for continuous reflection-on-action (Argyris & Schön, 1978) while demonstrating self-regulation during demanding situations and help the mentee develop options for responding in a variety of situations.

Proficient. A person can advance to the proficient stage if rules and principles are replaced by situational "intuition" and "know-how" from seeing similar situations from previous experiences (Dreyfus & Dreyfus, 1986, p. 28). Yet, despite using intuition in a new situation, the proficient person will still turn to analytic thinking to evaluate what to do. S. Dreyfus (2004) explained that at this stage the involved learner can perceive important aspects of a situation, but does not know how to react. The proficient performer has had sufficient experience with the outcomes of possible responses to a wide range of situations to be able to react automatically and effortlessly. Thus, a proficient teacher now has the skills to predict if a student may misbehave, if students are confused, or if a new approach must be used to regain the class's attention (Berliner, 2004). Their case knowledge aids them in reading the workings of the class; however, the teacher will still deliberate when making decisions.

Moving from proficient to expert. The goal for moving to the expert level is to increase the analysis of and reflection on situations the proficient person faces in their work. The mentoring relationship continues to be purposeful but the mentee may have become the primary initiator of the interactions. The mentee may need the mentor on a less frequent basis than in earlier levels as situational intuition replaces a rules-based approach to practice. Because they are not completely intuitive in their practice, the mentee may seek the mentor's advice when deliberating in the decision-making process.

Mentor actions. At this level, it will be important for the mentor to model strategies for reflection-in-action (Argyris & Schön, 1978). This type of reflection, as opposed to reflection-on-action (after the action has occurred) used while in the competent level, is done in the moment, during a situation, and can affect the outcome of the situation. According to Argyris and Schön (1978), reflection-in-action "serves to reshape what we are doing while we are doing it" (p. 26). The ability to reflect during action and change in mid-stream requires a certain level of intuition in practice. The mentor can be instrumental in developing the mentee's ability to use their intuition to make qualitative changes in practice as situations arise by providing regular feedback on reflections and actions.

Expert. At the final stage, from experience and deep involvement in a variety of situations, the expert sees and reacts immediately with "mature and practiced understanding" without detachment or planning (Dreyfus & Dreyfus, 1986, p. 30). From the wealth of past, varied experiences requiring different actions, the expert is able to respond intuitively to situations. However, intuition is not devoid of deliberation. If time is available or if the situation is serious, the expert will critically reflect on their intuitive judgment. The performance of the expert is based on involvement and experience to result in fluid, intuitive decisions. By the nature of the expert's gradual refinement of acquiring skill through facing risks and having experiences in the everyday world, an expert can respond to a difficult situation "in a more subtle way than a nonexpert can" (H. Dreyfus, 2004, p. 272). The expert's response is characterized by know how. Berliner and colleagues (1988, 2004) found that this know how also includes an awareness of the context and the needs of those being served. Interviews with the expert teachers revealed that through their deep involvement and shared history with their own students, the teachers knew the cognitive abilities of their students and the students were able to interact with the teacher according to mutually understood expectations. This level is achieved by a small number of teachers whose performance is exemplary (Berliner, 2004).

Mentor actions. In this level of practice, an expert can still be faced with challenges that may require them to transfer their experience to domains that are unfamiliar. For example, an expert teacher may be expected to implement reforms for which they have not been trained or take on the role of a teacher leader, perhaps as a department chair or program manager. The teaching practice they have developed may have served them well up to this point, but they may be less prepared to enact expected reforms or assume the myriad other duties of an instructional leader. The purposeful mentor can help the mentee pinpoint experiences that will transfer to the new responsibilities/role and those which will need to be learned. The expert has had much experience at this point with self-reflection and regulation of practice and will likely utilize the mentoring relationship as an opportunity for continuous discourse regarding practice in new situations.

CONCLUSIONS

The authors anticipate that the model may be used differently depending on circumstances and may not necessarily be followed in lock-step sequence. For example, a mentee may begin working with a mentor at a level other than novice or may work with multiple mentors over the period of their career(s) as their needs change. Workers can no longer assume a one-job or one-career professional life; professional learning is a life-long process (Watkins & Marsick, 1993); therefore, movement across the continuum may take different forms. This model is meant to supply a frame for purposefully thinking about, preparing for, and developing actions for the acquisition of higher levels of skill in any area of work. Those who desire forward movement from their current level of practice can use the model to think about their needs when seeking a mentor. Supervisors and managers of personnel can use the model to plan for the professional development of their staff. Current mentors can make their work more purposeful by utilizing the goals and suggestions for mentor actions as outlined in the model. While professional development in the form of mentoring has been practiced for many years (Daloz, 1986), we believe the purposeful nature of this model provides a dimension that will allow for more effective and efficient acquisition of higher skill levels.

REFERENCES

Argyris, C., & Schön, D. (1978). *Organizational learning: A theory of action perspective.* Reading, MA: Addison-Wesley.

Benner, P. (1984). *From novice to expert: Excellence and power in clinical nursing practice.* Menlo Park, CA: Addison-Wesley.

Benner, P. (2004). Using the Dreyfus model of skill acquisition to describe and interpret skill acquisition and clinical judgment in nursing practice and education. *Bulletin of Science, Technology & Society, 24,* 188-199.

Berliner, D. C. (2004). Describing the behavior and documenting the accomplishments of expert teachers. *Bulletin of Science, Technology & Society, 24,* 200-212.

Berliner, D. C., Stein, P., Sabers, D., Clarridge, P. B., Cushing, K., & Pinnegar, S. (1988). Implications of research on pedagogical expertise and experience for mathematics teaching. In D. A. Grouws & T. J. Cooney (Eds.), *Perspectives on research on effective mathematics teaching* (pp. 67-95). Reston, VA: National Council of Teachers of Mathematics.

Bransford, J. (2007). Preparing people for rapidly changing environments. *Journal of Engineering Education*, 1-3.

Daley, B. J. (1999). Novice to Expert: An exploration of how professionals learn. *Adult Education Quarterly, 49*(4), 133-147.

Daloz, L. A. (1986). *Effective teaching and mentoring: Realizing the transformational power of adult learning experiences.* San Francisco, CA: Jossey-Bass.

Dewey, J. (1910). *How we think.* Lexington, MA: D.C. Heath.

Dreyfus, H. L. (2004). What could be more intelligible than everyday intelligibility? Reinterpreting Division I of *Being and Time* in the light of Division II. *Bulletin of Science, Technology & Society, 24*, 265-274.

Dreyfus, H. L., & Dreyfus, S. E. (1986). *Mind over machine: The power of human intuition and expertise in the era of the computer.* New York, NY: Free Press.

Dreyfus, S. E. (2004). The five-stage model of adult skill acquisition. *Bulletin of Science, Technology & Society, 24*(3), 177-181.

Dreyfus, S. E., & Dreyfus, H. L. (1980). *A five-stage model of the mental activities involved in directed skill acquisition* (ORC 80-2). Berkeley, CA: University of California, Berkeley, Operations Research Center.

Lin, S. S. J. (1999, April). *Looking for the prototype of teacher expertise: An initial attempt in Taiwan.* Paper presented at the annual meeting of the American Educational Research Association, Montreal, Quebec, Canada.

Parker, P. (2008). Promoting employability in a "flat" world. *Journal of Employment Counseling, 45*(1), 2-13.

Schön, D. J. (1983). *The reflective practitioner.* New York, NY: Basic Books.

Schön, D. J. (1987). *Educating the reflective practitioner: Toward a new design for teaching and learning in the professions.* San Francisco, CA: Jossey-Bass.

Schmidt, S. W., Mott, V. W., & Lanoux, J. (2009). Using principles of adult learning to improve human performance. In V. C. X. Wang & K. P. King (Eds.), *Fundamentals of human performance and training* (pp.41-60). Charlotte, NC: Information Age Publishing.

van Driel, J. H., Beijaard, D., & Verloop, N. (2001). Professional development and reform in science education: The role of teachers' practical knowledge. *Journal of Research in Science Teaching, 38*(2), 137-158.

Vygotsky, L. S. (1978). *Mind in society: The development of higher psychological processes.* (M. Cole, V. John-Steiner, S. Scribner, & E. Souberman, Eds.). Cambridge, MA: Harvard University Press.

Watkins, K. E. & Marsick, V. J. (1993). *Sculpting the learning organization: Lessons in the art and science of systemic change.* San Francisco, CA: Jossey-Bass.

CHAPTER 15

IMPROVING FACULTY DEVELOPMENT THROUGH PEER COACHING, LEARNING COMMUNITIES, AND MENTORING

Kathryn McAtee and Catherine Hansman

Kara enthusiastically started her tenure-track position at a community college, ready to learn anything the faculty development program could teach her about instructing, student learning, and the college culture. Through the faculty development mentoring program for new faculty members, she was provided with a faculty mentor; eventually she had several mentors, all guiding and molding her to be the professor she eventually became. She participated in several faculty development sponsored events, and she even led a faculty conversation, where she facilitated a discussion with peer faculty members. Her interest in helping other faculty members become better teachers grew, so after teaching for 2 years, she became the campus faculty development coordinator. For the next 7 years, she was very involved in faculty development opportunities, presenting workshops and organizing college wide sponsored faculty events. She enjoyed her role in helping other faculty members, but as the faculty

Conversations About Adult Learning in Our Complex World, pp. 223–236

development coordinator, she experienced frustration after she and other peer faculty presenters spent extensive time readying presentations for only two or three faculty members who attended the faculty development sessions. Although Kara has experimented with various formats for the sessions, interactive methods such as peer coaching, learning communities, and mentoring seemed to be helpful to some faculty members, and Kara herself has found them useful for her professional development. However, she found little research that shows the effectiveness of interactive faculty development methods.

Kara's story may be typical of many community college or university faculty members' experiences with faculty development programs. Institutions of higher education have long sought to provide a variety of faculty development activities and programs to improve teaching practices, yet more research is needed to examine the effectiveness of the many different faculty development activities. The purpose of this chapter is to examine three faculty development programs that engage faculty members through interactive activities while addressing their individual professional development needs, focusing on examples of peer coaching, learning communities, and mentoring as types of faculty development programs at higher education institutions. In addition, we will highlight Kara's experiences as a faculty member in her community versions of each of these techniques in their faculty development program.

FACULTY DEVELOPMENT PROGRAMS

Recent research points to the need and rationale for good faculty development programs in institutions of higher education. Barlett and Rappaport (2009) contend that when higher education institutions invest in week-long or even as little as 2-day faculty development workshops, there is a robust effect on the faculty members' research innovation, interdisciplinary dialogue, and university quality of life. They further suggest that there is evidence that faculty teaching new topics and their use of new teaching methods is affected as well as the faculty member's level of engagement in research, interdisciplinary cooperation, and personal engagement. Furthermore, O'Meara and Terosky (2010) discovered that level of commitment, satisfaction, and retention rates of faculty increase when faculty feel that their academic environments are generative and genuine places for professional growth.

Barlett and Rappaport (2009) discuss that although there is collaboration between disciplines and engaging pedagogies in academic communities, it is rare for long-term measurements of faculty development program impact to exist. In addition, challenges of today's complex world influence the variety of faculty development programs that could be offered to faculty members. First, today's higher education classrooms demand university and community college faculty members to keep up to date with current trends in andragogy and technology in the classroom. Second, constantly evolving technologies challenges all educators to learn and adapt new applications to design academically sound courses (King & Lawler, 2003). Third, the higher education classroom, comprised of various generations and diverse students, requires faculty members to respond to the varied and complex needs of all students in their classrooms. Finally, due to the current bleak economic situation in the United States and elsewhere in the world that results in shrinking institutional budgets, university and community college faculty members are frequently required to continue their professional development activities with little support and funding from their institutions to cover the expenses of travel, conferences, and continuing education.

The challenges facing faculty members and their needs for professional development are many. Sorcinelli (2007) groups these into three categories; (1) the changing professorate, (2) the changing nature of the student body, and (3) the changing nature of teaching, learning, and scholarship. To address these challenges, faculty development programs require areas of emphasis. Boucher et al. (2006) contend that faculty development should concentrate on areas of: "(1) professionalism, including individual scholarship, (2) instructional, (3) leadership, and (4) organizational, such as time management. These focus areas may be addressed through workshops, seminars, teleconferences, electronic media, mini-courses, mentoring programs, sabbaticals, and directed publications" (p. 1). Likewise, O'Meara and Terosky (2010) identified four similar key aspects of faculty professional growth: (1) learning; (2) agency; (3) professional relationship; and (4) commitments. Boucher et al. (2006) further suggest that faculty development programs include three major characteristics to be effective: commitment to the program, flexibility of the program to meet the needs of faculty members, and institutional resource commitment.

These challenges raise several issues for the faculty and staff members who plan faculty development opportunities. The need for faculty development programs is broad, ranging from classroom pedagogical techniques to research and writing skills for publication; the programs and methods can be further complicated by the variety of faculty members' experience levels, from junior to senior faculty. Furthermore, involving faculty members in professional development activities requires that the opportunities offered to them meet their diverse individual needs for engagement with teaching and research skills. Finally, all of these challenges come at time when the complex economic and political climate around the world has resulted in reduced funding for development programs. Faculty development programs, then, have to be fluid and flexible enough to meet the needs of changing faculty and staff members as well as institutions.

THEORY TO PRACTICE

McLeod and Steinert (2009) contend that expert-led lecture type interventions are often ineffective and may put off participants in these sessions. Engaging faculty members in discussions and encouraging them to actively participate in learning that is tailored to their individual needs may be more effective than using lecture as a key faculty development methodology. As faculty members, our experiences point to faculty development programs based more on relationships built between facilitators and participants rather than on expert knowledge transmitted in a "telling" format. The need for faculty members to share their expertise with each other is evident in emerging types of faculty development which incorporates some self-directed learning principles (Knowles, 1975), allowing faculty members to formulate their own learning goals and to find value in the personal and professional learning they accomplish.

Merriam, Caffarella, and Baumgartner (2007) discuss self-directed learning as "a process of learning, in which people take the primary initiative for planning, carrying out, and evaluating their own learning experiences" (p. 110). Knowles (1975) includes six steps in his description of self-directed learning, including diagnosing learning needs, writing learning goals, applying suitable strategies for learning, and evaluating outcomes. Through applying self-directed learning principles to faculty development programs, faculty members may take ownership of their learning, and this ownership may help faculty members find the motivation to continue their professional development (Wlodkowski, 2003) throughout their academic careers. Including self-directed learning principles can be accomplished through planning development programs that include relational activities, such as peer coaching, learning communities, and mentoring. Pata (2009) states that workshops must address learners' self-directing competences by diagnosing their learning needs, formulating meaningful goals and objectives, developing and using a wide range of learning strategies, and monitoring performance to measure learning objectives.

Although self-directed learning can clearly play a large role in faculty development programs, the complex world in which we live require faculty members to reflect upon their own notions of teaching and learning, as well as the needs and issues of the diverse students in their classrooms, in order to transform their thinking to confront whatever challenges face them (Brancato, 2003; King & Lawler, 2003; Lawler & King, 2000). Faculty development activities can be planned to include faculty members' perceptions of what skills they need to develop, using concepts such as Wenger's (1998) communities of practice (CoPs). CoPs "involve self-directed learning by individuals as well as group learning through experiences and interactions" (Hansman, 2008, p. 294). In CoPs, "real world contexts, social relationships, and tools make the best learning environments" (p. 299). Faculty members may share their experiences in the classroom, and as researchers, with fellow CoP members, communicating with each other about, how their "experience in learning, context, culture, and tools play in shaping experiential learning" (Hansman, 2008, p. 298) furthering discussions and activities to nurture learning from each other that enrich their knowledge of teaching and research in academe.

There are many ways in which faculty development programs can be structured to incorporate concepts of self-directed learning, critically reflective practice and CoPs while meeting the various needs of the faculty members and their institutions in order to engage, encourage, and ultimately motivate faculty members to continue their professional development. Through relationship-based learning experiences, such as peer-coaching, learning communities, and mentoring, faculty members have an opportunity to control their learning environment and the context and content of their learning, encouraging them to be motivated and accountable for their own professional development while developing shared knowledge. The following sections focus on three types of faculty development methods designed to encourage faculty members' engagement, while at the same time meeting their individual needs: peer coaching, learning communities, and mentoring.

Peer Coaching

Huston and Weaver (2008) discuss peer coaching as a "collegial process whereby two faculty members voluntarily work together to improve or expand their approaches to teaching" (p. 19). They ascertain three steps typically utilized in peer coaching: identification of the area of coaching, peer classroom observations, and debriefing sessions. McLeod and Steinert (2009) discovered in their research that peer coaching "increased participant confidence in teaching, appreciation of exposure to new education ideas and an improved sense of institutional support and collegiality" (p. 1044). Zwart, Wubbles, Bergen, and Bolhuis (2007) take peer coaching a step farther and describe reciprocal peer coaching as peer coaching turn-taking, where the faculty members take turns, first as a teacher coach, and then as a coached teacher. Aligning with concepts from both self-directed learning (Knowles, 1975) and critically reflective practice (Brookfield, 1995), Zwart et al. (2007) explain that "Reciprocal peer coaching takes place in the workplace, where teachers learn by all kinds of day-to-day teaching experiences without planning. For example, they spontaneously learn by taking notes of remarks made by students or colleagues" (p. 167).

A model of a successful peer coaching program piloted at Seattle University recently is provided by Huston and Weaver (2008). The first year of the program was designated for planning, reviewing literature, and conducting research about other institutions which had similar programs, while at the same time, faculty members were nominated by their deans to participate in the Seattle University program. From the nominations, 10 faculty members expressed interest and were available to participate as coaches in the pilot program. During the second year of the program, the coaches were introduced to each other and discussed the roles, responsibilities, and skills required for coaching. The faculty coaches came from various disciplines, allowing them to expand their observations from their own disciplines across other disciplines and to develop their abilities to reflect, observe and provide feedback to others. The coaches also participated in a reciprocal relationship, where they had the opportunities to coach and be coached by another faculty member coach. Year two ended with a reflective exercise to assist the faculty coaches find closure to their experiences. During this workshop, the coaches reflected on their understandings and provided suggestions to improve the program, including how they would like to continue their coach roles in the program. Year three focused on the now experienced faculty coaches providing their skills to other faculty members in a one-way coaching experience.

The program had some major successes, as 8 of the 10 original coaches returned for year 3 and evaluated their experiences as positive. A ninth original coach participated after returning from sabbatical. All the coaches believed that the workshops and activities were helpful to them as faculty members. During the third year, 18 additional faculty members were reached through the program and also spoke highly of their experiences. Some of these faculty members had never before participated in faculty development opportunities. The final program success was that the professional development office staff had the opportunity to meet and become well-acquainted with many excellent faculty members.

Despite the successes experienced during the Seattle University program, two obstacles had to be overcome. The first obstacle was scheduling times when everyone could meet. To help with this challenge, meeting times were scheduled several months in advance, and faculty members' attendance at workshops was required. The second challenge was connecting faculty members to coaches in a timely manner. For example, sometimes the classroom issue that a faculty member wanted to discuss with a coach was no longer occurring by the time the coach was available to observe his or her class. To make the connections between coaches and faculty members timelier, the professional development office had to develop an efficient and effective system to more quickly connect faculty members with coaches.

Kara and Peer Coaching

Kara's experience with peer coaching in her community college's faculty development program was somewhat different than the experiences described by participants in the Seattle University program. Kara's community college has informally incorporated a peer coaching component into the tenure and advancement in academic rank processes. A formal review of a faculty member's teaching and classroom management is conducted at various times during their career by the department dean, as outlined in the faculty union contract. In addition, a strongly suggested yet not a required component of the tenure and academic rank processes allows faculty members applying for tenure and/or academic promotion of rank to also request a peer review conducted by a faculty member of their choice. Both the formal review and the peer review use the same forms and processes. The faculty member chooses the class and time for both evaluations. The evaluator observes the faculty member teaching class and reviews the syllabus and other supporting classroom documents and completes the review form. The faculty member and the evaluator then discuss the evaluation, with the evaluator providing constructive feedback and suggestions to improve classroom management and student engagement.

Kara has taken advantage of both the formal and peer evaluation processes at her community college, not only for tenure and advancement in rank, but on multiple occasions she asked a colleague to observe a new course she has developed. Following the observation, she and the evaluator discussed how the course could be better structured and other ways of improving teaching. Kara sought out this opportunity on her own and was able to use the feedback to improve her course and her instructional skills. This was a valuable experience for Kara, one in which she would like to encourage other faculty members at her community college to engage.

Learning Communities

Learning communities comprise similar concepts as those of CoPs, and learning communities can provide a "safe" environment for faculty to reflect upon their teaching and profession. Phelps and Waalkes (2009) discuss the idea of faculty learning communities as having the emphasis on learning in small communities over an extended time period, focusing on targeted and measureable learning outcomes. Marshall (2005) presents three essential elements of a learning community training program: (1) cultivate transitory communities of scholar-teachers who are interested in examining their vocations as teachers, (2) develop experienced communities representing interdisciplinary and cross-institutional areas and (3) honor teachers for their vocations and encourage appropriate self-care. Marshall (2005) summarized Parker Palmer's (1998) description of learning communities used to structure faculty development:

> it is not a model where experts come to teach the novice and amateurs about teaching; rather it is that right and talented scholars and teachers bring their gifts and graces into a new community where risk and honesty are valued highly and teaching is a form of art. In the context of these communities of teacher-scholars, faculty member talk about the struggles and pains of their own teaching experiences, as well as about the joys and celebrations. (p. 33)

An example of a university incorporating a learning community as a faculty development opportunity is provided by O'Meara and Terosky (2010). Michigan State University's faculty learning community (FLCs) program fosters learning through peer-to-peer extended conversations in areas of interest or need. In this faculty learning community, eight to twelve group members, consisting of faculty administrators and support staff, volunteer for a year-long commitment to hold discussion groups around specific topics. The topics of choice are determined at the beginning of the year, as well as the goals and specific outcomes of the learning community. The group is led by two faculty members who facilitate and organize the monthly meetings, communicate to the other members, and manage group logistics.

The importance of the faculty learning community to the university is evident by the amount of support they are provided. The university's Office of Faculty and Organizational Development provides the learning community both staff and financial support, such as room reservations, stipends for the faculty facilitators, and food allowances as well as grant-writing or publishing services and training in facilitation and communication skills. At the end of the academic year, the hard work accomplished by the faculty learning community is highlighted at the university's spring institute poster session. In some cases, the learning community is able to get their work published as research articles and make it available to general audiences.

Kara and Learning Communities

At Kara's community college, learning communities are actively employed at the student level, but they have been neglected as a viable concept at the faculty level. The closest opportunity Kara has had to participate in a learning community is the college sponsored faculty conversations. The faculty conversation format is a faculty driven development program, where faculty members come together three times an academic year in off campus locations for lunch on a Friday afternoon. At the beginning of the academic year, a topic, such as student engagement, is chosen by the faculty development coordinators. Once the topic is determined, faculty members are identified and asked to volunteer to lead one or more of the discussions. Both attendance and leading a conversation is voluntary, and faculty members can choose to participate in all, some, or none of the three discussions throughout the year. The community college supports these conversations by providing funding for the space and food requirements. The conversations are held off-site, rather than on a campus, and include a casual meal in hopes of providing a more conducive environment for discussing topics. Kara found participating as both a discussion leader and faculty attendee worthwhile. The topics were current and relevant, so Kara was able to apply what she learned her classroom and in her overall professional development.

Mentoring

Formal and informal mentoring relationships "have been unquestioningly and uncritically accepted as fundamental to foster learning in the workplace, advance careers, help new employees learn workplace culture, and provide developmental and psychological support" (Hansman, 2002, p. 39). Since "mentors can play key roles in their protégé's personal and professional development" (Hansman, 2009, p. 53), some faculty development programs include both formal and informal mentoring programs. Sorcinelli and Yun (2007) present emerging models of mentoring that take the mentoring relationship from a top-down, one-to-one relationship to associations based on "flexible networks of support, in which no single person is expected to possess the expertise required of someone to navigate the shoals of a faculty career" (p. 58). Planners of faculty development formal mentoring programs must consider various characteristics of the potential faculty participants, both as mentors and protégés. Cariaga-Lo, Dawkings, Enger, Schotter, and Spence (2010) state that successful faculty mentoring programs "are attentive to differences across gender, race, ethnicity, culture and generational lines" (p. 21). The diverse characteristics of the participants in the mentoring relationship can affect how individuals participate and benefit from their mentoring experiences. At the conclusion of faculty development formal mentoring programs, mentoring relationships may morph into informal structures, based on the individual needs and the expertise and availability of the faculty in the network. Borders et al.(2011) uncovered that faculty members appreciate informal and spontaneous mentoring relationships, and "these pairs are seen by some as more effective, meaningful, comfortable, relational and enduring" (p. 173)

Borders et al. (2011) discussed their development of a mentoring program incorporating Sorcinelli's (2000) 10 principles of good practice for supporting junior faculty in their career journey. The 10 principles they used were

1. communicate expectations for performance;
2. give feedback on performance;
3. enhance collegial review processes;
4. create flexible timelines for tenure;
5. encourage mentoring by senior faculty;
6. extend mentoring and feedback to graduate students who aspire to be faculty members;
7. recognize the department chair as a career sponsor;
8. support teaching, particularly at the undergraduate level;
9. support scholarly development; and
10. foster a balance between professional and personal life.

Using these 10 principles allows the mentoring program to have both a formal and informal structure. It also encourages senior faculty members to mentor junior faculty members, but at the same time, may encourage faculty members to engage in peer-to-peer mentoring.

Angelique, Kyle, and Taylor (2002) provide an example of how they developed a peer mentoring program at Penn State Harrisburg. Out of frustration of unmet needs from the formal mentoring program, Angelique asked other untenured faculty members if they would be interested in starting a peer faculty mentoring program. The group began with 4-6 regular attending members. None of these members were originally from Pennsylvania, they were predominantly White males, their ages ranged from 35 and 55, and all of the members earned graduate degrees from Research I universities, although they came from different disciplinary backgrounds. Most members were single, three were married and one was a single parent. As the group met and matured, they established grounds rules. The first set of ground rules focused on meetings and faculty members. Two monthly scheduled meetings were open to all new/ untenured faculty members, and every year new faculty members were invited to join the group. The first meeting was a more social event, while the second meeting focused on tasks. Other ground rules centered on establishing roles and responsibilities of the group. They were to provide support, advice, suggestions, and ideas for joint research proposals. The final ground rule identified two offices, the president who provided an agenda for the meetings, and a secretary who sent out meeting reminders. Outcomes emerged from this group, including greater emphasis on professional development, which increased collaborative efforts by faculty members in participating at conferences, workshops and qualitative research projects, as well as, eased the transition to postgraduate school life while helping new faculty members understand the political climate of the institution.

Kara and Mentoring

Kara also participated in mentoring programs at her institution. Her mentoring relationships were both formal and informal and in many cases were peer mentoring relationships with other faculty members. Unlike the peer mentoring program at Penn State Harrisburg, there was no person acting as a formal organizer to begin a peer mentoring program for Kara to attend. During Kara's first year at her institution, she was provided a faculty mentor by the college campus faculty mentoring coordinator. This was a formal mentoring relationship focused on learning about the institution, both physically such as the locations of the copy center, student resources, and campus life, as well as politically, which included what choice committees to join, carefully chosen meetings to attend, and what faculty, staff, and administration members with whom to associate. From her first year, Kara established long lasting mentoring relationships both inside her institution as well as outside it. She also participates in mentoring relationships at with faculty and staff members at various levels of the institution, including senior and newer and untenured faculty members as well administrative staff. In faculty peer mentoring relationships, Kara and other faculty members share teaching ideas, course work concepts, and committee and meeting responsibilities. Through her staff and administrators mentoring relationships, Kara attends meetings and participates in groups that help with institutional processes and new programs. Kara had to search out and establish these relationships. When Kara needed guidance, advice, or support, she was able to fill that need from a network of professionals she had established.

Kara's community college provides financial support for the formal mentoring program to the new faculty members, faculty mentors, and faculty mentoring coordinators. A stipend for the new faculty member is for their participation in a mandatory orientation program, which focuses on helping the new faculty member acclimate to the college. A stipend for the mentoring faculty member is for providing the new faculty member guidance and advice on classroom management and teaching techniques. A third stipend is available to the faculty mentoring coordinator for orchestrating the meetings of the faculty mentor and the new faculty member, as well helping with scheduling meetings and completing reports that highlight the relationship of the faculty mentor the new faculty member.

CONCLUSION

As illustrated by the programs described in this chapter, the ever changing and complex world requires that faculty development programs be more than lecture-based workshops and "expert" led discussions. Evolving faculty development programs should encompass theories and principles of adult learning, such as self-directed learning, critically reflective practice, transformational learning, and engaging in communities of practice. Adult educators, through their work as program planners and teachers of adults, can further develop and expand adult learning techniques and best practices in effective faculty development programs, designing programs that are inclusive of faculty members' needs and objectives.

Faculty development programmers face many challenges in helping faculty members meet their professional development needs. Faculty members struggle to find development opportunities that meet their individual needs; furthermore, they wrestle with finding the personal motivation to engage in professional development to continue their individual career trajectory. To help meet these challenges, emerging types of faculty development techniques, peer coaching, learning communities, and formal and informal mentoring are a means to encourage faculty to critically reflect upon their practices as teachers and researchers while engaging with other faculty members to share knowledge. Many institutions of higher education are adopting these faculty development program strategies, demonstrating that they are beneficial to the institutions while meeting individual faculty development needs.

Final Note: Kara's Faculty Development

Through her community college, Kara discovered ways to engage herself in professional development, finding opportunities to work with other faculty members both within and outside the formal structure of the college's faculty development program. Even though Kara's community college did not provide structured and formal peer coaching, learning communities and peer mentoring programs, but provided similar types of programs, she took the initiative to engage with other faculty members and design her own individual professional development. However, the struggle remains to communicate and share with their colleagues the importance of taking the initiative and finding opportunities for faculty development both inside and outside the formal structure of faculty development programs.

REFERENCES

Angelique, H., Kyle, K., & Taylor, E. (2002). Mentors and muses: New strategies for academic success. *Innovative Higher Education, 26*(3), 195-209.

Barlett, P. F., & Rappaport, A. (2009). Long-term impacts of faculty development programs: The experience of Teli and Piedmont. *College Teaching, 57*(2), 73–82.

Borders, L. D., Young, J. S., Wester, K. L., Murray, C. E., Vilalba, J. A., Lewis, T. F., & Mobley, A. E. (2011). Mentoring promotion/tenure-seeking faculty: Principles of good practice within a counselor education program. *Counselor Education & Supervision, 50,* 171-188.

Boucher, B. A., Chyke, P. J., Fitzgerald, W. L., Hak, L. J., Miller, D. D., Parker, R. B., Phelps, S. J., Wood, G. C., & Gourley, D. R. (2006). A comprehensive approach to faculty development. *American Journal of Pharmaceutical Education, 70*(2), 1-6.

Brancato, V. C. (2003). Professional development in higher education. *New Directions for Adult & Continuing Education, 98,* 59-68.

Brookfield, S. (1995). *Becoming a critically reflective teacher.* San Francisco, CA: Jossey-Bass.

Cariaga-lo, L., Dawkings, P. W., Enger, R., Schotter, A., & Spence, C. (2010). Supporting the development of the professoriate. *Peer Review Summer,* 19-22.

Hansman, C. A. (2002). Diversity and power in mentoring relationships. In C. A. Hansman (Ed.), *Critical perspectives on mentoring: Trends & issues* (pp. 39-48). Information series no. 388. Columbus, OH: ERIC Clearinghouse on Adult, Career, and Vocational Education (ERIC Document Reproduction Service No. ED99CO0013).

Hansman, C. A. (2008). Adult learning in communities of practice: Situating theory in practice. In C. Kimble, P. Hildreth, & I. Bourdon (Eds.), *Communities of practice: Creating learning environments for educators, 1* (pp. 279-292). Charlotte, NC: Information Age Publishing.

Hansman, C. A. (2009). Ethical issues in mentoring adult learners in higher education. *New Directions for Adult and Continuing Education, 123,* 53-64.

Huston, T., & Weaver, C. (2008). Peer coaching: Professional development for experienced faculty. *Innovative Higher Education, 33,* 5-20.

King, K. P., & Lawler, P. (2003). Trends and issues in the professional development of teachers of adults. *New Directions for Adult & Continuing Education, 98,* 5-13.

Knowles, M. S. (1975). *Self-directed learning.* New York, NY: Association Press.

Lawler, P. A., & King, K. P. (2000). *Planning for effective faculty development.* Malabar, FL: Krieger.

Marshall, J. L. (2005). Learning about teaching in communities: Lessons for faculty development. *Teaching Theology and Religion, 8*(1), 29-34.

McLeod, P. J. & Steinert, Y. (2009). Peer coaching as an approach to faculty development. *Medical Teacher, 31,* 1043-1044.

Merriam, S., Caffarella, R., & Baumgartner, L. (2007). *Learning in adulthood* (3rd ed.). San Francisco, CA: Jossey-Bass.

O'Meara, K., & Terosky, A. L. (2010). Engendering faculty professional growth. *Change,* 44-51.

Palmer, P. J. (1998). *The courage to teach: Exploring the inner landscape of a teacher's life.* San Francisco, CA: Jossey-Bass.

Pata, K. (2009). Modeling spaces for self-directed learning at university courses. *Educational Technology & Society, 12*(3), 23-43.

Phelps, M. P., & Waalkes, S. (2009). Christian friendship and faculty development: A narrative account. *Journal of Education & Christian Belief, 13*(2), 125-139.

Sorcinelli, M.D. (2000). Principles of good practice: Supporting early-career faculty-guidance for deans, department chairs, and other academic leaders. In R. E. Rice, M. D. Sorcinelli, & A. E. Austin (Eds.), *Heeding new voices: Academic careers for a new generation.* Washington, DC: American Association for Higher Education. Retrieved from http://eric.ed.gov/PDFS/ED450634.pdf

Sorcinelli, M. D. (2007). Faculty development: The challenge going forward. *Peer Review.* 4-8.

Sorcinelli, M. D., & Yun, J. (2007). From mentor to mentoring networks: Mentoring in the new academy. *Change,* 58-61.

Wenger, E. (1998). *Communities of practice: Learning, meaning and identity.* Cambridge, England: Cambridge University Press.

Wlodkowski, R. J. (2003). Fostering motivation in professional development programs. *New Directions for Adult & Continuing Education, 98,* 39-48.

Zwart, R. C., Wubbles, T. C., Bergen, M. & Bolhuis, S. (2007). Experience of teacher learning within the context of reciprocal peer coaching. *Teachers and Teaching: Theory and Practice, 13*(2), 165-187.

CHAPTER 16

TECHNICAL AND TEACHER TRAINING CHALLENGES IN UGANDA

An Instructional Technology Approach to a 21st Century Development Issue

Charles K. Kyobe and Kathleen P. King

With the steadfast increase in Uganda's primary school enrollments over the past decade (currently 83.2% of its primary school age population), This nation now has a shortage of qualified teachers to meet the demands of their students. International organizations have sought to provide a solution for the need by enrolling qualified Ugandan adults in western designed and managed distance education teacher training programs. However, these distance education programs frequently carry Eurocentric bias that has little or no sensitivity to social, cultural, and educational differences among learners (Gunawardena & LaPointe, 2008). The resulting dependency on expatriate teachers and Western learning materials is mainly due to the lack of the native experts in instructional technology. This situation leads to learning experiences which are not specific to local learners, their culture, context, or needs.

Conversations About Adult Learning in Our Complex World, pp. 237–253

Given this gap in relevant and appropriate instruction, teacher training and technical education are two sectors of Ugandan higher education which could positively impact the country's economic development. Effective education of the nation would increase with indigenously developed and culturally appropriate instructional materials and instructional technology tools. Yet currently, there is little capacity to prepare Ugandans in these areas.

When instructional technology is infused in the curriculum, it can play a substantial role in educating adults in rural communities regarding activities that promote and sustain human and economic development. It is powerful because instructional technology is a subarea of the larger field of technical education, and focuses on how to use technology to increase the effects of teaching and learning. Certainly, technical education has a direct impact on the world of work and economic development. However, in today's technologically driven global economy, policymakers and educators need to embrace and leverage technology to increase the effectiveness of teaching and learning in Uganda.

Clouding this issue is the fact that there have been considerable efforts to implement information and communication technology (ICT) tools in Ugandan higher education sectors. However, ICT has not included the design and use of technology for instructional purposes (instructional technology).

In addition, another issue arises: most technical colleges in Uganda are located in rural areas and offer academic concentrations that are directly related to the economic activities of the respective communities. However, due to lack of employment opportunities in these communities, graduates from these colleges often move to larger cities and towns in search of jobs. It is a form of rural "brain drain" which nations worldwide have experienced for many years.

This chapter proposes recommendations and a strategy to alleviate poverty and improve livelihoods in developing countries. Simply stated, the education systems must prepare students with skills that are critically needed in their rural areas. Infusing instructional technology into the technical education curriculum is one way of achieving both that goal and others. A graduate from the farm tractor mechanics or water resource management academic program, for example, would also learn how to design electronic learning materials in a specific local language that he or she can use to educate other adults in the area. In addition, the resources would be quickly scaled. According to popular practice in these settings, the electronic materials would be welcome to be viewed by entire communities in their outside "theaters." Moreover, this opportunity provides graduates with valuable and viable roles for staying to serve in their communities as self-employed instructors or employees of international organizations who focus on educating adults in rural communities. However, at the crux of all obstacles to this plan is the general, systemic lack of instructional technology expertise in the country.

Figure 16.1 illustrates the three overarching issues discussed in this chapter and how they intersect with the proposed solution. Considering the importance and potential these sectors pose to economic development, the main concern presented in this chapter is the level and quality of technological input in the teaching and learning process in teacher education, as well as the economic development potential of instructional technology infusion in technical education. The chapter presents a practical approach to developing an educational institution that is focused on media technologies, specifically for the education sectors. Instructional technology where the institution's students and graduates will provide indigenous resources, instruction, and support are also described in this chapter. As discussed by Thakrar, Zinn, and Wolfenden (2009), given similar economic and human development issues in sub-Saharan Africa, suggestions offered here can be replicated in the region as well. There are abundant indigenous artistic resources in Uganda; if tapped through instructional technologies, they can effectively contribute to 21st century human and economic development strategies.

THE NEED: EDUCATION AND ECONOMIC DEVELOPMENT

Alleviating extreme poverty and improving livelihoods in sub-Saharan countries has been one of the greatest challenges for the international community since this countries independence in the 1960s (Barret, Carter, & Little, 2006). However, the goals and intervention strategies were given a significant push in 2000 when the United Nations Organization member heads of state and governments of 189 countries developed a compact of eight millennium development goals (MDGs) to be achieved by 2015 (United Nations Development Programme Uganda, 2010). The eight MDGs of the UNO's compact are to (1) eradicate extreme hunger and poverty, (2) achieve universal primary education, (3) promote gender equality and empower women, (4) reduce child mortality, (5) improve maternal health, (6) combat HIV/AIDS, malaria, and other diseases, (7) ensure environmental sustainability, and (8) develop a global partnership for development.

Education plays a vital role in human development and it is the reason why universal primary education (UPE) was emphasized in the MDGs as the main strategy to eradicate abject poverty, improve human rights, and increase overall economic development in developing nations. According to United Nations Children's Fund (UNICEF) (2010), accelerating the

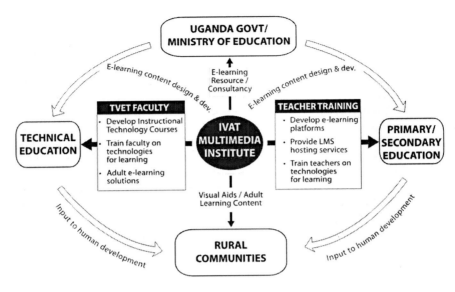

Figure 16.1.   Overview of proposed solution and critical issues.

movement towards UPE would lead directly to an acceleration of many of the other MDGs, especially those focusing on poverty reduction and general improvements in health. Critical factors to consider in the impact of the UPE on relieving poverty include the fact that people who have been to school are more likely to find work, look after their health, and demand that governments act in their interests (King, McGrath, & Rose, 2007). Uganda has been acknowledged as one of the few developing countries that has made concerted efforts towards UPE with 83.2% of Ugandan children enrolled in primary schools (United Nations Development Programme Uganda, 2010). While this is a an improvement there is is still an inadequate number of higher education institutions to provide educational opportunities for the increasing population. Specifically, according to Liang (2004), Uganda's 28 universities can accommodate slightly below 2 percent of all primary school graduates. Moreover, the cost of continuing education for primary school graduates have not been addressed; it remains financially out of reach for the majority of these graduates. Together, these factors contribute greatly to the fact that 98% of the target group does not have access to university education. As this population grows into adulthood and reside mainly in rural areas, technical institutions in those areas can play a significant role when they prepare their graduates to become educators of related economic activities instead of seeking jobs in urban areas.

Today's global economy and need for economic development requires far more than a primary school certificate (the equivalent of a U.S. Middle School education). This recognition has compelled a number of international agencies (King et al., 2007), including the World Bank, to broaden their focus and address the role other aspects of education play in reducing poverty. Teacher education has received much attention and assistance from internationally-based open and distance education organizations in Uganda, and this situation has challenged Uganda's teacher education institutions to develop distance learning options (Kato et al., 2007). However, no higher education institution in the country offers instructional technology as a separate field from information communication technology (ICT). This prompts the question as to who evaluates the specific educational needs for teacher education among the Ugandan population, as well as who in Uganda is capable of using existing distance learning research, practice, and standards to design, develop, deliver, and maintain the planned online learning content and platforms.

TEACHER TRAINING SECTOR CHALLENGES

The rapid increase in enrollment in primary education has not been adequately reciprocated with government resource funding, resulting in concerns of deteriorating quality as well as increased demand for secondary education (Oketch & Rollestone, 2007). As sub-Saharan countries continue to increase their UPE enrollments, it is estimated that approximately 4 million additional teachers will be needed to fill both new posts in light of other challenges such as effects of HIV/AIDs and the migration of teachers to other countries outside the region (Thakrar, Zinn, & Wofenden, 2009, p. 2). Moreover, one must understand the challenges of teaching in Uganda when we realize the average teacher has 49 pupils and each classroom has 68 pupils (Uganda Bureau of Statistics, 2010). With UPE-initiated primary enrollments steadfastly increasing from 2.9 million in 1996, to 5.3 million in 1997, to 6.5 million in 2007, and to the 2009 figure, the 46 primary teachers' colleges have an acute challenge to effectively train and fill enough teaching positions to bring these ratios down (Kahiigi, Ekenberg, Hanson, Danielson, & Tusubira, 2008). Two-thirds of primary school teachers in Uganda's urban schools are qualified; however, only 50% of teachers in rural schools are qualified (Bennell, 2004).

Distance education is being recognized both in the country and internationally not only as an alternative, but also an training option for adults seeking for adults seeking to join this important profession. Even as of 2007, distance and open education provided by Ugandan institutions, international organizations, or partnerships of both have gained real credibility as a method of providing training to teachers and as a way of up-skilling and increasing national workforces (Kato et al., 2007, p. 1). In developing world, distance learning for teacher education has several advantages for enhancing the effective, efficient, and equitable provision of education with less costs and more time flexibility than face-to-face education (Danaher & Umar, 2010, p. 1). Distance education also allows teachers to continue working as they train, thereby enabling them to pursue their education without having to forego their earnings or requiring employers to replace them (Adem, 2009). One may in fact consider that there is a dual advancement occurring because of this dynamic: (1) students continue to advance with their qualified teachers guiding them, and (2) the teachers advance professionally through the online classes as well.

DISTANCE EDUCATION CHALLENGES

Open and distance education are not without their own challenges in Uganda and throughout sub-Saharan Africa. Each country has developed different forms of open and distance learning alternatives to meet demand for education (Gulati, 2008). While Uganda is one of the few African countries that has provided successful and large-scale distance teacher education (Sikwibele & Mungoo, 2009), the more specific issue is whether increasing the number of teachers guarantees the quality of teacher education and whether there are adequate resources to allow that.

Quality of Training

Increasing the number of teacher trainees is a commendable goal, but there are issues related to the format and quality of the training in which they engage. First, the Uganda education system has long been limited to pedagogy and curriculum developed from pre- and postcolonial times modes of teacher education (Lauglo, 2009). Second, there are abundant inefficiencies in the current educational administrative systems. Gross lack of infrastructure to support online learning in terms of reliable electricity supply, technology/computer resources, overbearing cost of Internet through service providers, and high speed Internet access are some of the structural factors that constrain any efforts towards implementing effective online education platforms. These factors, coupled with inadequate local expertise to effectively develop, deliver, and maintain media technologies, are serious impediments towards implementing effective teacher training through distance education (Leary & Berge, 2006). Considering that most primary schools in Uganda are located in poverty-stricken rural areas where these resources are least available, these are crucial challenges.

Resources and Expertise

There are isolated cases where international open and distance education providers have effectively tackled some of these issues. However, the reality is that Ugandan educational systems will have neither the expertise nor the resources to eventually become self-reliant if this dependency continues. Specifically, Ugandans need expertise in effective development of learning technologies which incorporate learner characteristics that are best suited for the country's academic sectors. In order for teacher training using technology to be designed and sustained with the learner in mind, the instructional technology field needs to be developed indigenously. Specifically, Ugandans skilled in this field will be more likely to develop more culturally and pedagogically effective online learning platforms than international developers who address divergent learners globally.

Sociocultural Contexts and Theoretical Concerns

According to Vygotskian theory of teaching and learning, knowledge acquisition is a sociocultural process. Whereas, Kozulin, Gindis, Ageyev, and Miller (2003) refer to conceptual change from an introductory overview of the subject matter, in the context of education, which can be achieved to the extent that new learning experiences impact learners corresponding to their prior knowledge. Piaget goes further to refer to knowledge acquisition as social transmission of the collective representation of the society and the reconstruction of it as a function of social engagement in which a sense of self and other is constructed (Müller, Carpendale, Budwig, & Sokol, 2008). Specific to adult learning, Illeris's three-dimensional learning model—cognition, emotion, and society—provides that all three aspects are always present in a learning activity and that adult learning is always within the social context in which the learner lives and interacts with other members of society (Merriam, Caffarella, & Baumgartner, 2007). The social context is an influential determinant of the characteristics of the adult learner as it embodies prior knowledge, events, and circumstances that influence the learning process (Galbraith, 2004, p. 31).

Learning is contextualized in our own cultures and experiences within society, international. Therefore, distance educators need to be aware of the fact that technology connects us, but that it is not culturally neutral.

This perspective enables educators to address the fact that the problems of education in the developing world are more complex that what technology alone can solve (Gunawardena & LaPointe, 2008). For example, Ugandan culture tends to be an oral culture; thus, students feel pressured when they are expected to read and write for extended periods of time (Basaza, Milman, & Wright, 2010). Moreover, a multitribal society like Uganda increases in the complexity of cultural considerations that international organizations need to address in designing instructional content. Although external organizations may be better technologically equipped, it is impossible for them to design instruction for delivery across diverse populations in developing world because they have not effectively addressed the cultural nuances and intricacies of the complex Ugandan cultural differences.

This misplaced, high dependency on expatriate teachers and learning materials developed in the West can lead to learning that is not specific to the local populations and their learning needs (Gulati, 2008). Fahy and Ally (2005) point out that when students do not participate in accordance to their learning styles and preferences, the requirement for online interaction becomes a potential barrier (as cited in Gunawardena & LaPointe, 2008). Additionally, virtual programs developed overseas that depend on an existing digital infrastructure in homes, businesses, and institutions that do not yet exist in Africa lead to frustrations and attrition, especially in rural areas (Wolff, 2002).

Moreover, even though English is the main language of communication in the Ugandan education system, it is the second language to all Ugandans and therefore accurate interpretation of online content developed in the West may be problematic to some students. It is not uncommon, especially in rural areas, for teachers and students in classrooms to express themselves in both English and their native language considering that world views and cultural values are a product of the society's ways of thinking, speaking, and cognition, which are then expressed articulately in the society's language (Pincas, 2001). This issue drives the need for Uganda's development of expertise to design and sustain its own quality teacher training.

TECHNICAL EDUCATION AND ECONOMIC DEVELOPMENT

The 2005 United Nations evaluation of countries engaged in MDGs indicated nearly half of the sub-Saharan population is living below the international poverty line of a dollar a day (Mondal, 2009). About 70% of this region's poor live in rural areas, and the majority of the rural work force makes a living based on subsistence agriculture. This fact has convinced many economic development scholars that poverty reduction will require agricultural development in most African countries. Uganda is a very good reflection of this scenario where 70% of the work force is in agriculture and substantial government revenues are derived from this sector (Uganda Bureau of Statistics, 2010). Effective technical education is instrumental if policymakers are seriously dedicated to developing agriculture into a 21st century globally competitive level.

A number of teacher training issues so far discussed are similar to the technical education sector, considering that most institutions are located in rural areas. An assumption may be made that increased enrollment in higher education should translate into higher human and economic development as graduates are able to find jobs and better their lives. It is the reverse in Uganda, where the formal market has been unable to keep pace with the ever-growing demand for employment, with only 36% of university graduates gainfully employed (Kimani, 2011); of the 400,000 Ugandans who enter the labor market each year, only about 80,000 have been absorbed into the existing workforce (Uganda Bureau of Statistics, 2010). This situation poses serious questions regarding government and international organizations' tendencies to relate education-based skills development to formal labor market needs, especially where statistics show that the majority of employment in sub-Saharan Africa is in informal structures such as subsistence agriculture. It has also brought about the belief among rural youth that education is a ticket that will take them away from their home village—to the capital city or even to one of the great global metropolises—rather than as a means of transforming and enriching their home environment (Parry, 2009). Training students from rural areas in skills that are employable in urban centers draws students away from the rural communities, thereby weakening any potential for increasing government revenue through agriculture.

Dr. Lourdes Quisumbing, a renowned scholar on technical education, stated that, "If education is the key to development, vocational and technical education is the master key that opens the door to the world of work and the economy, alleviate poverty, save the environment and improve the quality of life" (Park, 2005, p. 1). Indeed, education encompasses the ability to accelerate economic growth, provide a marketable labor supply, minimize unemployment and underemployment, infuse technical knowledge, and reduce poverty (Park, 2005). Since technical and vocational education and training (TVET) is the education sector in Uganda best suited to quickly and directly contribute to economic development, policymakers ought to invest more in modernizing technical and vocational institutions with technological and skill development strategies that will directly contribute to human and economic development rural communities. Since TVET institutions are more spread out around the country and in rural areas than universities, their education curricular and skill development can be tailored with the right education enhancing technologies to address youth and rural community development needs in the respective locations, and thereby, help keep technical education graduates employed within their communities. As discussed in the next section, the proposal to infuse instructional technology in the technical education curriculum provides new opportunities. Indeed, the goal is to increase Ugandan technology skills through indigenous efforts and enter competitive production for a 21st century global economy.

Instructional Technology

Whereas information and communication technology (ICT) is the technical field of computer and technology communications systems, instructional technology is the design and use of technology for instructional purposes. However, worldwide, ICT and instructional technology are often confused by nontechnical people (such as government officials, educators, and media). Reiser (1987), a prolific author on the history and definition of instructional technology, explained the contrasting definitions as a set of instructional media versus systems process approach. His 2001 work clarifies the term further as "instructional technology and design" and offers this definition:

> The field of instructional design and technology encompasses the analysis of learning and performance problems, and the design, development, implementation, evaluation and management of instructional and noninstructional processes and resources intended to improve learning and performance in a variety of settings, particularly educational institutions and the workplace. (Reiser, 2001, p. 53)

This definition of instructional technology is well-rounded and encompasses the broader field of educational technology. The Association for Educational Communications and Technology (AECT) defines educational technology as "the study and ethical practice of facilitating learning and improving performance by creating, using and managing appropriate technological processes and resources" (Richey, 2008, p. 24). Facilitating learning and improving performance are byproducts of effective evaluation and management of instructional and noninstructional processes and resources. The design, development, and implementation process require someone with not only creative and communication technology skills, but also the ability to analyze the learners' characteristics, needs, and limitations. It is therefore important to develop instructional technology skills in Uganda consistent with the communications infrastructure, financial resources, and sociocultural contexts as serious considerations to bring about effective learning outcomes at all levels of education. Indigenous skilled personnel will be the most effective at accomplishing these goals as they implicitly understand the broad and nuanced details of the sociocultural context.

Given the dominance of technology in the 21st century global marketplace, it is no surprise that almost every university in Uganda, in addition to some lower level institutions, offer ICT certificates, diplomas, undergraduate, and graduate programs in this area. As a result, the ICT employment market is more or less saturated. However, the interest in technology has not adequately connected with the education sector, and hence instructional technology. Therefore, few graduates, if any, are skilled in this critical field. At the same time, Uganda is endowed with abundant artistic skills that can be infused with media design technologies that are much needed to design cutting edge effective e-learning (video, graphic design, simulations, virtual worlds, etc.).

PROPOSAL: ESTABLISH A UGANDAN MEDIA ARTS AND TECHNOLOGY INSTITUTION

The project proposed here is real-life and in its initial stages of development. The purpose of the project is to advance Ugandan economic development by infusing readily abundant indigenous artistic human resources with technology within the education sector. The proposed "Institute of Visual Arts and Technology" (IVAT) will be a unique educational self-sustaining institution. Unlike other higher education institutions in the country offering 3-year undergraduate programs and relying on enrollment numbers for financial resources, IVAT will be a 4-year institution with a total of 120 students (30 students in each year of study). In an innovative design, IVAT will operate an educational wing and a for-profit business entity to benefit all stakeholders, including students.

IVAT will be a multimedia institute that will enroll artistically talented university-bound students and enable them to convert their talents into marketable skills in various electronic mediums of communication. In IVAT's business wing, the acquired academic skills will be combined with innovative strategies. Based on sound business ethics and plans to foster organizational sustainability and growth, this business wing will generate revenue and provide an effective internship during enrollment. Another objective is for graduating students to be highly competitive, not only regionally, but also globally. The vision is that they would be able to compete as either self-employed individuals or employed by business organizations worldwide.

This plan grows from the need that as developing countries become more sophisticated and technologies accessible and affordable, media content demand increase in all sectors of the economy. At the moment, these personnel needs are being filled by foreign agencies and organizations. Instead, Uganda could decrease its unemployment rate and fill its skilled personnel need through this proposal. The gap is that currently there is no institution strictly specializing in media communications. Therefore, the proposal provides this specific training and infuses multimedia technology with Uganda's young people's indigenous artistic skills in an academic setting. In the IVAT, students will study as well as contribute to the organization's sustainability by working for an income.

In this mutually beneficial design, the organization contracts projects from various businesses and institutions as well as creates its own. Students are then employed to work on these projects depending on their skill levels. In other words, they will be putting into practice what they are learning, and by the time the graduate, they will not need additional internships. Additionally, through these programs, students will work with clients to a certain level and participate in the decision-making process of given projects. These experiences further build essential business skills for the students.

While higher education is expensive and beyond the reach of most Ugandans, a work/study system such as described here currently is nonexistent in the country. In IVAT, any artistically talented person with good academic undergraduate entry credentials can enroll irrespective of income so long as he/she is willing to work. Having a diverse student body with varied cultural, social, and economic backgrounds from across East Africa will be advantageous in providing varied points of view on any design solution. Additionally, this broad geographic representation enables IVAT to venture into income-generating projects that appeal to and are demanded in any of the East African regions which the students represent.

Figure 16.2 illustrates that IVAT will offer four major academic programs in Graphics and Interactive Media Design, Video Production and Special Effects, Media Arts and Animation, and Instructional Technology. There are similar course curriculum components in these majors, especially in the beginning stages. Approaches to design technologies tend to differ as students begin to specialize in the different programs. A student majoring in instructional technology, for example, will have acquired intermediate competencies in Graphic and Interactive Media Design and elective courses from Video production or Animation before moving on to theories, principles and best practices of e-learning development and delivery.

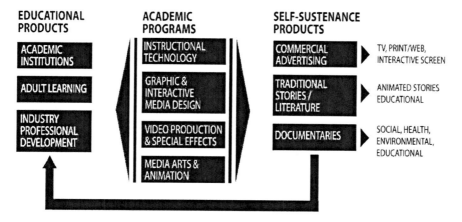

Figure 16.2.   IVAT academic and business services.

IVAT's Instructional Technology Services

For Teacher Training

Technology can play an instrumental role in creating effective learning communities (Riel & Fulton, 2001), increasing our ability to work with and learn from others and construct new shared understandings. This reality is not new to African societies with strong traditional ties and norms and if effectively incorporated in a technologically driven learning environment for desired learning outcome; it can also sustain cultures. As technology in education continues to permeate African education systems, and in this case adult learner settings (King, 2001), faculty must consider that we will have multiple skill levels in classes and must provide means to meet the needs of each student. In a study conducted on distance education teacher trainees in Botswana (Sikwibele & Mungoo, 2009), it was found that attrition rates were higher in the older participants who felt more frustrated with technology than their younger peers. For these trainees who, among other challenges, struggle with basic computing skills, sometimes under substandard infrastructures and learning in a second language, technology may become a hindrance to the learning process instead of being a supporting vehicle.

IVAT will seek to address this need by seeking contracts with teacher training institutions to design and develop e-learning content customized to specific learner and delivery mode characteristics. Infrastructural limitations and education system policies will be weighed in the effort to provide effective learning products. IVAT will also provide learning management system (LMS) hosting services for institutions which need the capacity to manage and maintain their learning platforms.

By definition, instructional technology must go beyond training. Globally, classroom technology proves to be an effective method for enhancing learning; this trend needs to be discovered in contextualized forms for sub-Saharan educational contexts as well. While few primary and secondary schools in Uganda currently have computers in class-rooms, it is not a far-fetched prediction that most schools will have them in 10 years time. Teachers who are versed in teaching and learning technologies more effectively teach students to use them. IVAT will therefore provide educational programs to teachers on teaching and learning with media communication technologies, contributing to teacher quality across the Sub-Saharan region.

For Technical Education

Due to the role of technical colleges in offering ICT, IVAT will seek to collaborate with them to develop complementary instructional technology courses as part of their program curricula. Because most technical institutions are in rural areas and students come from the same communi-ties, building their technological skills can be directly applied to valuable local projects. For example, they may create electronic learning materials in local languages with powerful visual media. Such indigenously designed and contextually appropriate instructional materials can be widely viewed many times, based on the community practice of viewing materials at local community centers, churches, or movie viewing halls commonly found in community trading centers.

As another example, a student majoring in tractor mechanics and maintenance may produce an electronic portfolio that teaches others how to repair a farm tractor. According to Donaldson (2009), the University of Northern Iowa's instructional technology program demonstrated that creating an e-portfolio increases students' retention of learning material. In this case, students followed a rubric based on AECT instructional tech-nology definition stages of design, development, utilization, manage-ment, and evaluation to construct an e-learning presentation appropriate to their delivery mode choice (Donaldson, 2009).

The constructivist methods of learning using instructional technology illustrated in the examples above would not only enable technical education students to gain a firmer grasp of the profession, but also empower them as job creators upon graduation. Specifically, they would have the skills and experience to become self-employed instructors in their local communities instead of fleeing the rural communities and failing to secure one of the scarce jobs in the cities. As a result, graduates will contribute to educating their communities on issues and in activities that affect local human and economic development.

CONCLUSION

The proposed project is planned for the context of Uganda, but applicable for the sub-Saharan region. This chapter presented the opportunity for the proposed IVAT in the current Ugandan educational system, to contribute to addressing the shortage of quality teachers, and Uganda's economic and workforce needs. In addition, the proposal builds on the strengths of Uganda's artistic resources and tertiary educational system to provide expert and practical preparation in media technology. This proposed model includes the means to not only leverage indigenous talent and skills, but also to generate revenue, thus addressing the economic needs of most Ugandan students. The ultimate project goal is to advance Ugandan economic development by infusing readily abundant indigenous artistic human resources with technology within the education sector.

This programmatic model offers the opportunity to build natural human resources and enable Uganda to begin to compete in the 21st century global marketplace. Rather than continuing to utilize colonial models of Western instruction and expertise, the most efficient and long lasting solution provided here is to cultivate indigenous expertise and skill. Not only will such a solution help the nation advance in its slow economic climb, but also it will assure the most culturally relevant and fulfilling teaching, interpretation, development and decision making through indigenous educational, technical and economic development. We welcome your insights, feedback, and recommendations in a continuing dialogue about this project.

REFERENCES

Adem, A. E. (2009). Teacher training through distance education: IICBA's experience. *Africa Education Review, 6*(1), 174-184.

Barrett, C. B., Carter, M. R., & Little, P. D. (2006). Understanding and reducing persistent poverty in Africa. *Journal of Development Studies, 42*(2), 167-177.

Basaza, G. N., Milman, N. B., & Wright, C. R. (2010). The challenges of implementing distance education in Uganda: A case study. *International Review of Research in Open and Distance Learning, 11*, 2.

Bennell, P. (2004). Teacher motivation and incentives in sub-Saharan Africa and Asia. *Knowledge and skills for development*. Brighton, England: Eldis. Retrieved from http://www.eldis.org/vfile/upload/1/document/0708/doc15160.pdf

Danaher, P. A., & Umar, A. (Eds.). (2010). *Teacher education through open and distance learning*. Vancouver, BC, Canada: Commonwealth of Learning. Retrieved from http://www.col.org/publicationdocuments/pub_ps_teachered_web.pdf

Donaldson, J. A. (2009). Definition to practice: Translating the definition into a standards-based IT program. *TechTrends, 53*(5), 29-33.

Fahy, P. J., & Ally, M. (2005). Student learning style and asynchronous computer-mediated conferencing. *American Journal of Distance Education, 19*(1), 5-22.

Galbraith, M. W. (Ed.). (2004). *Adult learning methods: A guide for effective instruction* (3rd ed.). Malabar, FL: Krieger.

Gulati, S. (2008). Technology-enhanced learning in developing nations: A review. *International Review of Research in Open and Distance Learning, 9*, 1.

Gunawardena, C. N., & LaPointe, D (2008). Social and cultural diversity in distance education. In T. Evans, M. Haughey, & D. Murphy (Eds.), *International handbook of distance education* (pp. 51-70). Bingley, England: Emerald Group Publishing.

Kahiigi, E. K., Ekenberg, L., Hanson, H., Danielson, M., & Tusubira, F. F. (2008). *An explorative study of e-learning in developing countries: A case of the Uganda education system*. Paper presented at the IADIS International Conference e-Learning 2008. Amsterdam, Netherlands. Retrieved from http://www.iadis.net/dl/final_uploads/200805R100.pdf

Kato, H., Eron, L., Maani, J., Otto, A. Y., Okumu, S. A., Bunoti, S., & Cula, A. (2007). The impact of a one-year teacher training program in Uganda. *Journal of Distance Learning, 11*, 1.

Kimani, M. (2011, June 12). Huge East African budgets... but will they spur growth, create jobs, lower cost of living? *The East African Paper.* Retrieved from http://www.theeastafrican.co.ke/news/-/2558/1179086/-/o1vvbcz/-/index.html

King, K., McGrath, S., & Rose, P. (2007). Beyond the basics: Educating and training out of poverty. *International Journal of Educational Development, 27*, 349-357.

King, K. P. (2001). Educators revitalize the classroom "Bulletin Board": A case study of the influence of online dialogue on face-to-face classes from an adult learning perspective *Journal of Research on Computing in Education, 33*(4), 337-354.

Kozulin, A., Gindis, B., Ageyev, V. S., & Miller, S. M. (Eds.). (2003). *Vygotsky's educational theory in cultural context*. New York, NY: Cambridge University Press.

Lauglo, J. (2009). Research for TVET policy development. *International Handbook of Education for Changing World of Work, 4*(6), 891-904. doi:10.1007/978-1-4020-5281-1_60

Leary, J., & Berge, Z. L. (2006). Trends and challenges of eLearning in national and international agricultural development. *International Journal of Education and Development using Information and Communication Technology, 2*(2), 51-59.

Liang, X. (2004). *Uganda tertiary education sector report. African Region Human Development Working Paper Series*. Washington, DC: The World Bank. Retrieved from siteresources.worldbank.org/AFRICAEXT/Resources/no_50.pdf

Merriam, S. B., Caffarella, R. S., & Baumgartner, L. M. (2007). *Learning in adulthood: A comprehensive guide* (3rd ed.). San Francisco, CA: Jossey-Bass.

Mondal, W. I. (2009). Poverty alleviation and microcredit in sub-Saharan Africa. *International Business & Economics Journal, 8*, 1.

Müller, U., Carpendale, J., I., M., Budwig, N., & Sokol, B. (Eds.). (2008). *Social life and social knowledge: toward a process account of development.* New York, NY: Taylor & Francis Group, LLC.

Oketch, M.O., & Rolleston, C.M. (2007). *Policies on free primary and secondary education in East Africa: A review of the literature.* Centre for International Education: Sussex School of Education, University of Sussex [Research Monograph No 10, CREATE]. Retrieved from http://www.create-rpc.org/pdf_documents/PTA10.pdf

Park, M., G. (2005, September). Building human resource highways through vocational training. Responses to the challenges of the labor market and the workplace. Retrieved from http://www.unevoc.net/fileadmin/user_upload/docs/8-Park.pdf

Parry, K. (2009). The story of a library: Research and development in an African village. *Teachers College Record, 111*, 9.

Pincas, A. (2001). Culture, cognition, and communication in global education. *Distance Education, 22*, 1.

Reiser, R. A. (1987). Instructional technology: A history. In R. M. Gagne (Ed.), *Instructional technology: Foundations* (pp. 11-48). Hillsdale, NJ: Erlbaum.

Reiser, R. A. (2001). A history of instructional design and technology: Part 1: A history of instructional media. *Educational Technology Research and Development, 49*(1), 53-64.

Richey, R. C. (2008). Reflections on the 2008 AECT definitions of the Field. *TechTrends, 54*(1), 38-46.

Riel, M., & Fulton, K. (2001). Technology's role in supporting learning communities for the new millennium. *Kappan, 82*(7), 518-523.

Sikwibele, A. L., & Mungoo, J. K. (2009). Distance learning and teacher education in Botswana: Opportunities and challenges, *International Review of Research in Open and Distance Learning, 10*(4), 1-16.

Thakrar, J., Zinn, D., & Wolfenden, F. (2009). Harnessing open educational resources to the challenges of teacher education in sub-Saharan Africa. *International Review of Research in Open and Distance Learning, 10*(4), 1-15.

Uganda Bureau of Statistics. (2010). Statistical Abstract Report. Retrieved from http://www.ubos.org/onlinefiles/uploads/ubos/pdf%20documents/2010StatAbstract.pdf

United Nations Development Programme Uganda (UNDP Uganda). (2010). *Millennium Development Goals Report for Uganda.* Retrieved from http://www.undp.or.ug/mdgs/25

United Nations Children's Fund (UNICEF). (2010). *The central role of education in the Millennium Development Goals.* Paris, France: UNESCO. Retrieved from http://www.unesco.org/fileadmin/MULTIMEDIA/HQ/ED/ED_new/images/education_for_all_international_coordination_new/PDF/analyticalnote.pdf

Wolff, L. (2002). The African virtual university: The challenge of higher education development in sub-Saharan Africa. *TechKnowLogia, 4*(2), 23-25.

CHAPTER 17

LEARNING TO LEAD

Leveraging Social Capital, Social Learning, and Social Media in Leadership Development

Carmela R. Nanton

The task of leadership is not to put greatness into people, but to elicit it, for the greatness is there already.

—John Buchan

In the next decade, more than 60% of top managers and executives will be retiring as Baby Boomers continue their exit from the workforce (Kliesen, 2005). Organizations of all types are concerned at the looming prospect of losing their most valuable workers in an unprecedented knowledge drain across all sectors of society. Despite these projections, it would appear that many organizations are not prepared for this inexorable workforce transition as formal leadership development and succession planning programs are not in place. Bieschke (2006), for example, referring to a recent study where 94% of the companies surveyed were without a succession plan, posits that "many organizations are one step away from extinction" (p. 1). Bieschke contends that the lack of formal succession planning programs in contemporary organizations places many of them on a fast track to insignificance. In a dynamic, ever-changing external environment, it then becomes imperative for organizations wanting to remain viable in today's complex economic environment, and into the future, to provide developmental frameworks. Within these organizational frameworks, promising or high potential workers can engage in learning how to lead, or leadership development.

THE CHALLENGE OF
LEADERSHIP DEVELOPMENT IN THE 21ST CENTURY

How then can organizations prepare for the inevitable? Strategic leadership is going to be required because leadership in contemporary society is occurring in an unprecedented volatile, complex, and dynamic context. Griffin (2008) contends that strategic leadership has the "capability to understand the complexities of both the organization and its environment and to lead change in the organization in order to achieve and maintain a superior alignment between the organization and its environment" (p. 341). A vital part of this strategic organizational milieu is leadership development, the nexus where social learning, social capital, and social media converge. Leadership development, according to Nanton (2011), is "the personal or organizational initiative(s) put in place utilizing strategic relational partnerships between leader and follower to impart leadership knowledge" (p. 3).

Therefore, the purpose of this chapter is to highlight social cognitive learning as a critical form of adult learning in leadership development. The chapter further explores the roles that social capital networks and social media play as agentic facilitators of the leader development process. The discussion will focus on how leadership knowledge can be acquired and retained, and it will address how leaders locally or globally can leverage social cognitive learning as a learning method for acquiring that knowledge (Bandura, 1969; Latham, 2007; Merriam, Caffarella, & Baumgartner, 2007). Then the roles of social capital networks (Burgess, 2009; Falzer, 2007; Nanton, 2009), and social media (Considine, 2009; Hare, 2009; Jue, Marr, & Kassotakis, 2010; Wenger, 2009) will be presented as two essential methods for leadership development for succession planning in contemporary organizations.

Leadership Theory and Leadership Development

One of the reasons for the dire state of organizational succession planning today is the decades-old but enduring debate over whether leadership is premised on innate traits or whether it is based on that which is learned and developed. This debate continues to persist even though highly successful and effective leaders have emerged or arisen over the years who did not necessarily fit the typical trait approach to leadership. According to Northouse (2010), there is value to this trait approach to leadership because "the average individual in the leadership role is different from an average group member with regard to the following eight traits: intelligence, alertness, insight, responsibility, initiative, persistence, self-confidence, and sociability" (p. 16). The focus on leader traits has also survived the discipline's transitions to skills theories, and relational theories. Today, according to Northouse, leader traits are enjoying a resurgence of interest if we consider the emphasis on *social intelligence* as a leader characteristic in charismatic, transformational, and servant leader theories.

Zaccaro's (2002) definition of social intelligence includes both capabilities and abilities. Zaccaro, (as cited in Northouse, 2010), states that leaders have such "capabilities as social awareness, social acumen, self-monitoring, and the ability to select and enact the best response given the contingencies of the situation and social environment" (p. 18). The significance of this skillset to leadership development is that social intelligence is an essential component for strategic leadership effectiveness, and it is a critical component of the learning that occurs in leadership development programs.

The challenge this poses for the leadership development is that the personal capabilities are not so easily taught and or developed. For the most part, these characteristics, along with work experience and educational preparation, are usually already evident in high-potential candidates. However, the abilities listed in the second part of the definition can be modeled and acquired by high potential candidates through social learning and are better placed in the skills theories category because they "can be learned and developed" (Northouse, 2010, p. 39).

When social learning is introduced into the discussion, there is further acknowledgment that in leadership development, whether in formal or informal settings, some form of teaching and learning is taking place. Thus, in keeping with the focus on leadership development, aspiring leaders need to have one additional characteristic or trait not usually added to the list of leadership characteristics: *teachability*. A thought-provoking opportunity for linking leadership development and adult learning is readily apparent.

LEADERSHIP DEVELOPMENT AND ADULT LEARNING

The intent of leadership development for succession planning is the strategic transfer of knowledge, skill sets, and leader behaviors from leaders to followers. This knowledge transfer is to prepare the next generation of leaders to seamlessly transition into leadership positions when the opportunity arises and to ensure the organization's viability. Even though there is no systematic way or universal leadership development program applicable across all disciplines and organizations, there are some overarching concepts that can be tailored to fit each situational context. One of these is the type of adult learning that is taking place.

There is no doubt that contemporary leadership development is occurring in a fluid, complex, dynamic, and sometimes volatile social environment. Thus, it is imperative that the complexity of the learning process that is occurring, and the learning context in which the learning occurs, are addressed. Greeno (1997) captures this complexity by arguing that "... all learning involves socially organized activity" and, as such, the focus needs to be on "what kinds of complex, social activities to arrange, for which aspects of participation, and in what sequence to use them" (p. 10). Leadership development is the acquisition of skills needed for leading in an increasingly complex social environment. The adult learning theory that specifically integrates learning and the environmental context is social learning.

SOCIAL LEARNING AND LEADERSHIP DEVELOPMENT

Organizations have utilized learning methods over the years that have required observation of modeled behaviors and decision making in specific situations. This form of observational learning is called social learning (Bandura, 1969, 2000). Familiar formal and informal forms of social learning in today's organizations include techniques like on-the-job-training, collaborative problem solving teams, the pairing of new hires with seasoned mentors, or membership in an interdisciplinary team (Lassiter & Zervas, 2007). Each of these forms involves the learning by individuals through exposure to another's behavior, decision making and experience in a social context.

Social cognitive learning theory (Bandura, 2000) provides a realistic method for follower development through observation, modeling, and feedback on leadership behaviors in specific situations and contexts. Social learning also incorporates the salient social and relational elements of leadership development and presumes prerequisite experience and knowledge in the high potential candidate. The social cognitive learning orientation, according to Merriam, Caffarella, and Baumgartner (2007), is an integrative blend of the change in behavior expected in the behaviorist orientation and the mental processes and social environment in the cognitivist orientation.

Thus, social cognitive learning as a basis for succession planning is appropriate, arguably because the skills and characteristics of leadership behavior for specific organizational contexts are not based on objective knowledge alone. Rather, they are directly influenced by and dependent on, the mentor, the behavior to be learned, and the nuanced situational context in which it is occurring. The social learning relationship is the place where new knowledge is transmitted and acquired from integrating experiences, the opinions of the model-expert, and feedback on judgments and decisions made or observed (Marsick, & Watkins, 1999; Senge, 2006). This knowing involves the "competence that our communities have established over time ... and our ongoing experience of the world as a member (in the context of a given community and beyond)" (Wenger, 2009, p. 227). Wenger (2009) further points out that "socially defined competence is always in interplay with our experience. It is in this interplay that learning takes place" (p. 226) and new knowledge is translated into competence. According to Marsick and Watkins (1999) "powerful mental filters help people to select and interpret stimuli to create meaning from what they experience" (p. 80), allowing them to personalize their knowledge. This personalized knowledge, acquired in the social learning process, is that which translates into personal development. Candidates' acquisition of new mental filters and new skill in interpreting stimuli from the experience also expands their potential for making new meaning from the learning that is taking place.

The Social Cognitive Learning Process

Social cognitive learning (Bandura, 2000) fosters follower development through observation of modeled leadership behavior. The salience of this theory in the leadership development setting is the overt recognition of the reciprocal interaction between learning, behavior, and context. Bandura's (1986) model of *"triadic reciprocality,"* where the individual's "behavior, cognitive, and other personal factors and environmental events all operate as interacting determinants of each other," is the basis of this form of learning (p. 18). A leadership candidate's behavior is often the cumulative effect of internal and external factors interacting in a reciprocal way. For example, personal factors, such as the individual's education, previous experiences, or intuition serve to inform their reaction to the surrounding environment and or the events that are occurring. The resulting knowledge that he or she accumulates from integrating these elements is the ability to make the appropriate decision or take the desired action. Neither of the three components operates independently as the decision or action occurs; rather, the behavior (decision or action) is the cumulative result of all three elements. Personal factors coupled with the individual's knowledge base serve to inform the behavioral response in a particular situation: what they know shapes how they behave in a given situation. The relationship between these three components is interactive and reciprocal in their effect on each other and ultimately on the eventual outcome. Latham (2007) presents it as "reciprocal determinism among a person's cognitions, behavior and the environment" (p. 119), where it is recognized that manifested behavior can also be the result of external causation. Consequently, social learning that is based on observing another's behavior can serve in professional settings to shed light on "social role acquisition and the nature of mentoring" that occurs in the leadership development process (Merriam, Caffarella, & Baumgartner, 2007, p. 290).

The Observational Process of Social Learning

Upwardly mobile individuals or those aspiring to future leadership responsibility will work consciously or unconsciously to emulate the behaviors of their leaders (Bandura, 1969). Individuals engage in social learning by endeavoring to learn, adopt, or take their cues from the behaviors of those who are in power, believing that those behaviors will grant them the same recognition, power, and control over the same or similar resources that the leader has. The context of leadership development it is no different: the lure of power, management, and responsibility for departments, divisions, resources, or the entire company is a powerful incentive. In the three-part observational process, responses are created from underlying cues picked up by the observer who categorizes and stores the behavioral patterns and responses in such a way that they can be easily retrieved and demonstrated at the appropriate time; here is also where the observer begins to identify with the one who models the behavior (Bandura, 1969). The observational sequence includes attention, retention, and motoric processes.

Attention Processes

The observer pays close attention to the behavior being modeled in order to recognize relevant stimuli and to accurately perceive cues. The observer then must take incoming information, codify it into words and or images, and translate it into a format (mental models) that can be personalized, linked to memory, retrieved and reproduced (Bandura, 1969).

Prior training and knowledge, along with repeated exposure to modeling stimuli, reinforces candidates' development of situational factor priorities. Once individuals can identify which factors take priority, prior experience can make creating the appropriate perceptual sequences easier and facilitate future demonstration of the desired behavior.

Retention Processes

During this phase, the candidate internalizes and translates observed behavior into symbolic codes that are associated with the behavior *and* situational factors. This allows for easy retrieval of the actual and observed behavior under the right conditions (Bandura, 1969). In leadership development, the retention process is particularly relevant because much of the observed behavior learned by the candidates is for future demonstration. The knowledge that is created is personalized, internalized, and sifted through cultural, gender, and generational filters, which can have significant influence on how that behavior is codified and whether it is effectively reproduced in real life or similar situations.

Motoric Reproduction

Here the content codes created during the retention process are used for self-instruction during overt performance opportunities, demonstrating the learner's ability to correctly combine and sequence newly acquired behaviors into the development of new behavioral patterns. This is known as a "response sequence" (Bandura, 1969, p. 223). The response sequences are added to the repertoire of the observer, remaining there as part of new mental models that are created. It is here that the social learning process can be aborted if the candidate does not get an opportunity to reproduce learned behaviors. However, if the candidate has developed or been introduced to social capital networks, career advancement and opportunities for reproducing newly acquired behaviors have greater potential to occur.

SOCIAL CAPITAL NETWORKS AND LEADERSHIP DEVELOPMENT

One of the most advantageous outcomes of social learning and leadership development is the social capital network(s) that the high-potential candidate develops as part of the experience. Social capital, according to Putnam (1993), refers to the "features of social organization, such as networks, norms, and trust that facilitate coordination and cooperation for mutual benefit" (p. 35). Lin (2001) points out that individuals engage in networking and interactions for specific returns on their investment. The networks can be formal or informal means by which individuals can gain access to resources "through affiliations, contacts, and services allowing them to gain knowledge and information essential for achieving their goals" (Nanton, 2009, p. 14).

For aspiring leaders, information benefits in the organization can include upcoming projects or anticipated organizational changes, new behavioral criteria, or advancement opportunities. Benefits can also include increased bargaining (and decision making) power to key players in well-connected networks. Membership in networks can also strengthen credibility, by making "visible individual's assets that may not be apparent to those who do not hold membership in that person's networks and social relations" (Lin, 2001, p. 7). This network membership makes them more visible to those who would otherwise not know that they can bring benefit to the organization.

Falzer's (2007) *structural holes theory* illustrates the concept of social capital from the comparative framework of dense and weak ties. Weak ties are non-redundant, nonintense loose social networks. Falzer contends that individuals' social capital is based on their "ability to traverse this patchwork and establish nonredundant interpersonal relationships" (p. 36). The nonredundant relationships create a broader network which can potentially result in greater opportunity for career advancement. Nanton (2009) notes that "a collaborative context of social networks enhances, rather than diminishes, the [individual's] self-determination and ability to self-manage" (p. 16). Thus, social networks can improve the high potential candidate's ability to develop effective behaviors, and provide the greatest potential for attaining desired goals.

Social networks then are a vital part of the learning context for the individual being prepared through succession planning. The mentor-model, for example, becomes part of the protégé's dense network ties, contributing to his or her personal development. The mentor model also provides a critical link in response to the protégé's need for loose ties networks, that ensures connectedness, a sense of belonging, credibility, and the creation of similar perceptions and attitudes in the emerging leader (Nanton, 2009). In leadership development settings, high potential candidates could be strategically assisted with, and connected to, networks that are structured and durable enough for them to engage in and learn specific norms and behaviors that translate into beneficial relationships and recognition for them. By combining social cognitive learning with social networking, high-potential leaders can also be taught how to leverage the network relationships for their benefit and advancement. One rapidly growing source of social capital networks in leadership development is social media. How this phenomenon can enhance leadership development is the next focus of attention.

SOCIAL MEDIA AND LEADERSHIP DEVELOPMENT

Over the last decade, social media has grown rapidly and exponentially. Technology and social media (Facebook, Twitter, blogs (web-based logs), chat, or professional communities) have facilitated extensive formal and informal social networks for millions (Jue, Marr, & Kassotakis, 2010; Woog, 2009). The entire landscape of learning has been transformed, and the learning that takes place in the leadership development process is not excluded. According to Burgess (2009), "social networking sites are inter-active, user-driven, and spontaneous" (p. 65). Membership is based on self-enrollment, and there is constant communication "via chat, email, and other media forms" such as video technology (p. 65). With access to net-works and learning communities through weblogs or videos on YouTube, leadership development programs can be creative in the methods that are used for designing learning based on the communities of practice.

Wenger's (2009) concept of *communities of practice* clearly links social cap-ital and social media to social learning. Wenger contends that in commu-nities of practice "social units of learning" are developed along three dimensions of importance: "joint enterprise, relationships of mutuality, and shared repertoires of communal resources" (p. 229). These social units become network resources for members of the community, or network.

These communities of practice can emerge locally or globally as social learning systems for leadership development. For example, they can be collaborative structured forums for selected candidates to participate in leadership development programs, or they can be local or global virtual groups that engage in thought leadership and simulated decision making exercises within or outside the organization. Wenger (2009) explains that "mutuality: the depth of social capital" is based on reciprocated mutual engagement, trust, and norms" and that the three dimensions are interac-tive "basic building blocks of social learning" (p. 229).

Social Media and Social Learning

The learning that can occur in social media settings has a level of immediacy, transparency, speed, and exponential reach that none of the other forms of learning can equally emulate. A different leadership devel-opment context is created when unlimited access via the Internet is included. Participants are free to engage in learning to lead whether they are local or global. Social media has the potential to abbreviate the social cognitive learning cycle, even as it fulfills all the requisite theoretical com-ponents originally outlined by Bandura (1986). The learning is for the most part vicarious as the parties are usually at a considerable distance from each other. Yet, because of technology, the individuals in the per-sonal videos that are published world-wide can become real-time models. The self-regulation is based on the consequences that result from the behaviors, though the ability to self-regulate is not as easily managed "through observation of other people's behavior and its consequences for the observer" (p. 392). In this case, imitation is not necessarily separated from the observation, which is one of Bandura's central arguments as it relates to social learning. Rather, the observed behavior and learning is immediately imitated by the observer based on observed consequences.

Social Media and Social Capital

Communities of practice also become the emerging leader's social capital network. Beyond the learning that occurs, the members in the community also become facilitators of career advancement providing opportunities to practice newly acquired leadership skills. Social media can certainly be conceptualized as an agent for social capital development if Wenger's (2009) communities of practice is considered as contributing to "the social perceptions of reality" (Considine, 2009, p. 66). It is imperative that businesses and society become media literate for survival. Woog (2009) points out that social media serves as a communication tool that allows organizations and individuals to collaborate, access, and exchange information.

The powerful impact of social media on all aspects of contemporary society has resulted in significant and crucial impact on leadership practice. The changing nature of follower expectations of leadership and the implications for leadership development and succession planning is starkly evident on the world stage in the Middle East. Zhuo, Wellman, and Yu's (2011) illustration make the link between social media and social capital and social learning. They contend that in Egypt the "internet helped to maintain strong and weak network ties for political mobilization" (p. 6), and that social media was used to "form linkages with kindred networks elsewhere" (p. 7). In this context of change and emerging leadership, Zhuo, Wellman, and Yu (2011) point out that social media "was naturally integrated into the movement" serving to "build a sense of community and minimize [the] feeling of isolation (p. 8) as the leadership transition took place. This critical situation sets up the context for social learning to take place where Bandura's *triadic reciprocity* (1986) can be revisited. Bandura points out that "behavior" [protesting against current leadership practice], "cognitive and other personal factors" [social media, living conditions, education, desperation and valor], "and environmental events" [neighboring countries' recent success in similar endeavors] all operate as interacting determinants of each other" (p. 18). Social media creates added value with a proliferation of some unlikely but very robust and viable social networks across many communities.

SOCIAL LEARNING THE NEXT GENERATION: IMPLICATIONS FOR LEADERSHIP DEVELOPMENT

With the advent of social media, the definition of social learning has been reconceptualized; social learning in the 21st century has come into its own! Bandura's initial conceptual vision of social learning also has effectively responded to the critiques leveled against it. Thus, social learning is still a relevant form of adult learning in leadership development settings. This generation has fulfilled all that Bandura envisioned it to be in terms of learning that comes from the interaction of the learner, the context, and the behavior, especially when using social media forums.

Learning via social media is virtual and vicarious with immediate application opportunity. The learner and model need not be present with each other during the observation process. The observer sees the model's behavioral consequences and engages in their own self-regulatory behavior, since there is limited ability to ask questions or to receive feedback. Social networks are considered to be essential for developing leadership skills and attaining leadership positions because of their role in facilitating and sustaining the learning which has been acquired and translating it into demonstrable skills.

A network of like-minded colleagues, learning communities, or groups can be formed to augment modeled or collaborative experiences. The networks can also provide opportunities to collaborate on projects, or practice thought leadership and decision making. Social capital networks now begin to function as *bridging capital* (Burgess, 2009). Bridging networks function as safety nets that mitigate the challenges of transitioning from the old networks to the new ones. As participants of leadership development programs acquire new skills, the bridging networks can also reduce the stress of re-negotiating preexisting network relationships. Bridging networks maintain and sustain newly formed leader identities as developing leaders prepare for the personal demands of the desired career advancement (Nanton, 2009).

Social media further provides a structured forum for learning communities, that may be beneficial if aligned with the vision of the organization. One practical utility of social media is as an effective way to seek and advertise career advancement positions. It also is a forum for collaborative learning communities, a structured space for facilitating thought leadership groups, and a private space for mentoring and leadership coaching in succession planning. Social media also makes it possible for the diffuse global networks, which are analogous to Falzer's (2007) loose ties, to be transformed into virtual dense ties. The result is that strong close and redundant relationships are developed with individuals that have never seen or interacted with each other outside social media learning communities.

Ultimately, strategic leadership demands being proactive about succession planning. In organizations where older workers are retiring, the knowledge that they have accumulated over time can be strategically transferred to high potential candidates. Contemporary leaders must leverage the new social learning possibilities both inside and outside the organization made available through social media. The social capital networks that are built can further be used for the benefit of high-potential candidates and the company as they continue to advance their careers.

REFERENCES

Bandura, A. (1969). Social-learning theory of identificatory processes. In D. A. Goslin (Ed.), *Handbook of socialization theory and research* (pp. 213-261). New York, NY: Rand McNally.

Bandura, A. (1986). *Social foundations of thought and action: A social cognitive theory.* Englewood Cliffs, NJ: Prentice Hall.

Bandura, A. (2000). Social cognitive theory: An agentic perspective. *Annual Review of Psychology, 52,* 1-26.

Bieschke, M. D. (2006). Five succession planning values to keep your organization alive. *Leadership Advance Online, 6,* 1-4.

Burgess, K. (2009). Social networking technologies as vehicles of support for women in learning communities. *New Directions for Adult and Continuing Education, 122,* 63-71. doi:10.1002/ace.335

Considine, D. M. (2009, March/April). From Gutenberg to Gates: Media matters. *The social studies.* Philadelphia, PA: Heldref Publications, Taylor & Francis.

Falzer, P. R. (2007). Developing and using social capital in public mental health. *Mental Health Review, Psychology Module, 12*(3), 34-42.

Greeno, J. G. (1997). On claims that answer the wrong questions. *Educational Researcher, 26*(1), 5-17.

Griffin, R. W. (2008). *Fundamentals of management* (5th ed.). Boston, MA: Houghton Mifflin.

Hare, B. (2009). Does your social class determine your online social network? *Social Media.* Retrieved from http://www.cnn.com/2009/TECH/science/10/13/social.networking.class/index.html?iref=allsearch

Jue, A. L., Marr, J. A., & Kassotakis, M. E. (2010). *Social media at work: How networking tools propel organizational performance.* San Francisco, CA: Jossey Bass.

Kliesen, K. L. (2005). The region [Review of the book *The Coming Generational Storm: What you need to know about America's economic future*]. Federal Reserve Bank of St. Louis.

Lassiter, D., & Zervas, M. (2007). *Grow your own—The way to get the best leaders.* Retrieved from http://www.leadershipadvantage.com/growyourown.html

Latham, G. P. (2007). *Work motivation: History, theory, research, and practice. Foundations for Organizational Science.* Thousand Oaks, CA: SAGE.

Lin, N. (2001). *Social capital: A theory of social structure and action.* Cambridge, England: Cambridge University Press.

Marsick, V. J., & Watkins, K. E. (1999). *Facilitating learning organizations: Making learning count*. Brookfield, VT: Gower.

Merriam, S., Caffarella, R., & Baumgartner, L. (2007). *Learning in adulthood: A comprehensive guide* (3rd ed.). San Francisco, CA: Jossey Bass.

Nanton, C. R. (2009). Ties that bind: Cultural referent groups and coping strategies for adult women as learners.*New Directions for Adult and Continuing Education, 122*, 13-22. doi:10.1002/ace.330

Nanton, C. R. (2011). Creating leadership legacy: Social learning and leadership development. *The International Journal of Learning, 17*(12), 181-193.

Northouse, P. G. (2010). *Leadership theory and practice* (5th ed.). Thousand Oaks, CA: SAGE.

Putnam, R. D. (1993) The prosperous community: Social capital and public life. *The American Prospect, 13*, 35-42.

Senge, P. M. (2006). *The fifth discipline: The art and practice of the learning organization*. New York, NY: Doubleday.

Wenger, E. (2009). Communities of practice and social learning systems. *Organization, 7*, 225-246. doi:10.1177/135050840072002.

Woog, A. (2009). *Mark Zuckerberg: Facebook creator*. Farmington Hills, MI: Cengage Learning.

Zaccaro, S. J. (2002). Organizational leadership and social intelligence. In R. E. Riggio, S. E. Murphy, & F. J. Pirozzolo (Eds.), *Multiple intelligences and leadership* (pp. 29-54). Mahwah, NJ: Lawrence Erlbaum Associates.

Zhuo, X., Wellman, B., & Yu, J. (2011, Jul/Sep). Egypt: The first internet revolt. *Peace Magazine, 27*(3), 6-10. Retrieved from http://www.peacemagazine.org/archive/v27n3p06.htm

SECTION V

MEANINGFUL ASSESSMENT OF PROGRAMS FOR ADULTS

CHAPTER 18

DEMONSTRATING THE VALUE OF LIFELONG LEARNING THROUGH OUTCOMES ASSESSMENT RESEARCH

Frank DiSilvestro and Henry S. Merrill

Today, increasing numbers of adult learners have a variety of reasons for pursuing lifelong learning by returning to college or university degree programs. These reasons include keeping or improving skills, learning new skills, requirements by employers, promotion or raise, change in job or career, or the need for a certificate or license (Boeke & Paulson, 2006). Yet, the U.S. Census (2009) reported that only 27.5% of the U.S. population age 25 and above had a bachelor's degree or higher. The Lumina Foundation for Education recognized these lifelong learning needs of adults and made a significant commitment to advance adult degree completion in higher education. The goal of the Lumina Foundation (2010) is to increase the proportion of Americans with high-quality degrees or credentials to 60% by the year 2025. This is an ambitious but important goal for the first quarter of the 21st century since recent employment projections from the Bureau of Labor Statistics (2009) suggest that 33% of all job openings and nearly 50% of all new jobs created between 2008 and 2018 will require a postsecondary degree or credential.

Conversations About Adult Learning in Our Complex World, pp. 271–286
Copyright © 2013 by Information Age Publishing
All rights of reproduction in any form reserved.

The need for lifelong learning is clear (Georgetown Center on Education in the Workforce, 2006; Lumina Foundation, 2010; U.S. Bureau of Labor Statistics, 2009). However, in the quest to address this need, it is not only important to develop lifelong learning programs, but equally important to assess the outcomes of these programs. An important research question, therefore, is how can we demonstrate the benefits and value of lifelong learning for adults through our efforts in higher education? The call for accountability in postsecondary education created a form of institutional research that became known as outcomes assessment. This shifts the focus from the input side of institutional resources to the output or outcomes side. Outcomes assessment research investigates what happens as a result of the expenditure of the resources during the educational process. The undergraduate education mission is the largest sector for most institutions, so the focus on outcomes assessment is primarily focused on this sector. Volkwein (1999) provides this useful description:

> Simply put, the institutional goal should be the improvement of student learning and growth. Campuses need to carry out assessment and self-evaluation not for external accountability but for internal enhancement. Outcomes assessment does not judge undergraduate education but improves it. Faculty, especially, identify with this emphasis. (p. 16)

In this passage, Volkwein describes a framework for continuous improvement cycles in the context of postsecondary education. Institutional programs and resources are reviewed in the context of effective learning outcomes at every level: school/program, department, degree(s), and even individual courses.

Alumni surveys are often recommended as a method of collecting data for outcomes assessment. Borden (2005) described the limited purposes of alumni surveys in the decentralized and segmented efforts of a large university. Indiana University, with its eight campuses dispersed across the state delivering a wide variety of degrees in traditional arts and sciences schools and professional schools, is one example. Borden described the development of an alumni survey for undergraduates used regularly since 1994 at the Indiana University Purdue University Indianapolis campus. Despite this example of a long-term undergraduate alumni research project, Borden notes that there has been little success in establishing nationally benchmarked studies. Alumni research seems to be done primarily at the school, program or department, or degree level.

One approach to demonstrating the benefits and value of lifelong learning for adults is studying the important question of what graduates do with an undergraduate degree or a graduate degree designed for adult learners. The research described in this chapter describes two outcomes assessment research studies focusing on degree programs designed for adult learners. The first study focuses on alumni of the Indiana University undergraduate general studies degree. The second project focuses on alumni of an Indiana University master's degree in adult education. Both studies shed light on the value of lifelong learning for adults.

The General Studies Degree

The Indiana University general studies degree is offered at two levels; the 2 year associate's degree (associate of arts in general studies, AAGS) and the 4 year bachelor's degree (bachelor's of general studies, BGS). The general studies degree is an option that is particularly appealing to adult learners who may have full time jobs or family responsibilities, who need greater freedom in timing and pacing their education, and who need a variety of learning options.

The degree has no major; rather, it is an interdisciplinary degree that includes courses from the arts and humanities, social and behavioral sciences, and mathematics and natural sciences within a flexible degree requirement structure. This allows students to develop their own individualized plan of study to meet their unique goals. This highly flexible degree allows students to transfer previously earned college credit and to earn college credit for self-acquired competency through prior learning assessment. In addition, students may earn the degree in a variety of ways: entirely at a distance through the university-wide office, at one of the eight campuses throughout the state, or by combining distance learning with on-campus instruction.

Research Study One: What Do Graduates Achieve With a General Studies Bachelor's Degree?

Research Study One investigated what alumni accomplished after completing an undergraduate degree in general studies and what they thought about the degree program. The two overarching research questions were: What do alumni do with a general studies degree in terms of employment and further education? What do general studies alumni think of the general studies degree program?

Methodology, Sample and Data Collection

This study utilized a mixed methods research approach to draw from the strengths of qualitative and quantitative research (Johnson & Onwuegbuzie, 2004). Written surveys were used to obtain data from both AAGS and BGS graduates and telephone interviews were used to obtain additional in-depth information from BGS graduates who volunteered to be interviewed. The specific questions asked of graduates both in the written survey and the volunteer interviews are described in the results section.

The print surveys, with enclosed self-addressed return envelopes, were mailed in 2005 to 4,572 Indiana University School of Continuing Studies general studies graduates at the associate and bachelor's degree levels. Included were graduates from all IU campuses, as well as graduates who had completed their degree at a distance. The Indiana University Alumni Association (IUAA) supplied the names and addresses of all graduates from years 2002, 2003, and 2004, plus names and addresses of those who graduated before 2002 who are members of the IUAA. The graduates were asked to provide information related to written survey questions. In addition, 29 BGS graduates volunteered and were selected for in-depth interviews.

The Respondents

Four hundred and seventy-eight (10.7%) general studies graduates who received the survey responded to the survey. The group of 478 respondents may be characterized as recent graduates in that 75.5% had graduated in 2000 or later. Bachelor's of general studies (BGS) degree recipients made up 80% (382) of the respondents, with 20% (96) of the respondents having received the associate of arts in general studies (AAGS). There were 319 (67%) women and 159 (33%) men. The median age at which students received the BGS was 34. The median age at which AAGS students received their degree was 44. Respondents were graduates of School of Continuing Studies divisions on all campuses and of the university-wide school of Indiana University. The university-wide school allows students to take courses at a distance to earn the general studies degree.

Results

Based on tracking of returned mail, it was determined that 98% of the surveys arrived at, or were forwarded to, their destinations. The return rate was 10.7% of delivered surveys. The data reported reflect the combined results of both the AAGS and BGS graduates unless otherwise noted. The following questions (followed by the results) were investigated via the written survey about what graduates did with their undergraduate general studies degree, and about their experience with the degree program.

What Do Graduates Do With a General Studies Degree in Terms of Employment? Three hundred and fifty-three distinct job titles were reported. For purposes of data analysis, information that respondents supplied about their occupations and workplaces was categorized using

the October 2001 standard occupational categories (SOC) of the U.S. Department of Labor Bureau of Labor Statistics (2001). The main SOC categories reported most often were: business and financial operations (20%), Middle Management (14%), office and administrative support (11%), education, library, and training (9%), healthcare practitioners and technician (7%), upper management (6%), Community and social service (5%). A variety of other job titles included categories such as computer and mathematical; sales; arts, design, entertainment, sports, and media (28%).

What Do Graduates Do With a General Studies Degree in Terms of Further Education? Two hundred and thirty-one (48%) respondents reported that they pursued further education after they completed their general studies degree. One hundred and seventy-one (36%) of those pursued further education after earning the BGS, and the remaining sixty (12%) pursued additional education after earning the AAGS. Of the 231 respondents who pursued further education, 107 (46%) reported they pursued further education at 52 colleges and universities. Approximately 40% of those 107 respondents pursued further education at Indiana University. Of the 231 respondents who pursued further education, 117 (51%) reported the specific academic areas they pursued. The data reflect the remarkable range of fields of graduate study pursued by general studies alumni. The area of general studies is included because many general studies AAGS recipients pursued further undergraduate work in the BGS program. The categories reported most often by respondents are: business (25%), liberal arts (16%), general studies (15%), education (12%), and public affairs (7%). A variety of other graduate disciplines included computer science, law, nursing, and library science (25%).

What Types of Postgraduate Degrees Were Earned by General Studies Alumni? Respondents reported earning a total of 85 additional degrees after earning their general studies degrees. The degrees were earned by 74 BGS graduates and by 11 AAGS graduates. Examples of the levels of additional degrees earned include the following:

DBA-Doctor of Business Administration	MLS-Masters of Library Science
Ed D-Doctor of Education	MPA-Masters of Public Administration
JD-Doctor of Jurisprudence	MS-Masters of Science
MBA-Masters of Business Administration	PhD-Doctor of Philosophy

Examples of fields in which additional degrees were earned include the following:

Accounting	Higher Education	Physiology
Business	Human Resources	Psychology
Computer Science	Law	Public Affairs
Education	Library Science	Sociology
Exercise Science	Nursing	Theology

Why Did Graduates Choose The General Studies Degree Program?   Three hundred and ninety-nine respondents (83%) reported a variety of reasons for choosing the General Studies Degree Program. Clearly the predominant reason was the degree's flexibility. Respondents reported choosing the general studies degree because of its flexible scheduling, location, and curriculum (33%), acceptance of prior learning (24%), breadth and options of the degree requirements (12%). A variety of other reasons reported included that it enabled them to graduate sooner, was a reputable degree from IU, and provided an undergraduate degree so they could pursue graduate study (31%).

What Did Graduates Like Most About the General Studies Degree Program?   Three hundred and thirty-eight respondents (71%) reported what they liked most about the general studies degree. Clearly, what the respondents liked most about the degree was, again, its flexibility. Respondents cited the flexibility of degree requirements, curriculum, scheduling, and location (41%), the breadth and options of the degree requirements (26%), and acceptance of prior credits and prior learning (9%). A variety of other reasons for liking the degree included support from faculty, academic advisors, and program administrators (24%).

What Did Graduates Say Contributed Most to Their Success in Earning The General Studies Degree?   Three hundred thirty-five respondents (70%) reported the factors that contributed most toward their success in earning the general studies degree. Respondents cited the support they received as the biggest contributor to their success. Their responses indicated that support from IU advisors, instructors, and staff, as well as support from family and friends, contributed to their success in the general studies degree (42%), the flexibility of the general studies degree requirements, scheduling, location, and selection of courses contributed to their success (20%), personal determination and desire for the degree (12%), and self-discipline and persistence (11%). A wide variety of other reasons for liking the degree accounted for the remaining 21% of responses.

Did the General Studies Degree Meet Their Expectations?   Four hundred and sixty-seven (98%) of the respondents answered the question "Did the General Studies Degree Meet Your Expectations?" As can be

Table 18.1.   Student Expectations of the General Studies Degree

GSD Meet Expectations	Total Respondents	Yes	Percent of Respondents	No	Percent of Respondents
AAGS	95	87	91.6%	8	8.4%
BGS	372	341	91.7%	31	8.3%
All	467	428	91.6%	39	8.4%

seen in Table 18.2 above, 92% of these 467 respondents reported yes while about 8% reported no.

Telephone Interview Research Component. Additional questions were investigated through in-depth telephone interviews with 29 general studies alumni who volunteered via the mail survey. The focus of the interviews was the impact of earning the general studies degree on their educational and career changes. The 29 BGS participants for the telephone interviews were a convenience sample from the survey respondents. In addition to the telephone interview, an analysis of their academic transcripts was completed to determine the specific number of institutions attended, amount of transfer credit, and types of transfer credit (from military service training, CLEP and DANTES examinations, prior learning assessment, as well as regular college credit). The results are organized and reported here by the general questions used for the analysis of academic transcripts and during the interviews.

What Were the Educational Patterns and Levels of Attainment of the BGS Graduates Prior to Enrollment in the BGS Program? Analysis of their academic transcripts showed that all 29 (100%) completed high school in the traditional pattern (no stop-outs or GED completions). After high school graduation, 14 (48%) started working, joined the military, or got married, and 15 (52%) began college coursework. Of these, four (14%) completed their undergraduate degrees within a traditional 4-year time-frame after high school. All 29 (100%) transferred credit from other colleges prior to enrolling in the BGS. Of these, nine (31%) were first generation college graduates. The average age at graduation was 39 (ages ranged from 19 to 67 years).

What Types of Employment Did BGS Graduates Have Prior to Enrollment in the Degree Program? Prior to enrolling in the degree program, the 29 participants had worked at jobs in various employment categories as defined by the U.S. Department of Labor occupational codes (2001). Employment was reported in these categories: 15 (52%) employed in technical/professional occupations, 4 (14%) employed in administrative support positions, and 8 (28%) employed in the labor or service sector. There were two respondents (7%) in their 20s and still establishing careers so they did not match any categories.

Did the Attainment of the BGS Degree Change the Types of Employment of General Studies Graduates?   After completion of their degree, these 29 graduates reported many changes in types of employment, increase in income, and completion of graduate degrees. A total of 20 (69%) had moved to executive, management, or professional specialty occupations, three (10%) were employed in administrative support occupations, five (17%) in service/labor occupations, and one (3%) in a sales occupation. Significant income increases (from 4-400% more than pre-AGS/BGS income) were reported by1 6 (55%) respondents. Nine (31%) reported going on to complete graduate degrees (MBA, MEd., PhD, JD). These results demonstrate a marked change in graduates achieving executive and professional specialty occupations and increased incomes. All participants had graduated with their BGS within the last 16 years, so a variety of factors were at work in terms of career progression in addition to degree completion.

Did the Attainment of the BGS Degree Change the Career Patterns of the Graduates?   Two-thirds of the participants reported that getting a degree allowed them to change their career path. Only a few of the respondents specifically attributed this change to the general studies degree, as might be expected due to the complex number of factors involved in career progression. However, participants reported that completing the degree did open the door to career paths and job opportunities not available previously. Executive leadership and other opportunities for promotion were cited as career path changes since graduation. Several cited going on for graduate study as an outcome of the BGS.

Was Completion of the BGS Part of an Intentional Life Change Strategy?   Several participants reported that earning the degree was part of a larger intentional change process. Respondents cited the following reasons as being most important to them when completing a BGS. The desire to have a degree was reported as most important by 26 (90%) respondents. Other important reasons cited included: desire for personal interest in learning by 23 (31%), convenience of location and times by 19 (66%), needed degree for a career change by 16 (55%). Career change was cited as an important force for over half of the study respondents. However, it should be noted that satisfaction factors of achieving degree completion, the desire to learn, and having accessible education were ranked as being more important to graduates.

The interviews gathered additional qualitative data from graduates about the flexible structure of the degree that enabled them to create a personalized academic path to meet their professional and personal learning goals using transfer credit and many types of course delivery options. These comments were very similar to the comments reported by those completing only the mail survey. This third research focus and telephone interview protocol were based on a multicase study of 12 BGS graduates conducted as dissertation research (Merrill, 1993). The results of this 2005 study showed very similar impact on educational and career patterns, changes in employment, career development, and whether completing the degree was part of an intentional change strategy as found in the earlier research.

Discussion and Conclusions for Research Study One.   Higher education can effectively respond to the need for lifelong learning for adults. It can respond by better matching course offerings and timetables with the needs of adult learners. The general studies degree program is one example of this kind of adult focused degree plan. This study described what graduates accomplished with a general studies degree. The study clearly showed that a general studies degree allowed these students to tailor their academic program to their career interests and prepared them to work in a wide variety of occupations. The graduates in this study reported 353 distinct job titles.

The general studies degree also prepares students to pursue further education. The graduates in this study continued their education in diverse areas, particularly business, liberal arts, and education. They completed advanced degrees at a variety of well-respected universities. The themes of degree flexibility, breadth and options of the degree requirements, support from advisors and faculty, and self-discipline were all factors that contributed to the general satisfaction and success these graduates experienced. Completion of the degree program opened the door to desired career changes, engaged respondents in continuous learning, and empowered graduates by satisfying previously unmet educational goals.

Research Study Two—What Do Graduates Do With a Master's Degree in Adult Education?

The outcomes assessment literature is less often focused at the graduate degree level except for medical and other clinical education. The principles of effective outcomes assessment for undergraduate programs, however, can be adapted to graduate programs. The literature on alumni surveys of graduate programs suggest there are many reasons for gathering information about the impact of degree completion: career development and quality of life; effectiveness of the curriculum and teaching on developing knowledge, skills, abilities and values; accountability for effective use of institutional resources; impact with employers in the field; and gauging alumni satisfaction and interest in continuing engagement with the institution (Borden, 2005; Cabrera, Weerts, & Zulick, 2005; Volkwein, 2010).

There is only one document that focuses on assessment of graduate education for use at the Indiana University Purdue University Indianapolis campus where the degree is located. It is titled "Questions for Departmental Self-Assessment of Graduate Programs" (Queener, 2000). The questions provided in this self-assessment process are divided into these categories: recruitment, academic credentials of matriculated students, placement, advising and mentoring, financial resources, curriculum, and national reputation of the graduate program. The questions in these categories focus on a mix of inputs (recruitment, academic credentials, and financial resources) and the processes that lead to educational outcomes (advising and mentoring; curriculum) and evidence of student learning as judged by placement. Since the rankings and national reputation of a graduate program are influenced by so many factors (inputs, educational processes, a range of faculty accomplishments and student achievement) it is difficult to know how to characterize that category (Volkwein, 2010). The questions in the Indiana University Purdue University Indianapolis campus self-assessment posed about placement category are (Queener, 2000):

- List graduates of your program by current position, title and employing institution; also identify mentor for graduate work.
- How many of your graduates worked full time while pursuing their graduate degree? Part time?
- Did these students receive tuition assistance from their employer?
- How are students advised for placement?
- How typical of your field is your placement record?
- How could your placement be improved? (p. 2)

This is a relatively limited list of questions that seems to identify evidence of learning only by factors related to placement. We know from research on the Capstone Portfolio completed by each adult education graduate in the last 7 years that most of our students are employed full-time while they are working on the degree (Merrill, DiSilvestro, & Johnson, 2008). The few students working part-time or not employed at the time are usually in the process of making a career or life transition. The completion of the MS in adult education is usually an intentional part of that transition. The workforce sectors where these students are generally employed are: postsecondary education (40%); business-HR/training (25%); government/military (10%); and self-employed/consulting (10%). The remaining students (15%) are employed in health/clinical education, positions in non-profit organizations, retail sales, or other transitional jobs.

Methodology, Sample, and Data Collection

The IU School of Continuing Studies used a survey developed by this research team, described above, to gather data on the bachelor's of general studies (BGS) alumni. The survey used for the BGS alumni research project was adapted for this adult education alumni survey project. In May 2010, a two-page survey was mailed to 655 adult education graduates. The mailing list, provided by the IU Alumni Association, included graduates of the program from when the program was offered by the School of Education (approximately 1950-1995) as well as from the years when the School of Continuing Studies has been the location of the program (1996-2011 graduates). The letter mailed to graduates with a paper copy of the survey contained a link for those who wished to complete the survey online.

The IU Adult Education Program has three distinct groups of graduates. Those in the first two groups graduated when the program was located in the IU School of Education. They include: 1) graduates of a doctoral degree program active from the 1950s through the 1980s (program closed in 1983), and 2) graduates of a MS degree program delivered through 1995 in typical evening class meeting format with some weekend classes. The third group contains graduates of the online MS in adult education degree located in the School of Continuing Studies from 1996 to the present. The IU Alumni Association provided valid addresses, and surveys were sent to 655 graduates in all three categories. The response rate was 117 graduates (18%) responding to the survey. The number in each category was: School of Education Doctorates 37 respondents (32%), School of Education MS 40 respondents (34%) and School of Continuing Studies MS 40 respondents (34%).

Current Involvement in Adult and Continuing Education. Graduates were asked to list ways they were currently involved in adult and continuing education. Eighty-seven respondents (74%) reported 101 types of involvement. Thirty respondents (26%) left the question blank or indicated no involvement. We were able to get a detailed look at the types of involvement reported by the 74% who answered the question positively. Their open-ended responses were categorized as follows: teaching/training 47 (48%), counseling/advising 5 (6%), Online learning technology and course design 5 (6%), Volunteering 26 (31%), Part of daily life 17 (20%), taking courses 5 (6%). Note: Respondents gave more than one response so categories will not total to 100%.

The respondents from the early years of the program in the school of education include many graduates who are now retired. We were able to take a closer look at the responses of retirees. There were 34 retired respondents (29% of all respondents), and 17% indicated ways they were involved in adult and continuing education. Ten percent of those mentioned some sort of volunteer work. Thirteen percent did not respond to the question or indicated they were not involved. We noted that two respondents reported disabling illness, and it is fair to assume that some other retirees may be limited by diminished energy or poor health.

The teaching/training involvement was one area of continuity. This category of responses (48%) was distributed across all three groups of alumni respondents, ranging from 43% of the school of education masters alumni to 55% of the SCS MS alumni. Volunteerism was another area of continuity, ranging from a low of 24% for SCS alumni to a high of 38% of the doctoral alumni. Some of this variation might be due to the fact that the more recent SCS alumni are younger, employed, and have less time for volunteer activities than the older alumni who earned doctorates and many are now retired.

There are three areas of discontinuity between the groups in this category of engagement. Only the more recent graduates from the SCS alumni group are employed to this extent in academic counseling/advising roles and engaged in online learning technology and course design. The latter is not surprising since they are graduates of an online degree program and this technology is more prevalent in their careers. A puzzling discontinuity is that only nine percent of the SCS alumni group responded with open-ended comments that were included in the category of being engaged with adult education activities in other types of work or as part of their daily life. The two school of education groups ranged from 23-29%.

Participation in Further Education. The next section of the survey inquired about taking additional courses after completing their degree, about the types of courses completed, and/or enrolling in another degree. Sixty-eight of the respondents (59%) reported pursuing further education after earning the adult education degree. Of these, 64% took credit courses, 36% took noncredit courses, and 9% took both credit and noncredit courses. Overall, this is a group of people who appear to value further learning. The areas selected for further study were education (18%) and a variety of others, including business, management, religion/ministry, nursing and counseling. It is interesting to note that the SCS alumni group participated less (45%) in further learning. However, this group is the only one with respondents who indicated they are pursuing other degrees (21% of this group). This again is not surprising since they are the younger alumni, more likely to be working full-time and pursuing career development strategies.

Reasons for Selecting IU Adult Education Degree.   When asked why they selected this adult education program, 112 people offered 150 reasons. The largest number of respondents (61%) indicated that learning adult education theory and practice relevant to current job responsibilities and career development was most important. The reasons were categorized as follows: learn and acquire skills relevant to current employment (61%), advance or change careers (21%), reputation of the program or a recommendation by a friend or advisor (12%), online course offerings (11%) and the program's flexibility as to time and place (11%). A variety of other reasons included obtain a degree or credential, faculty and staff reputation, and program structure and curriculum. Note: Respondents gave more than one response so categories will not total to 100%.

Impact of Earning the Adult Education Degree.   The survey asked for information about the impact of the degree on employment or career plans as well as the impact of adult education on their life outside the workplace. When asked about the impact of the adult education degree on their employment or career plans, 113 people responded with 140 ways. These impacts were categorized and tabulated as follows: provided career enhancement and advancement opportunities (59%), imparted valuable knowledge and skills (39%), increased credibility and professional respect (6%), no impact (6%), and led to a salary increase (5%). Note: Respondents gave more than one response so categories will not total to 100%.

When asked about the impact of the adult education degree on their life outside the workplace, 81 people responded with 88 ways. These statements were categorized and tabulated as follows: providing intellectual growth and skills (48%), fostering personal growth and increasing self-confidence and esteem (46%), increasing their commitment to adult education (5%), and bringing credibility and increased respect (4%). Note: Respondents made more than one response so categories will not total to 100%.

There are two interesting areas of discontinuity among the groups in two of these categories. The SCS alumni responding indicated less impact in terms of intellectual growth and skills (36% vs. 58% of the school of education M. S. alumni and 52% of the doctoral graduates). In the area of personal growth and self-esteem, 54% of SCS alumni and 52% of doctoral alumni responding indicated impact. In contrast, 35% of the school of education MS indicated impact on their personal growth and self-esteem.

Satisfaction With the IU Adult Education Degree.   The last area to report is the responses when asked what aspects of the degree program they liked or were most satisfied with. In this section, 107 people responded with 149 aspects. It is important to note that some researchers warn of a "halo error" when considering the relationship between alumni reported perceptions of the educational experience and actual outcomes (Pike, 1999). These aspects were categorized and tabulated as follows: faculty and staff (32%), peer interaction and learning from fellow students (21%), application of adult education principles and practicality of the program(17%), flexibility and convenience in regard to time and place (14%), examples of specific courses and course content (12%), online courses (12%), intellectual challenge (8%), flexibility and adaptability of the curriculum (6%), and being respected and treated as adults (6%). Note: Respondents made more than one response so categories will not total to 100%.

DISCUSSION AND CONCLUSION

This second research study was completed in 2010. The results are being reviewed for ideas to strengthen the MS in adult education so it better prepares graduates for the profession. It is interesting to see the areas of continuity that connect the graduates in these three groups even with changes in types of course delivery over the last 50+ years. There are some notable areas of discontinuity across the groups of graduates such as perceptions of impact on intellectual and skills development as well as on personal growth and self-esteem. There are also areas where there appears to be continuity that links program focus, curriculum, and culture across the years between these groups even though faculty and delivery systems have changed over time. Additional research using in-depth interviews would probably yield additional suggestions for program improvements from the SCS alumni group.

The two research projects reported in this chapter focused on investigating the outcomes reported by the alumni of undergraduate and graduate degree programs in the Indiana University School of Continuing Studies. The importance of outcomes assessment to demonstrate the benefits and value of degree programs has become a major focus in higher education during the last three decades. These projects used learning outcomes measures such as where graduates are employed, whether the degree has been of assistance in their career, graduates' reflections on the value of the degree, what they liked about the program and suggested improvement for the graduate program. Overall, this research identified useful ways to investigate the outcomes reported by alumni of these degree programs. This research also demonstrates the variety of benefits on careers and values of lifelong learning reported by the adult learner alumni of these degree programs.

ACKNOWLEDGMENTS

Thanks to Joann B. Alexander, Lester Cook, Cynthia Proffitt, and Susan Tormey for assistance with these research studies.

REFERENCES

Boeke, M, & Paulson, K. (2006). Adult learners in the United States: A national profile, *Informed Practice*. Washington, DC: American Council on Education.

Borden, V. M. H. (2005). Using alumni research to align program improvement with institutional accountability. *New Directions for Institutional Research, 126,* 61-72. doi:10.1002/ir.148

Cabrera, A. F., Weerts, D. J., & Zulick, B. J. (2005), Making an impact with alumni surveys. *New Directions for Institutional Research, 126,* 5-17. doi: 10.1002/ir.144

Georgetown University News Release, (2010). *Report forecasts educated worker shortage by 2018.* Retrieved from http://explore.georgetown.edu/news/?ID=51240

Johnson, R. B., & Onwuegbuzie, A. J. (2004, October). Mixed methods research: A research paradigm whose time has come. *Educational Researcher 30*(7), 14-26.

Lumina Foundation Announcement (2010). *Lumina Foundation's adult degree completion commitment gives millions of recession-battered Americans a "second chance" at earning a degree.* Retrieved from http://www.luminafoundation.org/newsroom/news_releases/2010-09-29.html

Merrill, H. S. (1993). A multicase study of the employment and career patterns and intentional change strategies of adults who completed a nontraditional bachelor's degree. (Ed.D. dissertation, Ball State University, 1993) Dissertations & Theses: A&I database. (Publication No. AAT 9332550).

Merrill, H. S, DiSilvestro, F. D., & Johnson, J. (2008, October). *A capstone portfolio course as assessment in an online masters degree: Reporting on four years of experience.* Paper presented at the meeting of the Midwest Research-to-Practice Conference in Adult, Continuing and Community Education at the University of Western Kentucky, Bowling Green, KY.

Pike, G. R. (1999). The constant error of the halo in educational outcomes research. *Research in Higher Education, 40*(1), 61-86.

Queener, S. (2000). *Questions for departmental self-assessment of graduate programs.* Retrieved from http://www.planning.iupui.edu/assessment/

U.S. Department of Labor, Bureau of Labor Statistics (2009). *Economic news release: employment projections: 2008-2018 summary.* Retrieved from http://www.bls.gov/news.release/ecopro.nr0.htm

U.S. Department of Labor, Bureau of Labor Statistics (2001). *Standard occupational classifications.* Retrieved from http://www.bls.gov/oes/2001/appendix_a.pdf

Volkwein, J. F. (1999). The four faces of institutional research. *New Directions for Institutional Research, 104,* 9-19. doi:10.1002/ir.10401

Volkwein, J. (2010). Assessing alumni outcomes. *New Directions for Institutional Research, 145,* 125-139. doi:10.1002/ir.326

CHAPTER 19

THE POWER OF COLLABORATION IN PROMOTING ADULT STUDENT LEARNING OUTCOMES

Cynthia Tweedell and Audrey Kelleher

The Center for Research in Adult Learning was formed in 2007 as a partnership between the Council of Christian Colleges and Universities (CCCU) and Indiana Wesleyan University. Over 30 institutions have participated in the activities of the center, which include assessment projects, retention projects, an edited volume on best practices in integration of faith and learning for adult and online students, case studies on structuring adult education programs, a website of resources, teleconferences, and an annual conference. This chapter reviews two of these projects and shows how the center's work has been used by institutions to improve their adult learning programs.

According to the U.S. Education Department, 48% of students who started college in the fall of 2009 are nontraditional students who have transferred credits, attended part-time, or stopped out along the way (as cited in Lipka, 2012). The fastest growing sector in higher education is the degree completion program for working adults. Adult education is growing and flourishing, yet there are scant assessment tools designed to benchmark adult programs. In 1999 the Council for Adult and Experiential Education (CAEL) released the findings of a benchmarking study

Conversations About Adult Learning in Our Complex World, pp. 287–299
Copyright © 2013 by Information Age Publishing
All rights of reproduction in any form reserved.

pointing toward best practices in adult learning (Flint & Associates, 1999). This benchmarked institutional practices of "adult learning focused institutions," including the assessment of student learning, faculty roles, decision making, admission, student services, evaluation, and other aspects of program administration. In 2002, CAEL produced a self-evaluation workbook for colleges and universities who wanted to become more adult learning focused (Flint, Zakos, & Frey, 2002). This work sought to set standards for the organization and implementation of adult higher education. Several works have responded to these benchmarks (Bash, 2004; Kasworm, Polson, & Fishback, 2002) Later, CAEL collaborated with Noel-Levitz to produce an Adult Learner Inventory that measured adult student satisfaction (Noel-Levitz, 2011). While the data collected is quite useful to marketers and student service personnel, it does not specifically assess student learning in adult degree completion programs.

The Center for Research in Adult Learning launched projects that are based on this CAEL work, to look specifically at benchmarks for adult student learning outcomes. This chapter will describe two of these projects: A student learning outcomes benchmarking project, and a retention project.

ADULT LEARNING OUTCOMES PROJECT

Many standardized assessment tools exist to help colleges and universities compare their own student learning outcomes with a national sample of primarily traditionally-aged students. But there appear to be no tools that compare learning for students in adult degree completion programs with those in similar programs. This study is one of several projects designed to bridge that gap and provide adult programs the benchmarking information they need in order to maximize student learning outcomes. A task force from eleven colleges and universities with adult programs developed a writing prompt and scoring rubric to measure three learning objectives common to the eleven institutions' adult programs: critical thinking, written communication skill, and Christian world view development. The project has recently completed its fourth year of data collection, and schools are beginning to use the data to improve programs. This project began in 2007 with a conference call among several adult education professionals at schools affiliated with the CCCU. These educators had attended a brainstorming group at Indiana Wesleyan University where they expressed interest in collaborating on a tool to benchmark adult learning outcomes. The participants included: Cynthia Tweedell (Indiana Wesleyan); Karen Harder Klassen (Bluffton); Mary Moretto (Goshen); Shirley Roddy (Mid-America Christian); Julia Carpenter (Mid-

America Christian); Jeremy Roddy (Mid-America Christian); Jud Curry (North Park); Steve Holtrop (Huntington); Bradford Sample (Indiana Wesleyan); George Howell (Indiana Wesleyan). In subsequent phone conversations the following people were added to the task force: Wayne Dell (Master's), Dean Kroeker (Biola), Margie Conner (Trinity International), and Beverly Absher (Union). This task force was interested in benchmarking with one another on some common learning goals. After considerable discussion, it was agreed that each program could benefit by using a common writing prompt to assess written communication, critical thinking, and Christian worldview. Such a technique is supported by best practices in assessment (Huba & Freed, 2000; Palomba & Banta, 1999; Walvoord, 2010). The task force then collected sample rubrics and worked together to design the following simple rubric that would assess these three learning outcomes. This rubric was piloted over the first 3 years of the project and included in Table 19.1 here.

Table 19.1.   Rubric Used for Pilot Study

	Critical Thinking	Christian World View	Communication
5	Frequent analysis of issues Challenges assumptions Thorough analysis	Clearly demonstrates an understanding of a Christian perspective. (Frequent references to biblical principles)	No distracting spelling, punctuation, and grammatical errors. Very well organized Meaning is clear
4	General connections, analysis and identification of issues	Frequently refers to a Christian perspective. Student has a reasonable understanding of Christian perspective. (Some reference to biblical principals.)	Less than one spelling, punctuation and grammatical error per page. Fairly well organized A few places where meaning is a little unclear.
3	Some analysis Vague identification of issue	Makes some mention of a Christian perspective. Student indicates some understanding of a Christian perspective. (Biblical principles referred to somewhat.)	Most spelling, punctuation, and grammar are correct, though some errors remain. Organization may detract from meaning. Some places unclear.

(Table continues on next page)

Table 19.1.   (Continued)

	Critical Thinking	Christian World View	Communication
2	Incomplete analysis	Demonstrates little understanding of a Christian perspective. (Biblical principles hardly or not mentioned.)	Spelling, punctuation, and grammatical errors are distracting.
	Fragmented understanding of issue		Organization and meaning unclear.
1	Vague analysis	Makes no reference to a Christian perspective. Student does not appear to have an understanding of a Christian perspective. (Biblical principles not mentioned.)	Many spelling, punctuation and grammatical errors, making reader unable to follow ideas. (More than five errors per page.)
	Basic lack of understanding		
			Lacks organization.
			Meaning is very unclear.

Score:

In addition to collaborating on a rubric, the task force agreed on a writing prompt that would be given to all incoming and graduating students. This writing prompt would be an assignment embedded in regular coursework at each institution. Here is the writing prompt that was tested in the early years of the project:

Earlier this year, a successful and popular administrator at the Massachusetts Institute of Technology (MIT) lost her job after twenty-eight years when it was discovered that she had falsified her academic credentials on her resume thirty years before. Although she had earned an undergraduate degree from one college, she listed a different institution on her resume, and she included two other academic degrees that she had never earned. However, she was nationally recognized for her work and had risen to a senior position based on her extensive experience and ability. In response to her forced resignation, some have claimed that any falsification of academic credentials, no matter how old or inconsequential should be punished as unethical and fraudulent. Others, though, have suggested that if someone has proven her abilities through years of experience, success, and recognition, then the discovery of a misrepresentation of academic credentials from years ago is actually a minor matter.

ISSUE: What is the appropriate response to this or other similar situations? How should employers and the public respond to a discovery of misrepresentation or falsification of academic credentials after years of successful achievement?

Each participating institution collected essays from beginning and graduating students on this common writing prompt. The ungraded essays were sent to the Center for Research in Adult Learning for processing. Faculty at each institution also graded these assignments as part of their regular coursework, but these grades were for internal use only and did not become part of the data for this project. The Center for Research in Adult Learning removed all identifiers on each essay, assigning each a number which corresponded to the institution and the student status (beginning or graduating). The center also trained scorers who were drawn from the participating institutions. Each institution provided three scorers who read essays from another institution. Each essay was given three scores, and mean scores were calculated.

Statistics were calculated for each institution and for the sample as a whole. Each institution got a report on how their students scored against the benchmark group. *T*-tests were performed to investigate the differences between beginning and graduating students and between institutions and the sample as a whole.

After 3 years of using this rubric, another task force from the participating institutions came together to revise the rubric and develop a new writing prompt. This task force consisted of Kelly Lenarz (Trinity Christian), Karen Dieleman (Trinity Christian), Mary Moretto (Goshen), Mike Manning (Indiana Wesleyan), Kevin Cabe (Indiana Wesleyan), Kim Forbes (University of Mobile), Adele Hermann (University of Mobile), Svetlana Skhoklova (University of Mobile), and Shirley Roddy (Mid-America Christian). These people gave practical insights based on their own experience as scorers using this rubric. They had found that the Christian worldview criteria were particularly troublesome to score, since many students were not using particular biblical references. So there was an attempt to make these criteria more general, requiring reference to a biblical principle rather than a specific verse. The critical thinking criteria became more specific to require evidence of consideration of multiple issues arising from the prompt. The communication rubric was less focused on numbers of spelling and grammar errors and more focused on the flow of the essay (which also includes grammar and spelling). This revised rubric is included as Table 19.2.

In addition to collaborating on a rubric, the task force revised the writing prompt that would be given to all incoming and graduating students. It was felt that the original writing prompt did not evoke students to include a Christian worldview. There was also concern that the schools that had been using this same writing prompt for 4 years would now have seniors being asked to write on it again. Seniors might just dig out their old essay and turn it in again. The revised writing prompt is:

Table 19.2.   Revised Rubric

	Critical Thinking	Christian World View	Communication
5	Raises 3 or more insights on the issue.	Interprets and assesses from a well-developed Christian/biblical framework	Essay flows intelligently and smoothly from introduction through exploration of ideas through conclusion.
	Challenges assumptions	Raises multiple Christian/ biblical principles.	No distracting spelling, punctuation, and grammatical errors.
	Thorough analysis		Meaning is clear
4	General connections, analysis and identification of 1 or 2 insights on the issue.	Student demonstrates a reasonable understanding of Christian/biblical framework. Some Christian/biblical principles raised.	Essay flows well from introduction through conclusion.
			Minimal spelling, punctuation and grammatical errors.
			A few places where meaning is a little unclear.
3	Some analysis	Makes some mention of a Christian perspective.	Essay suffers from some disorganization of ideas across or within paragraphs
	Vague identification of issue	Student indicates some understanding of a Christian perspective.	
		At least one Christian/ biblical principle raised.	Most spelling, punctuation, and grammar are correct, though some errors remain.
			Some places unclear.
2	Incomplete analysis	Demonstrates little understanding of a Christian perspective. Christian/biblical principles hardly or not mentioned.	Organization and meaning unclear
	Fragmented understanding of issue		Spelling, punctuation, and grammatical errors are distracting.
1	Little analysis	Does not appear to work from a Christian/biblical framework at all	Essay consists of randomly collected sentences to fill space.
	Basic lack of understanding		Many spelling, punctuation and grammatical errors, making reader unable to follow ideas.
			Incoherent

At the completion of graduation requirements for a baccalaureate degree, two students with identical academic attainment are competing for the award as the graduate most likely to use knowledge to benefit society. What character traits, values, and ethical issues could be assessed to determine the awardee?

The specific institutions which have chosen to participate have varied from year to year. During the first year of the project, there were six participating institutions. In the second year, there were five institutions. In the third year, there were seven participating institutions. Only one institution has participated every year. Another institution has participated 2 years. Most institutions, however, participated only once. The reported reasons for the sporadic participation include the challenges of communicating the importance of the project to faculty and collecting the essays from students taught by adjunct professors.

Since the institutions vary from year to year, it is not surprising that the results have varied from year to year. Table 19.3 show the results. Results in Table 19.3 are for all institutions together. Each school also received a copy of their institution-specific scores compared to the sample as a whole. In this way, they could benchmark critical thinking, written communication, and Christian worldview with other similar adult programs. It is encouraging that each year showed a significant difference between beginning students and graduating students on critical thinking and written communication. This indicates that adult students make gains in these areas. However, it is a little disappointing that the degree of gain, though statistically significant, is rather small.

All the institutions were quite disappointed with the Christian worldview scores, which seemed to be disturbingly low for both beginning and graduating students. This project has highlighted the challenge many faith-based institutions face in implementing the integration of faith and learning. Follow up projects have focused on techniques to enhance this integration and some institutions have seen an improvement of these scores. For example, some of the institutions now make a more deliberate attempt to include faith integration writing assignments and other activities in their curriculum. There are more class discussions that integrate the subject matter with Christian principles. Finally, as mentioned earlier, the revised writing prompt was designed to allow students more opportunity to integrate Christian ideas. The rubric was also revised to make reference to Christian principles in general rather than Bible references specifically.

While institutions have been encouraged by the significant improvement in critical thinking and written communication scores, they seem to agree that these scores, overall, need to be higher. The results have sparked much conversation about ways to enhance critical thinking and written communication among adult students.

Table 19.3. Student Learning Outcomes Project Results

Criteria	Pre/Post	6 Adult Programs 2008			5 Adult Programs 2009			7 Adult Programs 2010		
		N	Mean	SD	N	Mean	SD	N	Mean	SD
Critical Thinking	pre	109	*3.27	0.80	107	*3.10	0.61	125	*3.28	0.74
	post	127	*3.49	0.72	84	*3.34	0.73	136	*3.56	0.73
Christian Worldview	pre	109	1.92	0.97	107	1.77	0.80	125	*1.90	0.83
	post	126	1.83	0.92	84	1.97	0.82	136	*2.25	0.98
Written Communication	pre	109	*3.06	0.83	107	*2.82	0.77	125	*3.18	0.83
	post	126	*3.36	0.70	84	*3.49	0.75	136	*3.54	0.76

*t-tests indicate a significant difference between pre- and posttests ($p < .05$)

294

PERSISTENCE IN ADULT PROGRAMS

A second project that was coordinated by the Center for Research in Adult Learning focused on retention. At the 2007 brainstorming meeting of adult educators from the Council of Christian Colleges and Universities (CCCU), there was a desire to investigate retention of adult students in adult-focused programs. Who drops out of adult completion programs and why? Institutions were asking the Center for Research in Adult Learning about how they might benchmark retention and graduation rates. How good was good enough when it came to graduation rates? The commonly accepted practices of the U.S. Department of Education did not seem to help here because their statistical retention and graduation rates were based on first time freshmen—a category few returning adult students fulfilled. Instead, adult degree completion programs were measuring the completion rates in their own programs, from start to finish. How many adult students starting the degree completion program in a given cohort were graduating four years later? The center collected statistics from eight different adult degree completion programs and found an average completion rate of 79%. Still, many institutions thought they could do better and sought to find the reasons for students not completing.

A task force of representatives from adult focused CCCU institutions was formed and participated in several phone conferences. Members of this task force included Cynthia Tweedell (Indiana Wesleyan), Scott Ray (LeTourneau), Deb Wade (Colorado Christian), Kevin Jones (Indiana Wesleyan), Lori Scrementi (Trinity Christian), Sonia Strevy (Indiana Wesleyan), Erica Woolridge (Indiana Wesleyan), and Frank Zeng (Indiana Wesleyan). They were led by John Kulaga (Spring Arbor). In discussing what they were doing on retention, it was found that most institutions contact nonreturning students to try to uncover some ways an institution may improve on these completion rates. Getting accurate data on nonreturning students is problematic, however. Former students are reluctant to speak to institutional representatives once the decision to leave has been made. They may be difficult to find or they may not give accurate or complete answers when asked why they left. Instead of focusing on why students leave, the Center for Research in Adult Learning conducted a project that focused on why students persist.

Cynthia Tweedell, from Indiana Wesleyan University, had developed entrance and exit surveys in collaboration with colleagues at Indiana Wesleyan who were interested in retention issues. These surveys were implemented at that institution in 2000. She suggested that these surveys (which had been placed online) could be opened to other institutions for participation from their students, too. These surveys included demographic, attitudinal, and behavioral variables. The URL was shared with ten institutions expressing interest in participating. The surveys included many identical variables that could be compared at entry and exit. What kinds of students were more likely to persist to the end of the program?

Results have indicated some interesting, though somewhat tentative, findings. While this method of research does not really tell us why non-persisting students leave, we can begin to make some predictions about what kinds of students are likely to stay. Four adult completion programs have implemented the surveys at both entry and exit. Data from 4,897 entering students were compared to 1,514 exiting students. Here are some of the highlights:

- **There are no statistically significant differences in completion rates by race.** Despite much discussion in higher education circles about low minority graduation rates, this study found that African Americans are present at the end of the program in statistically similar numbers as in the beginning of the program.

- **Persisting students compared to entering students tend to be more religious.** Students completing the exit surveys were more likely to report frequent church attendance and prayer. It is not known if perhaps these programs, which were all at faith-based schools, somehow influenced a change in religious behavior, or if students who are more religious are more likely to persist at faith-based schools than less religious students.

- **Persisting students compared to entering students tend to be more highly motivated by the adult-focused nature of the program.** When we asked students why they chose a particular college, students completing the exit surveys were more likely than entering students to report that they were strongly attracted by a program that is specially designed for adults.

- **Persisting students compared to entering students tend to be more altruistic than entering students.** Students completing the exit surveys were more likely to report that they volunteer frequently and they put others interests and well-being ahead of their own. Again, it is unclear if this is an effect of their attendance at a faith-based adult program or if this is a characteristic of students who are more likely to persist.

OTHER COLLABORATIVE PROJECTS

The Center for Research in Adult Learning has sponsored other collaborative projects among adult programs at institutions in the Council of Christian Colleges and Universities (CCCU). For example:

- **Collection of "best practices" in adult and online education.** Representatives from several institutions have contributed to a collection of teaching techniques to promote the integration of faith and learning in adult and online programs. This unpublished collection was disseminated to participants at a Center for Research in Adult Learning conference in 2010 (Florence, KY).

- **Benchmarking Associate Degree programs.** Four institutions shared curricula and learning outcomes to compare associate degree programs.

- **Structuring adult programs**. At a recent Center for Research in Adult Learning conference (Florence, KY, 2010) participants expressed interest in exploring the structures of adult programs. The Center facilitated the collection of examples of how institutions have structured their adult degree completion programs. These examples have been assembled into a book, which is a forthcoming Jossey-Bass publication in their *New Directions in Higher Education* series.

- **Study of African American persistence in adult programs**. Representatives from three institutions are currently collaborating to uncover the variables influencing the relatively high graduation rates for African Americans in faith-based adult programs. Interviews with faculty, administrators, and students will produce a case study analysis of these three institutions.

CLOSING THE LOOP: HOW DATA FROM THESE PROJECTS ARE IMPROVING ADULT PROGRAMS

Several institutions have benefitted from the research done by the Center for Research in Adult Learning. Indiana Wesleyan University, which sponsored much of this work, used the data to understand why students come, why they stay and what they learn. The student learning outcomes project resulted in an increased focus on curriculum materials that would enhance critical thinking among Indiana Wesleyan students.

Belhaven University benefitted greatly from the research done by the Center for Research in Adult Learning. After reviewing the retention study, they discovered that among participating institutions, 13% of students withdrawing from their program stated it was because of study group issues. Armed with this information they began a test pilot to allow our study groups (project teams) to collaborate virtually. The percent of students dropping out from the program because of study group issues has dropped to 3%.

The studies of best practices have also influenced key decisions for Belhaven. Looking at the study on employee student ratios, they discovered that their Orlando campus was understaffed in the student services area, based on data cited in that report. They were able to use this study to help justify an additional student services position. The study on orientation structures helped them develop their online orientation format. By comparing to other schools which topics are typically covered in orientation, they were able to incorporate those elements into their online orientation.

CONCLUSION

The Center for Research in Adult Learning is an example of a way adult education programs can collaborate to benchmark outcomes and improve adult programs. Since there are few standardized measures for learning outcomes in adult programs—particularly in faith-based institutions—this collaborative work has been very valuable to several institutions. As higher education changes from a focus on traditional 18- to 21-year-olds to adult focused degree completion and online programs, such benchmarking becomes increasing critical to manage the changes without sacrificing quality. We do not yet clearly know what counts for quality in adult higher education. Benchmarking with traditional programs, while giving evidence of comparable outcomes, may not give us an understanding of excellence in adult programs. Comparability with traditional programs may not be an assurance of quality. Collaborative work with other similar programs can inspire us to implement practices that promote quality in adult higher education at other institutions. Such collaboration can help achieve our goals of producing more college educated adults to meet the challenges of the future.

REFERENCES

Bash, L. (2004). *Adult learners in the academy.* Bolton, MA: Anker.

Flint, T. A., & Associates. (1999). *Best practices in adult learning: A CAEL/APQC Benchmarking Study.* New York, NY: Forbes Custom.

Flint, T., Zakos, P., & Frey, R. (2002). *Best practices in adult learning: A self-evaluation workbook for colleges and universities.* Dubuque, IA: Kendall-Hunt.

Huba, M. E., & Freed, J. (2000). *Learner-centered assessment on college campuses.* Boston, MA: Allyn & Bacon.

Kasworm, C. E., Polson, C. J., & Fishback, S. J. (2002). *Responding to adult learners in higher education.* Malabar, FL: Krieger.

Lipka, S. (2012). "Students who don't count." *Chronicle of Higher Education, 58*(27), A10.

Noel-Levitz & CAEL (2011). *National adult learners satisfaction-priorities report.* Retrieved from http://www.cael.org/pdfs/ALI_report_2011

Palomba, C. A., & Banta, T. (1999). *Assessment essentials.* San Francisco, CA: Jossey-Bass.

Walvoord, B. (2010). *Assessment clear and simple* (2nd ed.). San Francisco, CA: Jossey-Bass.

CONCLUSION

Kathleen P. King and Carrie J. Boden-McGill

Merry-go-rounds and ferris wheels, arcades and midway hawkers, for generations our societies have had their unique, but similar, venues where we could mix with people from different walks of life and cultures and be oversaturated by sound, smells, and new experiences. One of the differences today is that these experiences inundate our daily lives, rather than occurring once or twice a year at the regional festival.

Perhaps more than anything else, the rapid development of inexpensive and broadly implemented technology has led to a squeezing of diverse cultural experiences into many of our daily experiences (Enriquez, 2001; Levy, 2001). That is, from a handheld device we can click and choose to be connected in a moment with similar or dissimilar people. Whether looking for vintage collectibles, cutting edge technology devices, academic training, sports tips, international partnerships, or cultural arts, we can likely find not only resources, but also a community in which to participate.

We frequently hear people say the world has shrunken. Yet, how conscious are we of the great extent to which we engage in intercultural trade and communication daily? And where do we learn how to successfully navigate the multiple levels of understanding and communication entailed in each encounter? The truth is that some people learn how to do these things much more easily and better than others (Gardner, 2007; Wlodkowski, & Ginsberg, 2010). And indeed, some people are oblivious, or choose to ignore, the need to be inclusive and welcoming in their interactions with people different from themselves.

Conversations About Adult Learning in Our Complex World, pp. 301–307

INTERCULTURAL COMPETENCE

In the introduction to this volume, we mentioned recognizing intercultural competence as one frame across the volume. As we reach the last chapter, we ask you to reflect on this concept again and consider what intercultural competence means for adult learning across the many domains involved.

In thinking about *learning environments* and *classroom practices*, all of as educators and/or administrators can reflect on our ability to understand and address the needs of people different from ourselves (Cranton, 2001; Fink, 2003; Wlodkowski, & Ginsberg, 2010). For example, considering the needs of transnationals, immigrants, displaced workers, elders who need to retrain or upgrade skills later in life, or people who are disabled, illustrates our awareness of this issue.

Recently, a colleague and I discussed how social dominance is a relative and often quickly changing landscape. From Kathy's life experience growing up in southern New England, her multiethnic background was the norm, while when she moved to northern New England, it was not. This example is a matter of our identification with the dominant culture changes as we shift locations. However, sometimes we stand in one position, and as the people surrounding us change, so does our identification.

Consider that a White, gay male might be described in most setting as dominant /minority/dominant in relation to his societal acceptance. However, if this same person attends an exclusively African American woman's conference, he might be perceived as minority/minority/ minority. Alternatively, if he was there as an expert speaker on the history of African American coalition building, he might be considered dominant/dominant /dominant because of his status in the larger culture. This example illustrates not only the complexity, but also our potential to shift positions among being a member of the dominant or minority cultural group (Wlodkowski, & Ginsberg, 2010)

Intercultural competence includes being adept at reading status identity within specific contexts (Collier, 1989; Lustig & Koester, 1999; Redmond & Bunyi, 1993) and then, even more critical, knowing how to interact with persons based on different contexts and roles (Earley, 2002). Effective teachers and administrators have vigilant intercultural antennae and actively scan body language, comments, glances of students, faculty, and others with whom they interact. They use the information to create the most appropriate and meaningful learning activities so that people of all cultures and ways can have the full benefit of learning experiences and contribute valuably.

Fundamental to the ability to interact successfully with people different from ourselves is self-understanding and self-acceptance (Krieger, 2005;

Palmer, 1999). The literature of human relations tells us that the way we interact with others largely depends on our own self-perceptions and comfort level. Therefore, the reflective practitioner, as described by Schön (1983) and later Brookfield (1995) and Cranton (1994), considers and addresses the needs of adult learners best if they understand themselves. One might consider that it is hard to understand and interact genuinely with other people if you sufficiently resolved your own issues. As educators, although we might not share intimate details of our lives, it is difficult to separate who we are from what we teach: our lives become part of the message which people perceive (Brookfield, 1995; Cranton, 2001; Palmer, 1999). Therefore, if we have not successfully mastered or embraced intercultural competence, we will be less successful teaching and communicating with people different from ourselves.

Similarly, we have to consider whether our programs and institutions welcome all adult learners. Chapters in this book by Lockhart and Kelting-Gibson, Henschke, and Isenberg and Glancy are examples of those which clearly illustrate ways to serve all adult learners better and suggest that we need to continually reevaluate their needs. Higher education is slow to change, but as the distance education era demonstrated, if traditional colleges and universities do not step up to the opportunities and challenges, new institutional forms will (Allen & Seaman, 2008; Bok, 2003). Higher education has to become more responsive to current and prospective student needs, as well as community and business needs and expectations. If we do not effectively follow this charge, the traditional forms we know may face extinction.

In the midst of the rapid changes of global societal, economic, and political contexts, higher education stands on a precipice of change. And, intercultural competency and relevance may be among the largest collections of challenges which we face. A wide spectrum of stakeholders watch and wait to review the creative forms of programs and services we provide. These programs provide opportunities to reveal higher education's ability to thrive amidst constant and rapid change, or not. It is exciting to see that several institutions address these challenges and we earnestly anticipate more transformations ahead.

However, as institutions shift to address different student populations and needs, with new and old programs, the faculty will need to embrace the same intercultural competences. Obviously, the way to encourage and support such change is through professional development. However, just as our institutional programs and services for students have to change in order to address current and future student needs, so will faculty development. There needs to be a vital connection between not only teaching and learning with intercultural competence, but also the technology connection to these areas as well.

Fortunately, there is an increasing literature and investment in research related to applying adult learning principles to higher education faculty and their professional development needs. Several authors including Cranton (1996) and Lawler and King (2000) explored and applied the adult learning and transformative learning principles to faculty development. Several chapters in this volume provide further insight into how we need to assist faculty in continuing to understand and adapt to the changes and demands of our ever-changing complex world.

MENTORING AND PROFESSIONAL DEVELOPMENT

One of the powerful ways of continuing professional growth and success is found in the mentoring relationship. Now more than ever, it seems that many professional organizations, and higher education especially, have multiple layers of political and cultural complexity which we must learn and navigate to gain success (Birnbaum, 1991; Gardner, 2007; Lawler & King, 2000). We are fortunate when we find people willing to be supportive guides or mentors in discussing the issues, implications, and strategies for surviving in professional domains (Daloz, 1999). Peno and Mangiante provide valuable insight on the role and forms of mentoring throughout one's career. Moreover, their chapter illuminates the stages and needs experienced during the journey from novice to master, an essential understanding from both sides.

In a complementary chapter, McAtee and Hansman provide a comprehensive discussion of background literature on mentoring and faculty development, as well as keen insight into current and future challenges. Their focus is primarily higher education and provides compelling insight into address these challenges. Moreover, McAtee and Hansman's entire chapter- the literature review, illumination of challenges, and suggestions for alternative strategies, can be used either "as is" or as a springboard for further innovation. Here again, we can apply the dynamic model described in the Introduction of this volume, continuing to build upon the past, using information (evaluations or studies) to form future choices.

The last foray into professional development for our volume takes us to Uganda and invites readers to consider the many interrelating educational and economic needs of a country. Essentially rooted in issues of 21st century economies, policies, and politics, Kyobe and King tackle the pressing need for economic development in this nation. Beginning with an informative explanation of the background of colonialism in Uganda, they reveal a vision of indigenous educational models and programs to leverage native arts through technology. Intercultural competency is at the core of the issues that need to be addressed as the problematic Colonial model never validated nor supported indigenous cultural expressions for viable economic benefit. The chapter not only provides a model for cross-sector collaboration, interdependence, institutional development, and teacher training, but preliminary work will soon begin to test and research it on location. In a transferable dimension, this specific model has potential application to other nations in the Sub-Sahara region. More broadly, the model may stimulate exploration and development that will be appropriate to different contexts. Just as research commences in Uganda, our final book section is focused on assessment. Having read the many models, strategies, and theories this book presents, assessment is key to determining effectiveness and guide further efforts.

ASSESSEMENT AND ORGANIZATIONAL DEVELOPMENT

Concomitant with all of the topics discussed above is the need to be able to gather data and determine success. Whether one considers the domain of outcomes related to students, organizations, or faculty in higher and adult education, one needs assessment to provide answers. Moreover, our global and economically troubled society today relies heavily on data to guide decision making during lean cost cutting, or reorganization/mergers.

In the area of student outcomes and learning, our contributors Tweedell and Kelleher provide insight into assessing the critical 21st century skill of collaborative learning among adults. Their work opens new possibilities for research and practice and also models the essential nature of assessment to inform and guide our good intentions. Without valid and reliable assessment, we cannot know if our efforts need further refinement or redesign. What pilot would fly her craft without a means to guide and confirm the path? Assessment addresses this need for instructors, program developers, and administrators.

In a complementary fashion, DiSilvestro and Merrill address organizational development in order to better understand achievement of goals and outcomes. There is a symbiotic relationship between teaching and learning among individuals, groups, and organizations that provide those needed services. It is essential to be able to understand and communicate the value of our adult learning efforts within the scope, mission, and vision of the organization. When we have data to support our statements, we gain a better hearing with leaders and decision makers. Conversely, if our field fails to provide data supporting its outcomes and roles as critical in their organizations, we may fade away and be replaced by those which do.

CONCLUSION

At this stage of your reflections about this volume, we contributors and editors ask you to step back and consider whether any of your professional and personal ideas, practices, and/or assumptions have been illuminated or questioned. We also ask readers to consider how you may incorporate what you have read and understood into your educational practice. Furthermore, we hope that some readers will pursue any of the scores of research questions proposed in this volume. From intercultural competency to assessment, distance learning and beyond, adults coping, struggling, and thriving within our complex world of the 21st century urgently need the development of more strategies for understanding, success, creativity, and empowerment. We look forward to hearing from you as a possible future contributor to this series.

REFERENCES

Allen, I. E., & Seaman, J. (2008). *Online nation: Five years of growth in online learning*. Sloan Foundation Report. Retrieved from http://www.sloan-c.org/publications/survey/pdf/online_nation.pd

Birnbaum, R. (1991). *How colleges work*. San Francisco, CA: Jossey-Bass.

Bok, D. (2003). *Universities in the marketplace*. Princeton, NJ: Princeton Paperbacks.

Brookfield, S. (1995). *Becoming a critically reflective teacher*. San Francisco, CA: Jossey-Bass.

Collier, M. J. (1989). Cultural and intercultural communication competence. *International Journal of Intercultural Relations, 13*(3), 287-302.

Cranton. P. (1994). *Understanding and promoting transformative learning*. San Francisco, CA: Jossey-Bass.

Cranton, P. (1996). *Professional development as transformative learning*. San Francisco, CA: Jossey-Bass.

Cranton, P. (2001). *Becoming an authentic teacher in higher education*. Malabar, FL: Krieger Publishing.

Daloz, L. (1999). *Mentor: Guiding the journey of adult learners*. San Francisco, CA: Jossey-Bass.

Earley, P. C. (2002). Redefining interaction across culture and organizations: Moving forward with cultural intelligence, In B. M. Staw & R. M. Kramer (Eds.), *Research in Organizational Behavior* (pp. 271-299). Oxford, England: Elsevier.

Enriquez, I. J. (2001). *As the future catches you: How genomics and other forces are changing your life, work, health and work*. New York, NY: Three Rivers Press.

Fink, L. D. (2003). Creating significant learning experiences. San Francisco, CA: Jossey-Bass.

Gardner, H. (2007). *Five minds for the future*. Cambridge, MA: Harvard Business School Press.

Krieger, L. S. (2005). The inseparability of professionalism and personal satisfaction: Perspectives on values, integrity and happiness. *Clinical Law Review*, *11*(2), 425-445.

Lawler, P., & King, K. P. (2000). *Effective faculty development: Using adult learning principles.* Malabar, FL: Krieger.

Levy, P. (2001). *Cyberculture* (R. Bononno, Trans). Minneapolis, MN: University of Minnesota Press.

Lustig, M. W., & Koester, J. (2003). *Intercultural competence: Interpersonal communication across cultures* (4th ed.). Boston, MA: Allyn & Bacon.

Palmer, P. J. (1999). *The courage to teach.* San Francisco, CA: Jossey Bass.

Redmond, M. V., & Bunyi, J. M. (1993). The relationship of intercultural communication competence with stress and the handling of stress as reported by international students. *International Journal of Intercultural Relations, 17*, 235-254.

Schön, D. (1983). *The reflective practitioner.* New York, NY: Basic Books.

Wlodkowski, R. & Ginsberg, M. (2010). *Diversity and motivation: Culturally responsive teaching* (2nd ed.). San Francisco, CA: Jossey Bass.

ABOUT THE CONTRIBUTORS

Carrie J. Boden-McGill, PhD, is associate professor and chair of the Department of Occupational, Workforce, and Leadership Studies at Texas State University. She holds a PhD in curriculum and instruction with an emphasis in adult education from Kansas State University, MFA in creative writing from Wichita State University, and BA in English language and literature from Bethel College. Her memberships include the Arkansas Association for Continuing and Adult Education, American Association of Adult and Continuing Education, and Women Expanding Literacy Education Action Resource Network. Dr. Boden-McGill serves as a member-at-large for the Commission of Professors of Adult Education and as a director on the board of the Adult Higher Education Alliance. Dr. Boden-McGill's research is focused on teaching and learning strategies, transformative learning, mentoring, and instructional applications of technology. Her research has been presented at national and international conferences.

Teresa (Terry) J. Carter, EdD, is associate professor and associate dean for professional instruction and faculty development in the School of Medicine at Virginia Commonwealth University. She holds an EdD in executive leadership in human resource development from The George Washington University, MA in education and human development, also from George Washington University, and BS in food science from Clemson University. Her memberships include the American Association for Adult and Continuing Education, The Academy of Human Resource Development, and the Adult Higher Education Alliance. Dr. Carter's research is focused on teaching in medical education, transformative learning among professionals in the workplace, and teaching and learning with technology. She is also an affiliate faculty member in the Department of Teaching and Learning in the School of Education at Virginia Commonwealth University.

Xenia Coulter, PhD, after beginning her academic career at Stony Brook, spent the last 35 years as a mentor at SUNY Empire State College. A recipient of teaching awards from the college, the UUP, and SUNY, and currently professor emeritus, she has presented at conferences and published articles, a number in *All About Mentoring*, about her experiences with traditional aged students in the United States and abroad (particularly Lebanon) and with adult learners in a variety of settings. She has also published research reports related to psychology, technology, and statistics. With her coauthor, Alan Mandell, she has written an essay for the *Encyclopedia of Distributed Learning* (2004), a chapter in *Information Technology and Constructivism in Higher Education* edited by Payne (2009), and a number of other journal articles and book reviews related to adult education. She received her doctorate in experimental psychology from Princeton University.

Thomas D. Cox, EdD, is an assistant professor at the University of Central Florida. He teaches in the higher education and policy studies programs and is the coordinator of the master's program in Community College Education. Previously Dr. Cox was the founding program director of the master's in adult and higher education at the University of Houston-Victoria. He serves on the review board for *New Horizons in Adult Education and Human Resource Development* and *Administrative Issues Journal*. He has served as secretary/treasurer of the Commission of Professors of Adult Education within the American Association of Adult and Continuing Education. Dr. Cox's research focuses on adults and their experiences in higher education, specifically, barriers, retention, and learning styles. His research has been published and presented in national and international venues within higher education.

Ted Davis, MS, is an education specialist with the Alabama Department of Postsecondary Education. He has degrees in instructional technology (AS, Community College of the Air Force), general education (BS, Bluefield State College), adult education (MS, Troy University). Ted spent over 26 years in the United States Air Force with 18 years in aircraft maintenance, 6 years as an instructor at the Air Force Senior Noncommissioned Officer Academy, and over 2 years with the Educational Programs Cadre as a curriculum development specialist. He retired as a senior master sergeant in 2004. Ted's major responsibilities within the Alabama

Community College System include developing and implementing standardized curriculum and faculty professional development.

Frank DiSilvestro, EdD, is program coordinator and associate professor of adult education in the School of Education at Indiana University and associate professor, part time, of medical education. He served previously, for 8 years, as the director of the university-wide general studies degree at IU before joining the adult education faculty full-time. He served on the National University Continuing Education Board of Directors and Executive Committee, and edited A New Directions For Continuing Education volume titled *Advising and Counseling Adult Learners*. He frequently presents on the importance of listening and dialogue in teaching adults. He received his undergraduate and Master's degrees from Rutgers University and his doctorate from Indiana University. He is married and he and his wife Ruth have three children.

Emmanuel Jean Francois, PhD, is an assistant professor of human services and educational leadership at the University of Wisconsin Oshkosh. He earned a PhD in curriculum and instruction (adult and higher education) from the University of South Florida (USF). Dr. Jean Francois' repertoire of publications includes more than 30 titles in English, French, and Haitian Creole. His most recent books include *Transcultural Blended Learning and Teaching in Postsecondary Education (2012), DREAM model to start a small business (2011), and Global education on trial by U.S. college professors (2010)*. He has presented at various regional, national, and international conferences about his research on adult and continuing education, nontraditional college students, global education, transnational education, transcultural issues, globalization, international development, study abroad, transformative learning, scholarship of teaching and learning, and community based participatory research. He is on the editorial board of *Human Services Today* and the *International Interdisciplinary Journal of Education*.

Fletcher Glancy, PhD. is an assistant professor of management information systems at the School of Business and Entrepreneurship, Lindenwood University. He received his bachelor's of science degree in mechanical engineering from Missouri S&T in 1970, his MBA from Texas Tech University in 2006, and his PhD from the Rawls College of Business, Texas Tech University in 2010. He has 35 years of industry experience. His areas of interest include: business intelligence, text and data mining, linguistics, theory development, analytical methodology, e-learning, and e-mentoring.

Catherine Hansman, EdD, is professor of adult learning and development at Cleveland State University. She received the Cyril O. Houle Emerging Scholar in Adult and Continuing Education Scholarship recipient and was awarded a Distinguished Faculty Award for Research by Cleveland State University in 2005. Dr. Hansman is a past president of the American Association for Adult and Continuing Education (AAACE); she also chaired the Commission of Professors of Adult Education (CPAE) from 2004-2006. Her research interests include learning in adulthood, higher education, mentoring, communities of practice, qualitative research, and issues of diversity; these are reflected in the two books she has edited, *Understanding and Negotiating the Political Landscape of Adult Education* (with Peggy Sissel), and *Critical Perspectives on Mentoring: Trends and Issues,* and in the invited book chapters and articles published in journals such as *Adult Education Quarterly, Adult Learning, Journal of Adult Basic Education, Community College Review,* and the *Journal of Excellence on College Teaching*.

John A. Henschke, EdD, is associate professor of education, chair of the andragogy doctoral emphasis specialty, Lindenwood University, St. Charles, MO, U.S. Henschke is a board member of the International Adult and Continuing Education Hall of Fame (IACEHOF); visiting professor of The Beijing Radio and Television University, Peoples' Republic of China (PRC); past-president of the American Association for Adult and Continuing Education (AAACE); and, Missouri, U.S./Para, Brazil Partners of the Americas. Dr. Henschke has chaired 42 completed doctoral dissertations and served as a committee member on 38 other completed doctoral dissertations at Lindenwood University, University of Missouri-St. Louis, and four other Universities around the globe. John has been researching and testing his adult education (andragogical) ideas in the United States and 17 countries around the world since 1970; and has worked with adult educators from 85 countries. His andragogy website is: http://www.lindenwood.edu/education/andragogy and he may be reached at jhenschke@lindenwood.edu.

Jennifer Holtz, PhD, is visiting scholar at the University of Cincinnati and Cincinnati Children's Hospital. She holds a PhD in adult, continuing, and occupational education with an emphasis in medical education from Kansas State University, MA in gerontology from Wichita State University, and BA in biology, emphasis human biology, from Newman University. Her memberships include the American Association of Adult and Continuing Education, generalists in Medical Education, and International Mind, Brain, and Education Society. Dr. Holtz's research focuses on facilitating distance learning and assessment in the sciences, with particular emphasis on adult science literacy.

Susan Isenberg, PhD, is an assistant professor of education in the Doctor of Education-Andragogy Emphasis program at Lindenwood University. She was previously the Supervisor of Graduate Research. She earned a masters degree and PhD from University of Missouri—St. Louis. Her book, *Applying Andragogical Principles to Internet Learning* was published in 2007 by Cambria Press. Her research interests are e-learning/mentoring, self-directed learning, change, and merging business and education theories. In 2011, Isenberg and Glancy received the Best Theoretical Paper award for the EMCIS International Conference in Athens, Greece titled, Conceptual E-Learning Concept.

Carrie Johnson, EdD, has worked in higher education for over 30 years, working with adult students for the past 20 years. Carrie has been a faculty member as well as an administrator. She currently holds the position of director of the BA in general studies in the School of Continuing Education at Eastern Illinois University. Carrie is actively involved in the adult education community, previously serving on the board of the Adult Higher Education Alliance and chairing their conference planning committee in 2009. Carrie has published articles and has spoken internationally on her research which focuses on adult accelerated courses, adjunct faculty development, teaching adults, supporting underprepared adult learners in higher education, and positive aging. She earned her EdD in adult and higher education from Northern Illinois University. For additional information contact her at cejohnson@eiu.edu.

Audrey Kelleher, PhD, is vice president of adult and graduate marketing and development at Belhaven University. Her current responsibilities at Belhaven University include leadership of the adult program marketing, admission, and student services functions at multiple campuses throughout the southeastern United States. Dr. Kelleher has both a business and educational background with experience as a private school principal and formerly the central Florida men's division business planning manager for JC Penney Company. She has a BS in management and marketing, an MEd in educational leadership from the University of Central Florida, and a PhD in leadership and education from Barry University. Her dissertation focused on the adult learner in higher education. Kelleher is a graduate of Leadership Orlando and Lifework Leadership training program. She currently serves on the steering committee of the CCCU Center for Research in Adult Learning and is past president of the Central Florida Higher Education Association.

Lynn Kelting-Gibson, EdD, is a professor of classroom assessment in the Department of Education at Montana State University in Bozeman. Kelting-Gibson's areas of research include authentic teaching, assessment strategies, authentic assessment practices, assessment integration, curriculum design, and Indian education. As an award winning instructor, she teaches online and on-campus courses to both graduate and undergraduate students. Her recent awards include Outstanding Service and Teaching Awards for Education.

Kathleen P. King, EdD, is a department chair and professor of adult, career and higher education at the University of South Florida, Tampa. She is also coeditor of an international journal and series editor for three book series with Information Age Publishing. King's major areas of research and keynote speaking include distance learning, digital media, transformative learning, professional development, and instructional technology. She is the author/editor of 21 books and over 165 published articles and research papers. King's recent recognitions include induction into the International Continuing and Adult Education Hall of Fame (ICAE) in 2011, and the AERA Outstanding Research Publication in 2009. Her continuing international research spans Belize, Germany, and Canada. Prior to joining the USF faculty in 2010, for 13 years she was at Fordham University in New York City as a professor, program director and university administrator. Dr. King earned her EdD and MEd in Higher and Adult Education from Widener University, Chester, PA.

Charles Kyobe is a doctoral student of Higher Education Administration at the University of South Florida and expects to qualify for candidacy in Fall 2012. Since his teenage years in his mother country, Uganda, Mr. Kyobe has been a practicing fine artist, a talent that later became the foundation for his academic and professional careers in United States. He holds an MBA in technology management from the University of Phoenix–Pittsburgh campus and a BA in graphic design from Seton Hill University. He worked for a couple of corporations as a graphic and web designer before becoming an educator, and for the past 12 years, Mr. Kyobe has been an instructor at both high school and college levels in the field of visual communication technologies. It is the combination of these experiences and heritage that prompted his doctoral research focus on technology assisted teaching and learning practices that have a practical potential for improving human and socioeconomic conditions not only in Uganda, but also the Sub-Saharan region at large.

August Lamczyk, MA, is a graduate student at Eastern Illinois University in the master's of arts in gerontology program. August's areas of research include life satisfaction and happiness, retirement transition, caregiver burnout, and fiber consumption. He is an active member of Sigma Phi

Omega, Kappa Omicron Nu, and Eastern Illinois Student Veteran's. For more information contact him at atlamczyk@eiu.edu.

Dave Laton, MS, is the assistant director for career/technical education for the Alabama Department of Postsecondary Education. He has degrees in education administration (AAS, Community College of the Air Force), interdisciplinary management (BS, Southwest Texas State University), and adult education (MS, Troy State University). Mr. Laton has more than 27 years experience as an education and training manager, instructor, and curriculum developer for academia, heavy industry, military, governmental, and nonprofit organizations. His responsibilities include management of the curriculum and instruction unit of the Alabama Department of Postsecondary Education, and managing, designing, developing, and implementing curriculum to support education and training initiatives throughout the Alabama Community College System.

Marilyn Lockhart, EdD, is the interim director of faculty development and associate professor in the adult and higher education program at Montana State University in Bozeman, Montana. She was the president of AHEA during 2010-11. She has published numerous articles on faculty development and teaching best practices. Her previous work has been in the area of administration at University of Virginia and in various capacities in adult education.

Elyse D'nn Lovell, EdD, is a psychology instructor and student-parent program coordinator at Montana Tech of the University of Montana COT. Her research interests include college students who are parents, technology, and civic engagement in the college classroom, grandparents raising grandchildren, morale among seniors using technology, and non-offending parents. Her memberships include Northern Rocky Mountain Educational Research Association, Adult Higher Education Alliance, and Montana Alliance for Families Touched by Incarceration. Her awards include Outstanding Doctoral Student in Adult and Higher Education at Montana State University (2011) and Arthur Chickering Scholarship (2011). Her recent presentations include: My Homework or Yours? Student-Parents; American Indian Student-Parents; College Counselors Helping Student-Parents; Undergraduates' Technology and Social Connections; The Phenomenon of Facebook Journaling in the Classroom; Civic Engagement Across the Curriculum as It Relates to Change in Student Satisfaction and Participation; Grandparents Raising Grandchildren; Non-Offending Parents' Perceptions Differ from Professionals Working With Them. For additional information elysednnlovell@gmail.com

Kathryn A. McAtee, PhD, is associate professor of business administration the Cuyahoga Community College in Cleveland Ohio. She formerly served as the faculty development coordinator for the Eastern Campus of the college. Dr. McAtee's areas of research include faculty development, generations in the classroom, and women in higher education leadership. Examples of recent presentations include the 2011 AAACE International Conference, *A Discovery of Creative Professional Development Opportunities: Challenges to Faculty Development*, AAACE 58th International Conference Presenter, *Multiple Generations in Adult and Higher Education: Who are They?*, and presented and published a paper in the proceedings of the Adult Education Research Conference (AERC), *Women Leaders in Higher Education: Transformational VS Transactional Leadership Development*. Dr. McAtee earned her PhD in urban education from Cleveland State University in 2006.

Alan Mandell, PhD, is college professor of adult learning and mentoring at SUNY Empire State College, editor of *All About Mentoring*, and coeditor of the online journal, *PLA Insideout*. For the past 35 years, he has also served as administrator, mentor in the social sciences, and director of the college's Mentoring Institute. With Elana Michelson, he is the author of *Portfolio Development and the Assessment of Prior Learning* (2nd edition) (2004). With Lee Herman, he has facilitated workshops on adult learning and mentoring and written many essays, articles, and chapters, as well as *From Teaching to Mentoring: Principle and Practice, Dialogue and Life in Adult Education* (2004). A recent essay, "Mentoring: When Learners Make the Learning," is included in *Transformative Learning in Action* edited by Mezirow and Taylor (2009). With Xenia Coulter, he regularly writes about contemporary higher education, most recently, "Adult Higher Education: Are We Moving in the Wrong Direction?" for *JHCE* (2012).

Elaine M. Silva Mangiante, PhD, teaches in the teacher education programs at Salve Regina University and the University of Rhode Island. Her research interests include teacher development from novice to expert, urban education, science learning for critical thinking, and effective teaching practices. Her recent article, published in *Educational Assessment, Evaluation and Accountability*, addresses "Teachers Matter: Measures of Teacher Effectiveness in Low-Income Minority Schools" (2011). Elaine formerly served as a professional development specialist with The Education Alliance at Brown University for educational reform in high-poverty districts. As a science specialist and mathematics curriculum coordinator for a K-8 school, she mentored early career teachers, provided consulting services in science education to schools, and received the state-level Presidential Award for Excellence in Elementary Science Teaching. She has most recently completed a study of the planning practices of elementary teachers in urban schools identified as effective in teaching inquiry science.

Catherine McCall Marsh, EdD, MBA, is associate professor of management at North Park University in Chicago and principal of her consulting company through which she provides services related to diversity management, teambuilding and conflict resolution, as well as executive coaching. She formerly served as vice president of human resources at Kanbay, Inc. and held multiple positions from fund raiser to program developer with the Institute of Cultural Affairs in the United States, Japan, and Australia. Her research interests are in the fields of ethics, leadership, and diversity management. Catherine earned her doctorate in adult and higher education, with an emphasis on human resource development, from Northern Illinois University.

Henry S. Merrill, EdD, adult educator-at-large, became emeritus associate professor of adult education at Indiana University in 2010. During his career he taught theater at Earlham College and served as vice chancellor for student services and director of continuing studies at Indiana University East. At the Indiana University Purdue University Indianapolis campus, he served as chair of the MS in adult education in The School Of Continuing Studies. Research interests include adult development, instructional design, and distance learning, service on the board of directors of American Association for Adult and Continuing Education included director of the Commission of Professors of Adult Education and of the Commission of Affiliate Associations, and president in 2012. He earned a BA in drama-speech at Hanover College, an MFA in theater at UMass-Amherst, an MS in counseling psychology and EdD in adult and community education at Ball State University.

Lauren Merritt is a student in the Adult Education Graduate Program and works as the research assistant for the Office of the Provost at the University of Arkansas at Little Rock. Lauren earned a bachelor's of arts in psychology with a minor in sociology from the University of Arkansas at Little Rock. As an undergraduate, Lauren received the Chancellor's List Academic Excellence Award, and during her graduate studies, she has been recognized as a top student in her program and was recently a nominee for induction into the Alpha Epsilon Lambda Honor Society. Lauren is an active member of the Adult and Higher Education Alliance (AHEA), and she serves as an associate editor for *Adult Learning in Our Complex World*, a book published in 2012 in conjunction with the AHEA annual conference.

Carmela R. Nanton, EdD, is professor of education, Palm Beach Atlantic University, and chair of the Professional Education Program. In education she holds and EdD in organization and leadership, Columbia University, and cognate in adult education. She has master's degrees in human resource development and counseling psychology. Research interests include leadership development, adult education, social capital, women and leadership, cross-cultural competence. She has taught courses in China, the Czech Republic; and as visiting professor in Kenya, Hong Kong, and the Bahamas. Career background includes supervision in healthcare, training and staff development, online technology, program and curriculum design, performance improvement, and psycho-education. She has served as a regional accreditation assessor for healthcare and facilitated workshops in HRD, Allied Health, diversity, and cross-cultural communication. Dr. Nanton is a consultant, coach, international speaker and scholar and co-directs the HRD SIG for CPAE with AAACE. A recent co-edited publication is *Social Capital and Women's Support Systems: Networking, Learning and Surviving* (Alfred, 2009), Jossey-Bass.

Joann S. Olson, PhD, is assistant professor and program coordinator in the Adult and Higher Education program at the University of Houston-Victoria. She has also served as arts and sciences program chair and faculty specialist for the School of Online Studies and Graduate School at Crown College, west of Minneapolis. Olson's academic and research interests lie at the intersection of adult learning and higher education: exploring the transition from college to work—specifically for first-generation college students; the experiences of adult learners returning to and exiting from higher education; and the incorporation and development of contingent and adjunct faculty into the culture of the organizations where they teach. Joann earned her PhD in adult education from Penn State University.

Kathy Peno, PhD, is associate professor of adult education at the University of Rhode Island. Her research interests include professional development, mentoring, performance improvement along the novice to expert continuum, problem-based instruction, and organizational learning. A former banker, Peno combines her knowledge of corporate work practices with her educational foundation in adult learning to explore performance improvement strategies for a variety of practitioners. She also offers professional development to teachers on using problem-based instruction in the classroom to provide students with workplace context. Most recently, Peno worked with science educators and scientists on an NSF funded grant studying the development of preservice and in-service elementary teachers' use of inquiry-based science teaching. Along with Elaine Silva Mangiante, she recently completed a study on the factors that effect teacher development of expertise in inquiry-based science instruction. Kathy earned her doctorate in 2000 from the University of Connecticut.

Frederick Carl Prasuhn, PhD, is a recent graduate of the adult education program at the University of Georgia, Athens, GA, and is currently serving as an instructor at Athens Technical College. His research includes the University System of Georgia's Continuing Education impact and translation of asynchronous online education into credit hours. Fred is establishing himself in the academic community by presenting at national conferences, a current board member of Adult Higher Education Alliance, and a committee member for the Commission of Professors of Adult Education within the American Association of Adult and Continuing Education. For more information contact Fred: fprasuhn@gmail.com or www.FredPrasuhn.com.

Joe Reynolds, EdD, chairs the Department of Education at Troy University's Montgomery campus. He has degrees in electrical engineering (BS, USAF Academy), telecommunications science (MS, University of Colorado), general education administration (EdS, Troy State), and curriculum and instruction (EdD, Auburn). Dr. Reynolds spent 22 years in the United States Air Force as a Communications Engineer and, later, as an educator at the Air Command and Staff College. He retired as a Lieutenant Colonel in 2003. Dr. Reynolds teaches numerous graduate classes in adult education; chairs the Troy College of Education Graduate Academic Governance Committee; and oversees programs in general education administration (EdS), adult education (MS), postsecondary education (MS), and elementary education (MS).

Wytress Richardson, EdD, is an assistant professor of social and behavioral sciences at National-Louis University, Chicago. She has spent more than 20 years in the Human Services field where she has served as an administrator and clinician for public, private, and nonprofit organizations. She is a sought after conference speaker, facilitator, and lecturer. Richardson's area of research includes organizational leadership, mentoring, building effective relationships and adult education. She is a published author whose book, *Stress and Leadership: Voices of the Unheard* was published in 2009. Richardson is the president and founder of Girls of Grace Youth Organization (501c3) that is dedicated to mentoring and equipping girls and young women with valuable leadership skills. Wytress earned her doctorate degree in organizational leadership from Argosy University in 2006. For more information contact her at wytress.richardson@nl.edu or drwytressrichardson@gmail.com.

Annie Shibata, PhD, is a professor of communication at Walden University, and owner of Gemini Consulting. Shibata has been teaching communication and doing cross-cultural consulting and training since 1983, including 16 years in Japan, for such organizations as Hitachi Ltd., Fujitsu, Sanwa Bank, Shell Oil Japan, The Spencer Turbine Co., and ACORD. She has been certified as expert witness in court cases concerning Japanese cultural/communication issues, speaks Japanese fluently, and raised two bicultural/bilingual sons. She has held faculty and administrative positions at several institutions of higher learning in Japan and the United States and writes articles for academic as well as business audiences on cross-cultural and organizational communication issues. Her areas of interest include intercultural communication, Japanese culture, faculty development, and online teaching and learning. She is currently writing a cross-cultural memoir of her life as an American bride in Japan. For more information visit www.geminiconsultingdoc.com.

Gabriele Strohschen, EdD, completed her doctoral studies at Northern Illinois University-Leadership and Educational Policy Studies, with a focus on phenomenology and adult education. She serves as associate professor and faculty mentor at the School for New Learning, DePaul University in Chicago. She designed and implemented a teacher education program in Bangkok, Thailand, establishing the school's first international campus for graduate programs. Her research interests center on international/intercultural program design, teacher training, and popular education. She is has been engaged in action research projects and guest lecturing in Afghanistan, Germany, Kenya, China, Mexico, and Thailand. Her recent work is focused on community empowerment projects in Kenya and program design in China and the United States. Dr. Strohschen has worked for 20+ years in adult education and training within multiethnic, multinational populations in positions of director at not-for-profit and public community-based organizations, alternative high schools, and career and technical schools prior to entering academia full-time. She serves currently as president of Adult Higher Education Alliance and President of the Phi Beta Delta Honor Society—Delta Theta Chapter and is an active member of the American Association of Adult and Continuing Education and the Commission of Professors of Adult Education.

Dr. Jonathan Taylor, PhD, coordinates the adult and postsecondary education programs at Troy University's Montgomery campus. He earned his PhD in educational psychology and research at the University of Tennessee. Prior to his academic work, Dr. Taylor spent over a decade in public and private law enforcement training. His research interests are in the areas of learning resistance, workforce and professional training practices, and conceptual change theory.

Cynthia Benn Tweedell, PhD, is vice president for institutional effectiveness and planning at Mid-Continent University. She has conducted research and taught online and on site classes for over 30 years. She founded the CCCU Center for Research in Adult Learning, which facilitated collaborative research projects and conferences with schools. As vice president for institutional effectiveness and planning for Mid-Continent University, she assures quality of programs and services as well as overseeing compliance and accreditation. Dr. Tweedell is a frequent presenter on issues of adult student learning, retention, and innovative modes of delivery. She has coauthored two sociology textbooks, and *Systems of Excellence in Adult Education* (all with Triangle Publishing). Dr. Tweedell holds master's degrees from University of North Carolina-Greensboro and University of Chicago. She holds the PhD from Walden University.

CPSIA information can be obtained at www.ICGtesting.com
Printed in the USA
BVOW04s2004291013

334977BV00004B/35/P

9 781623 960766